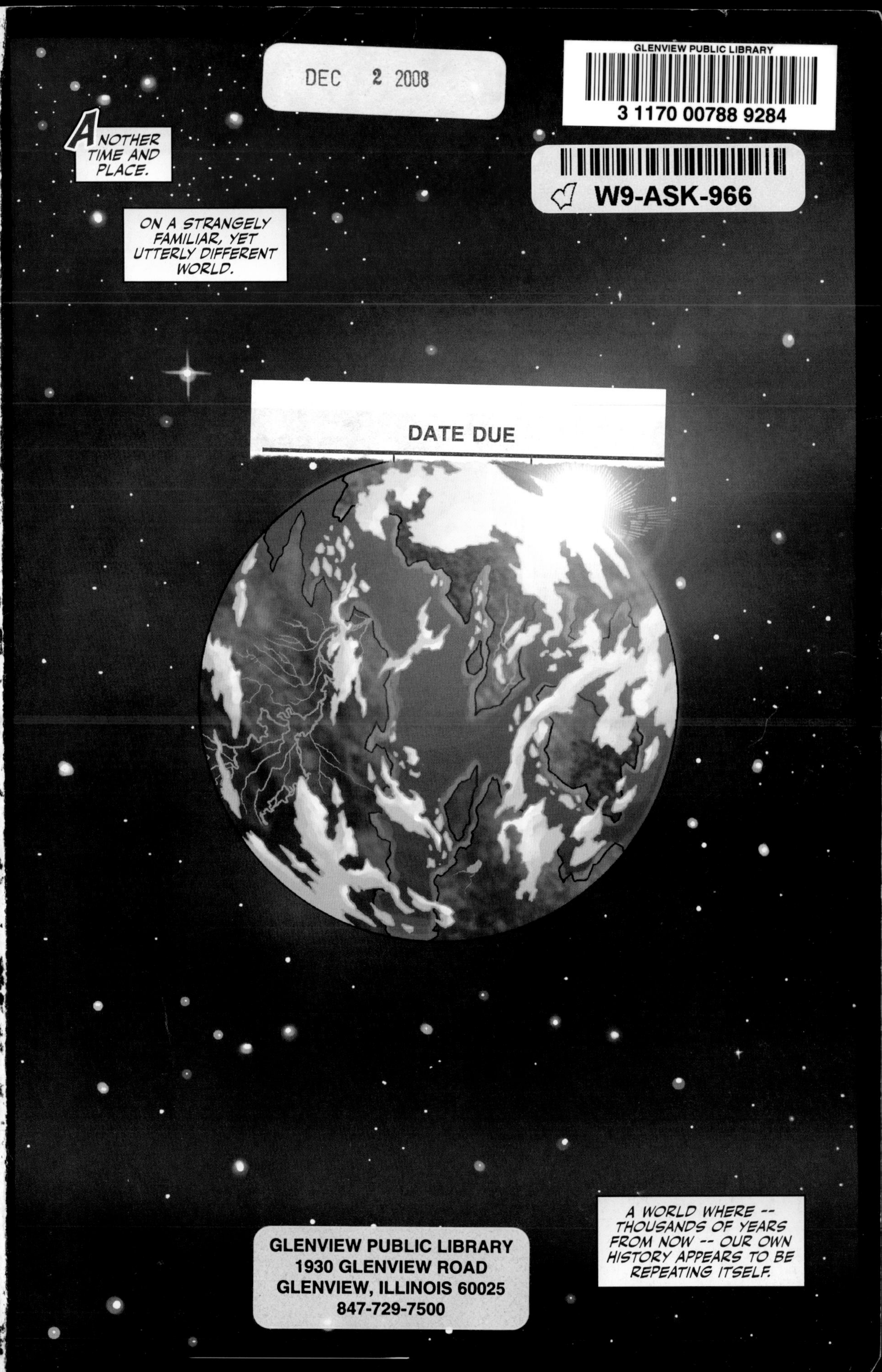
ANOTHER TIME AND PLACE.
ON A STRANGELY FAMILIAR, YET UTTERLY DIFFERENT WORLD.
A WORLD WHERE -- THOUSANDS OF YEARS FROM NOW -- OUR OWN HISTORY APPEARS TO BE REPEATING ITSELF.

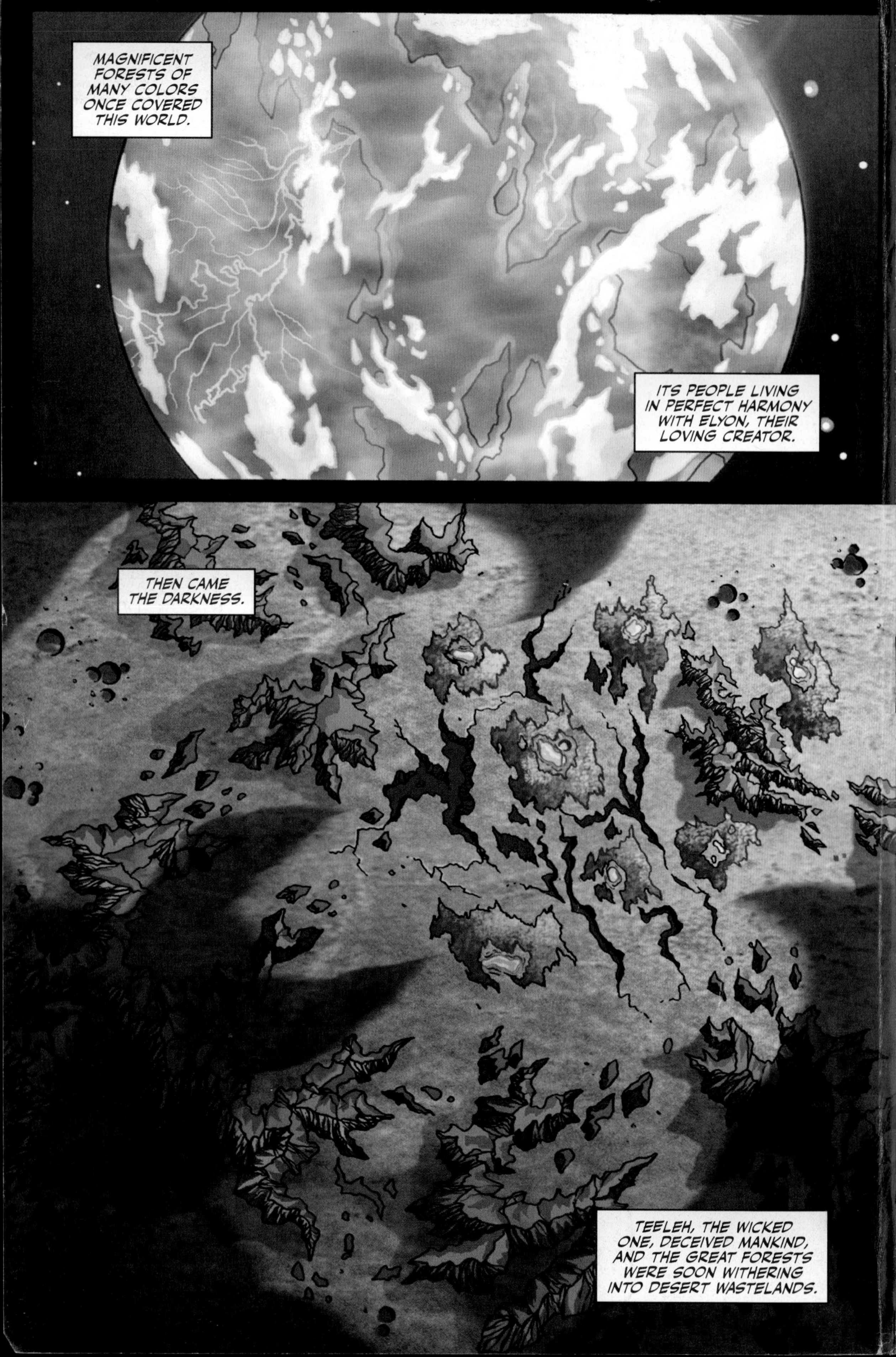
MAGNIFICENT FORESTS OF MANY COLORS ONCE COVERED THIS WORLD.
ITS PEOPLE LIVING IN PERFECT HARMONY WITH ELYON, THEIR LOVING CREATOR.
THEN CAME THE DARKNESS.
TEELEH, THE WICKED ONE, DECEIVED MANKIND, AND THE GREAT FORESTS WERE SOON WITHERING INTO DESERT WASTELANDS.

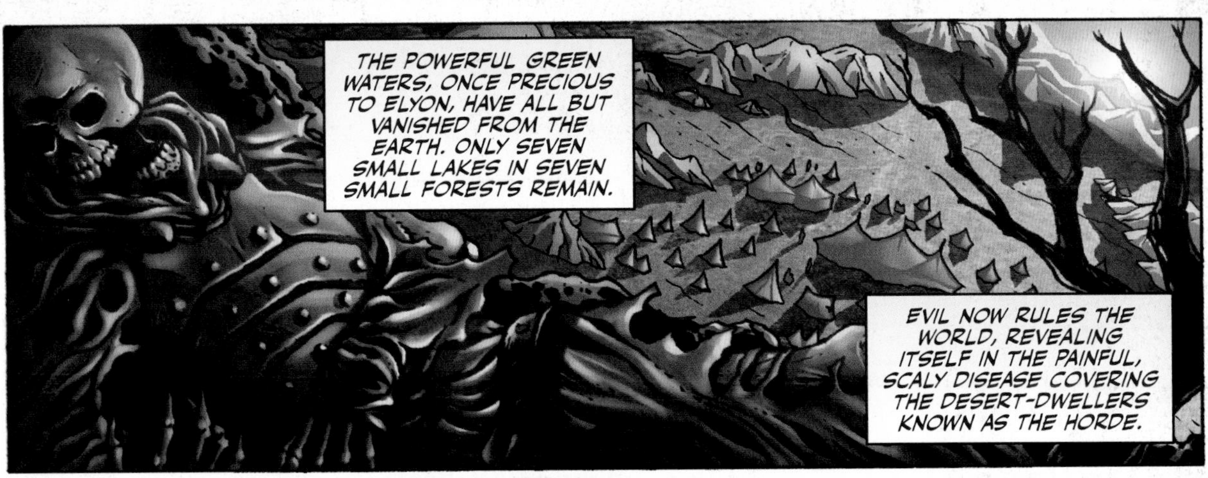
THE POWERFUL GREEN WATERS, ONCE PRECIOUS TO ELYON, HAVE ALL BUT VANISHED FROM THE EARTH. ONLY SEVEN SMALL LAKES IN SEVEN SMALL FORESTS REMAIN.
EVIL NOW RULES THE WORLD, REVEALING ITSELF IN THE PAINFUL, SCALY DISEASE COVERING THE DESERT-DWELLERS KNOWN AS THE HORDE.

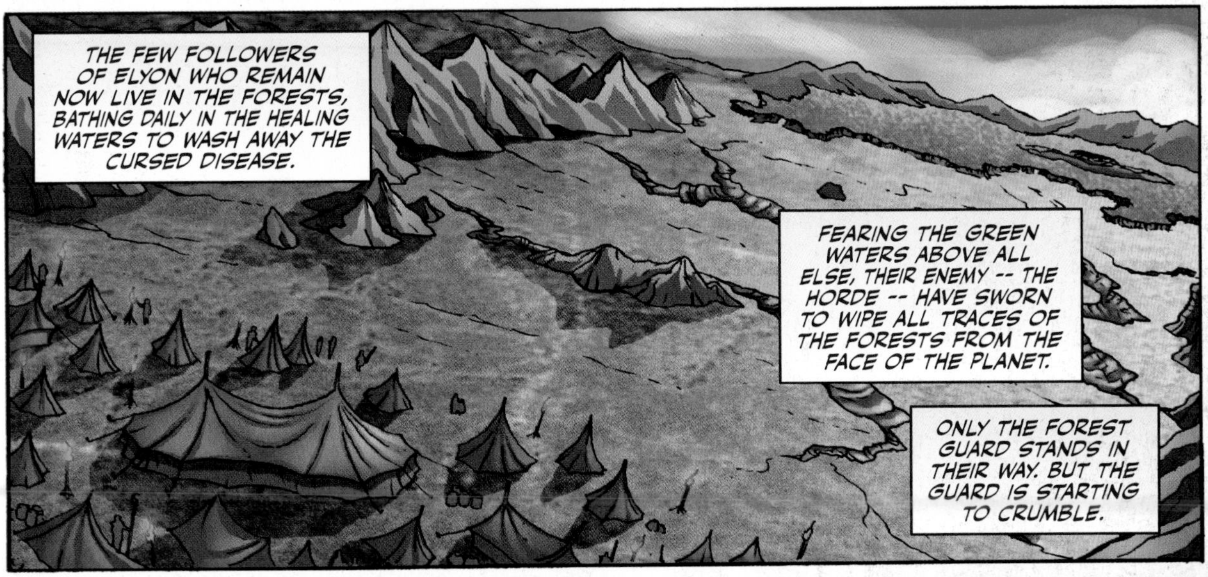
THE FEW FOLLOWERS OF ELYON WHO REMAIN NOW LIVE IN THE FORESTS, BATHING DAILY IN THE HEALING WATERS TO WASH AWAY THE CURSED DISEASE.
FEARING THE GREEN WATERS ABOVE ALL ELSE, THEIR ENEMY -- THE HORDE -- HAVE SWORN TO WIPE ALL TRACES OF THE FORESTS FROM THE FACE OF THE PLANET.
ONLY THE FOREST GUARD STANDS IN THEIR WAY. BUT THE GUARD IS STARTING TO CRUMBLE.

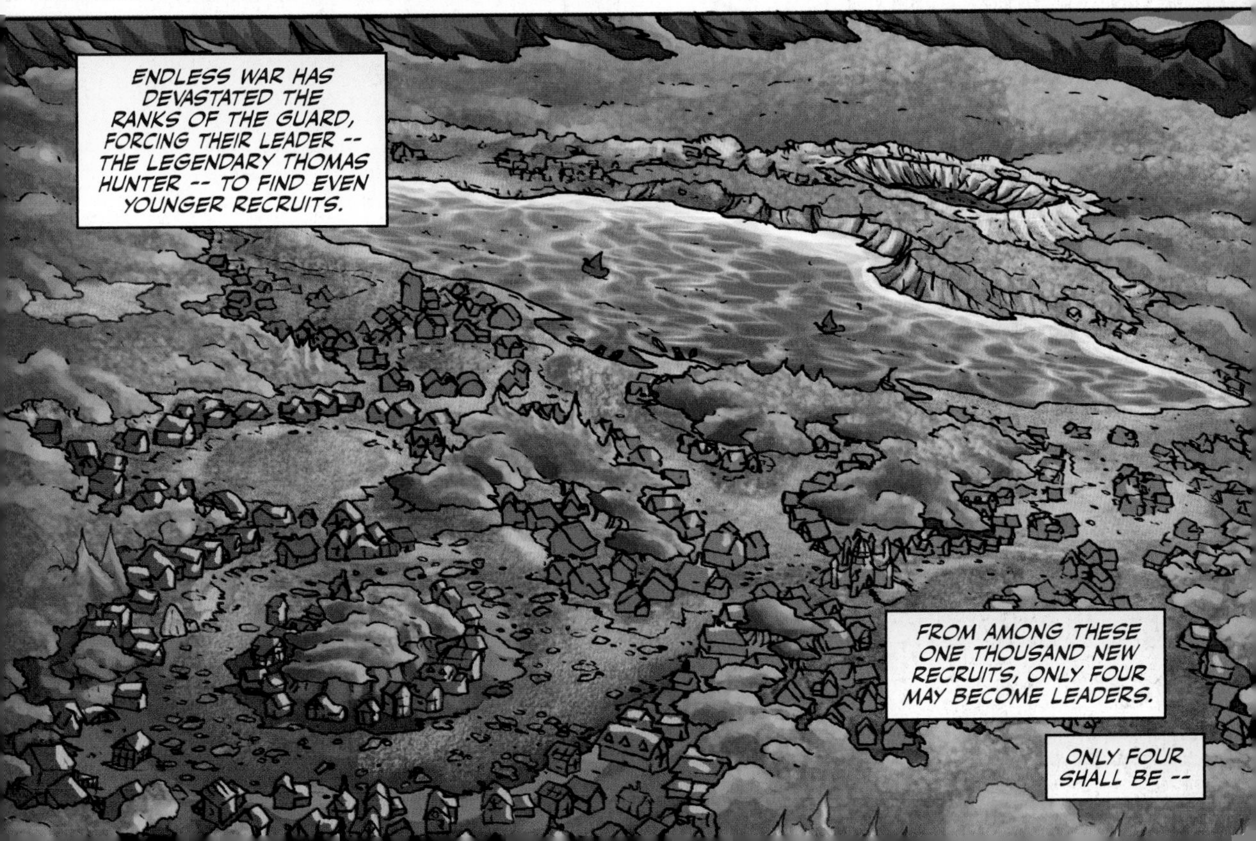
ENDLESS WAR HAS DEVASTATED THE RANKS OF THE GUARD, FORCING THEIR LEADER -- THE LEGENDARY THOMAS HUNTER -- TO FIND EVEN YOUNGER RECRUITS.
FROM AMONG THESE ONE THOUSAND NEW RECRUITS, ONLY FOUR MAY BECOME LEADERS.
ONLY FOUR SHALL BE --

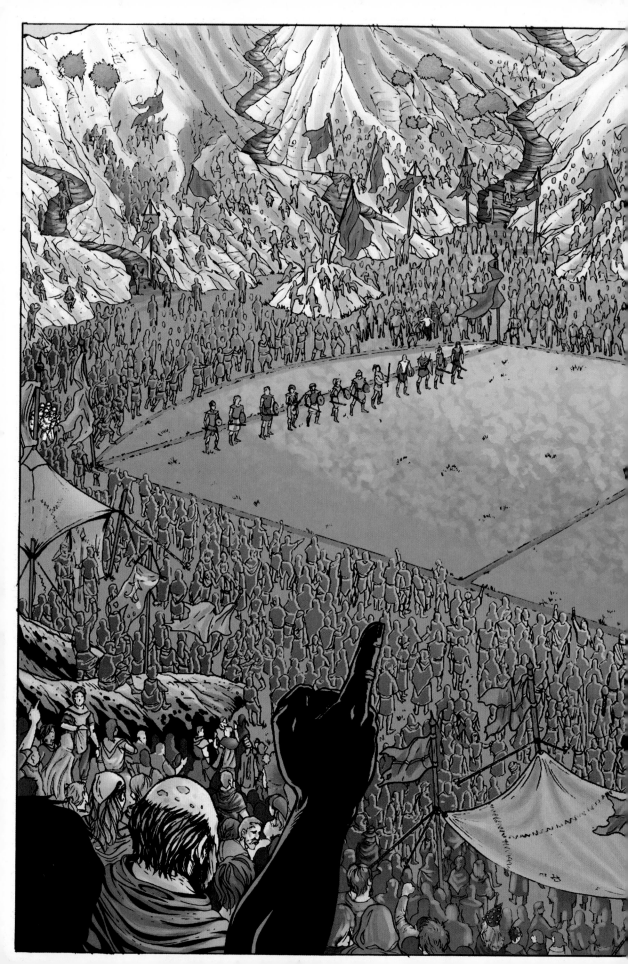

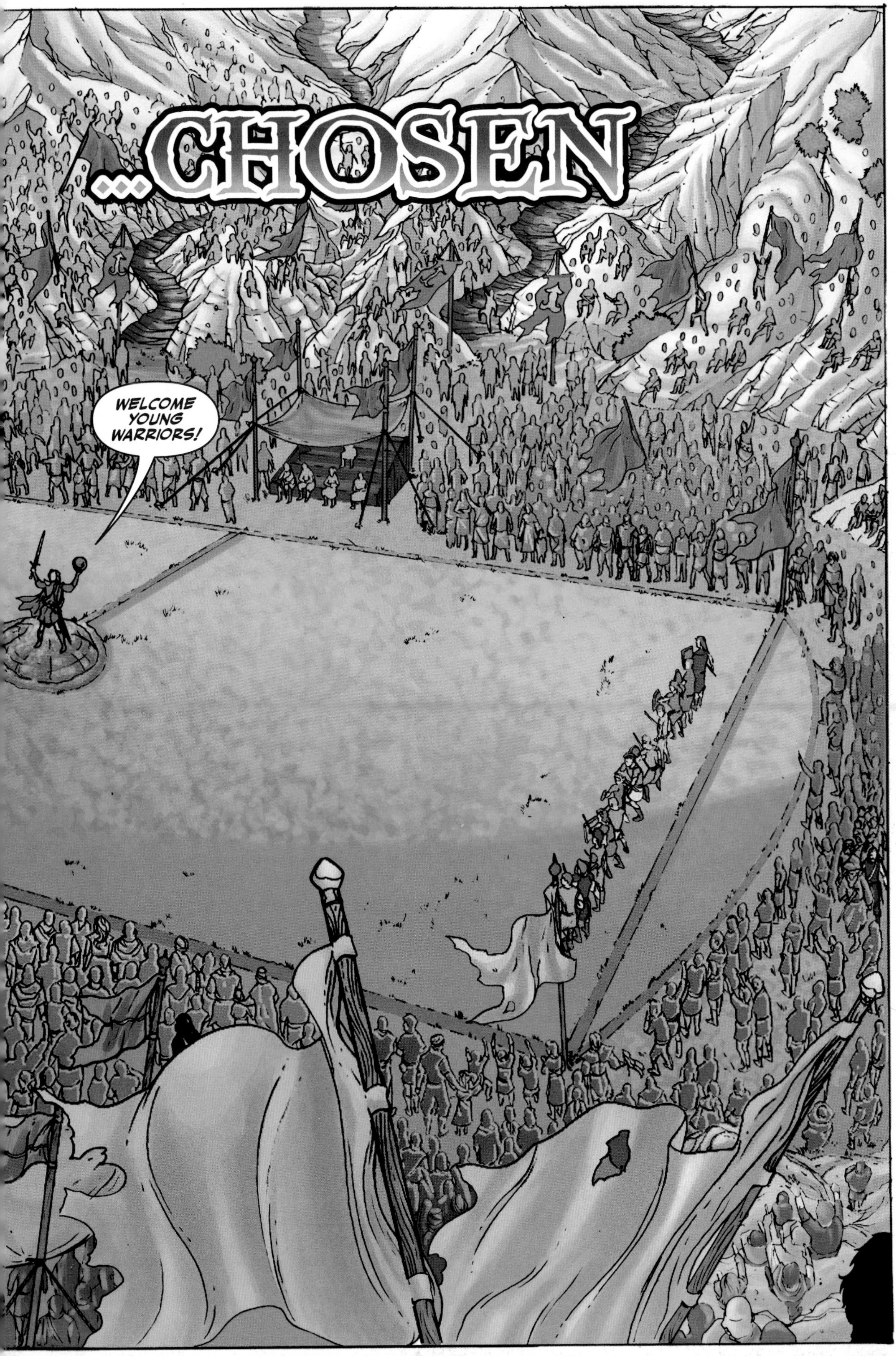
...CHOSEN
WELCOME YOUNG WARRIORS!

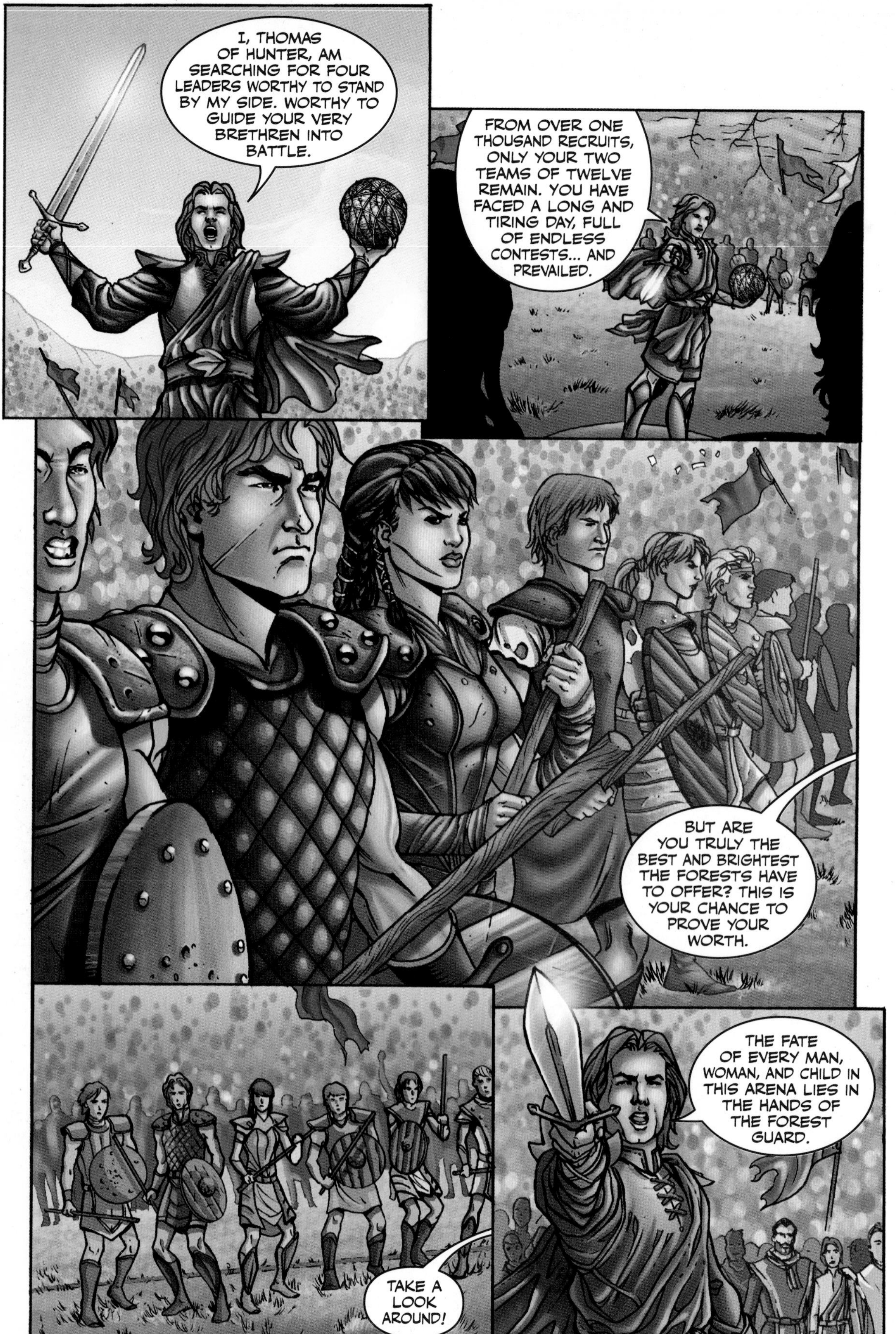
I, THOMAS OF HUNTER, AM SEARCHING FOR FOUR LEADERS WORTHY TO STAND BY MY SIDE. WORTHY TO GUIDE YOUR VERY BRETHREN INTO BATTLE.
FROM OVER ONE THOUSAND RECRUITS, ONLY YOUR TWO TEAMS OF TWELVE REMAIN. YOU HAVE FACED A LONG AND TIRING DAY, FULL OF ENDLESS CONTESTS... AND PREVAILED.
BUT ARE YOU TRULY THE BEST AND BRIGHTEST THE FORESTS HAVE TO OFFER? THIS IS YOUR CHANCE TO PROVE YOUR WORTH.
TAKE A LOOK AROUND!
THE FATE OF EVERY MAN, WOMAN, AND CHILD IN THIS ARENA LIES IN THE HANDS OF THE FOREST GUARD.

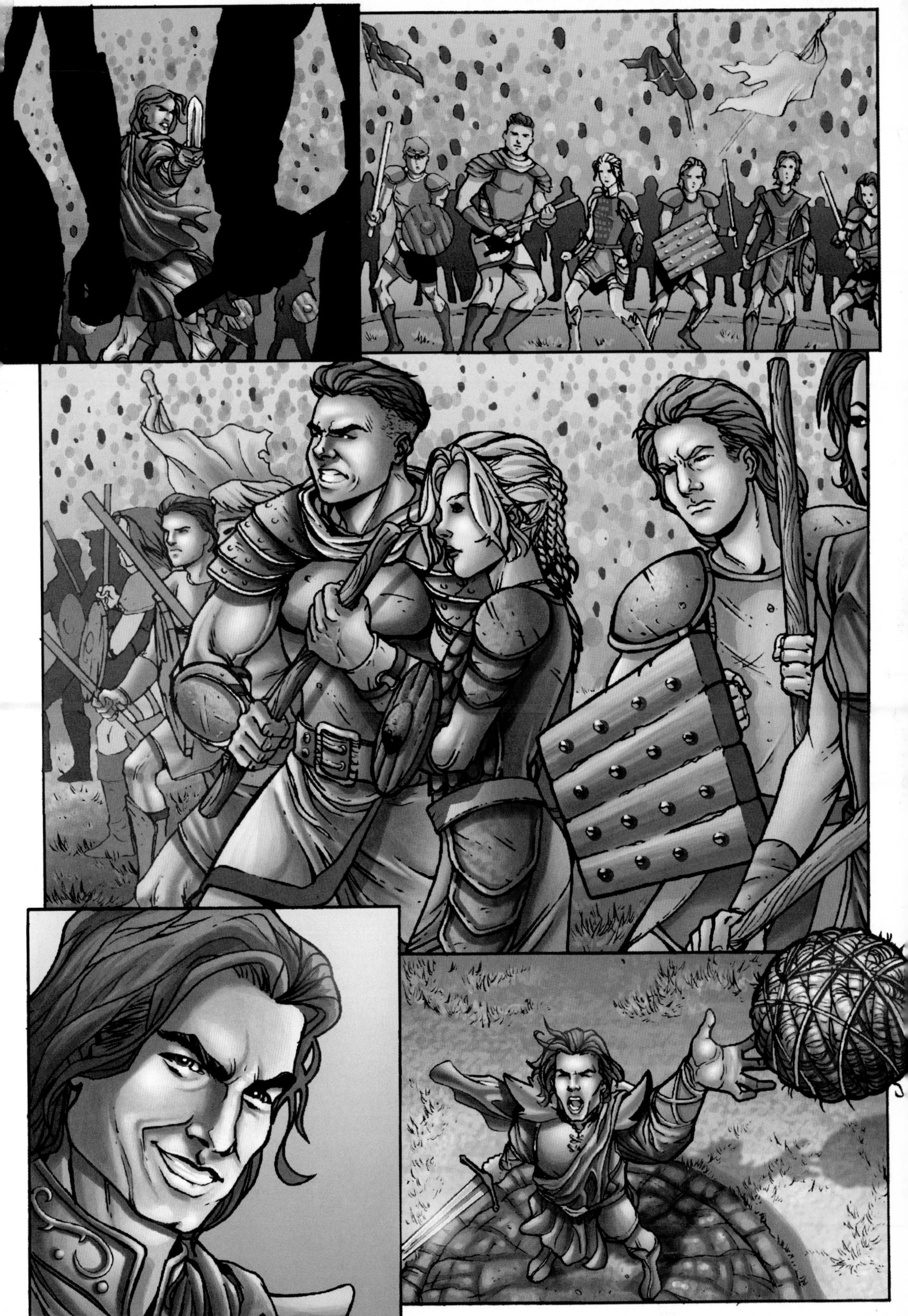

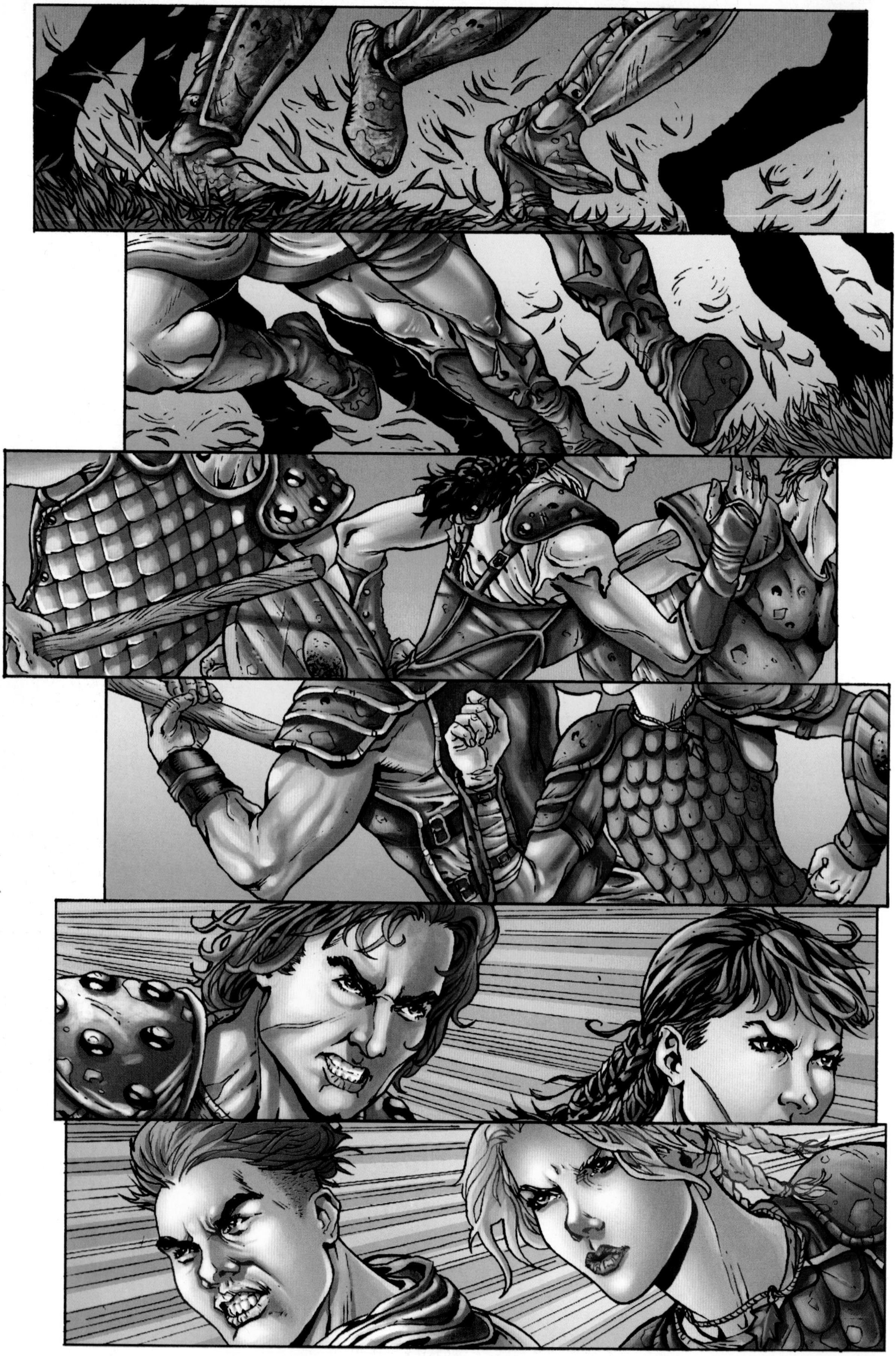

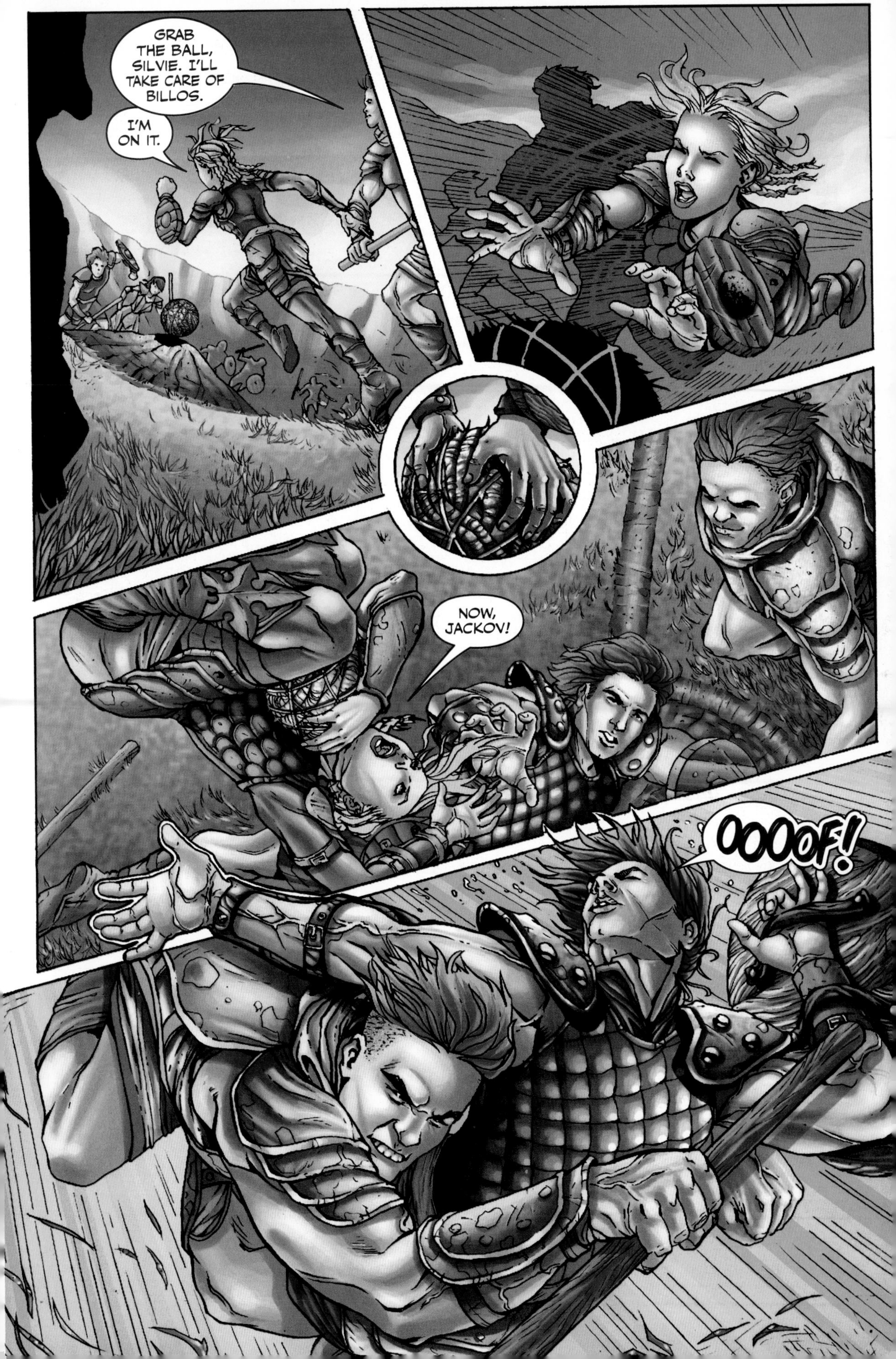
GRAB THE BALL, SILVIE. I'LL TAKE CARE OF BILLOS.
I'M ON IT.
NOW, JACKOV!
OOOOF!

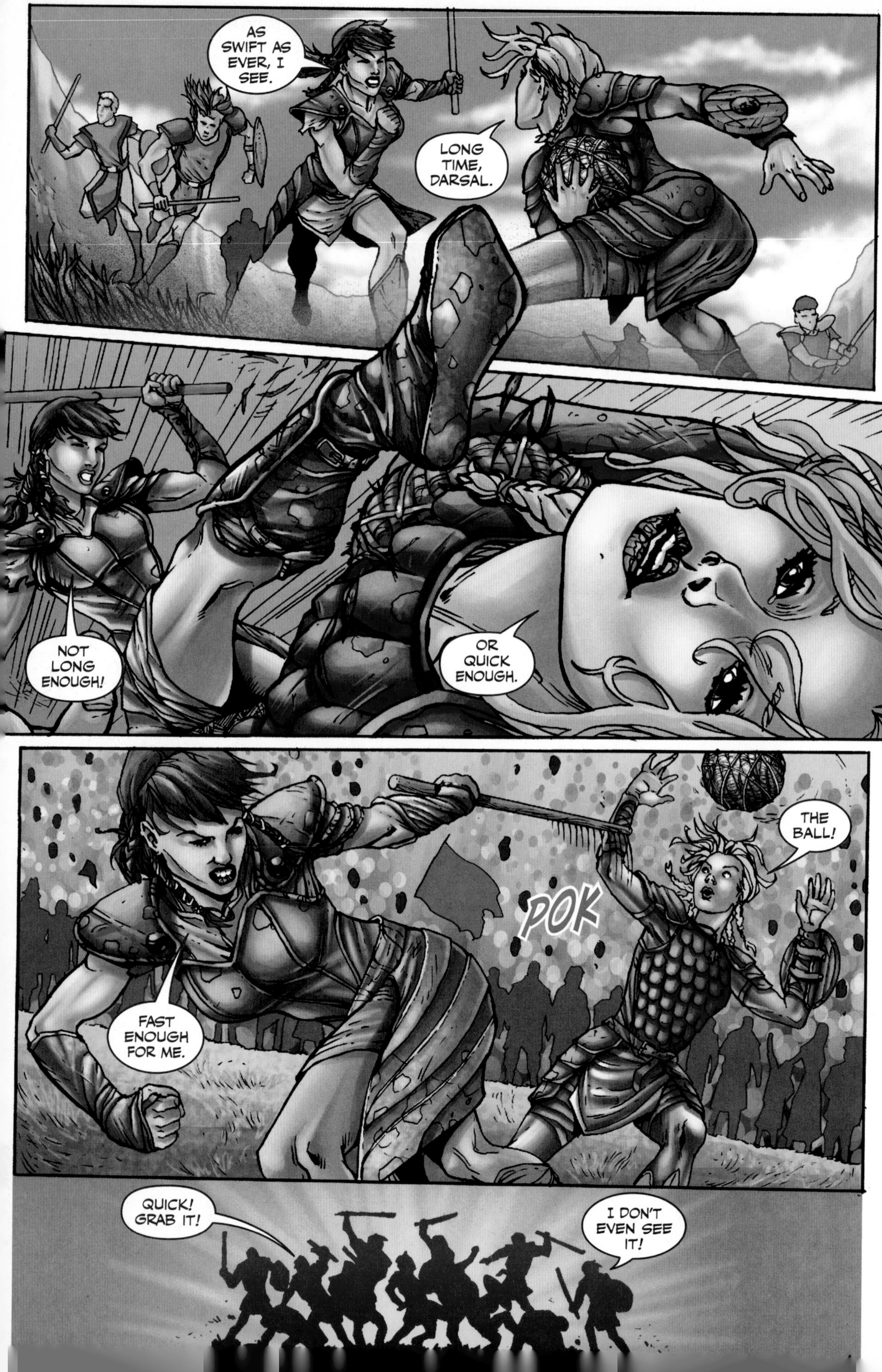
AS SWIFT AS EVER, I SEE.
LONG TIME, DARSAL.
NOT LONG ENOUGH!
OR QUICK ENOUGH.
FAST ENOUGH FOR ME.
POK
THE BALL!
QUICK! GRAB IT!
I DON'T EVEN SEE IT!

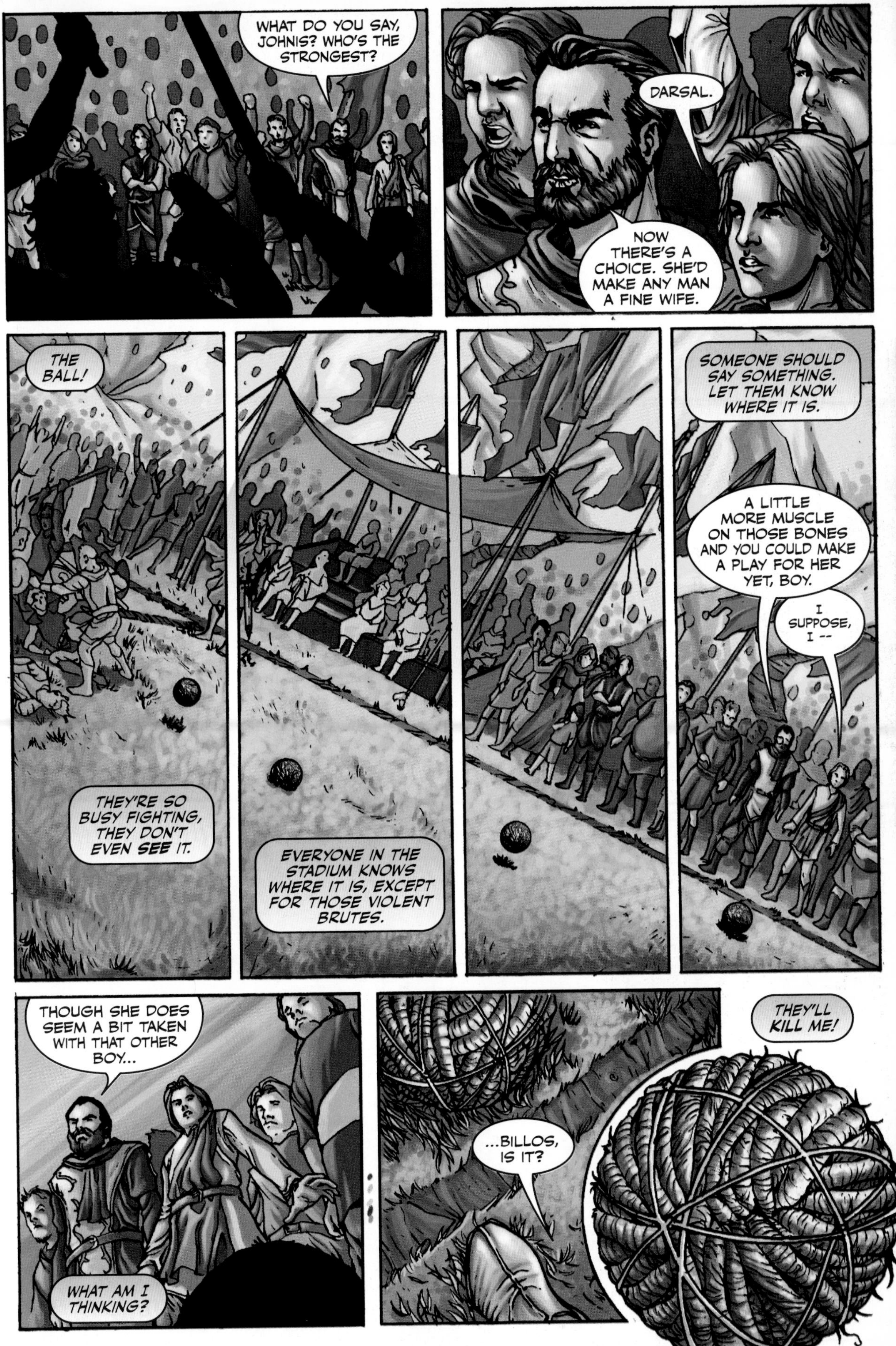
WHAT DO YOU SAY, JOHNIS? WHO'S THE STRONGEST?
DARSAL.
NOW THERE'S A CHOICE. SHE'D MAKE ANY MAN A FINE WIFE.
THE BALL!
THEY'RE SO BUSY FIGHTING, THEY DON'T EVEN SEE IT.
EVERYONE IN THE STADIUM KNOWS WHERE IT IS, EXCEPT FOR THOSE VIOLENT BRUTES.
SOMEONE SHOULD SAY SOMETHING. LET THEM KNOW WHERE IT IS.
A LITTLE MORE MUSCLE ON THOSE BONES AND YOU COULD MAKE A PLAY FOR HER YET, BOY.
I SUPPOSE, I --
THOUGH SHE DOES SEEM A BIT TAKEN WITH THAT OTHER BOY...
WHAT AM I THINKING?
...BILLOS, IS IT?
THEY'LL KILL ME!

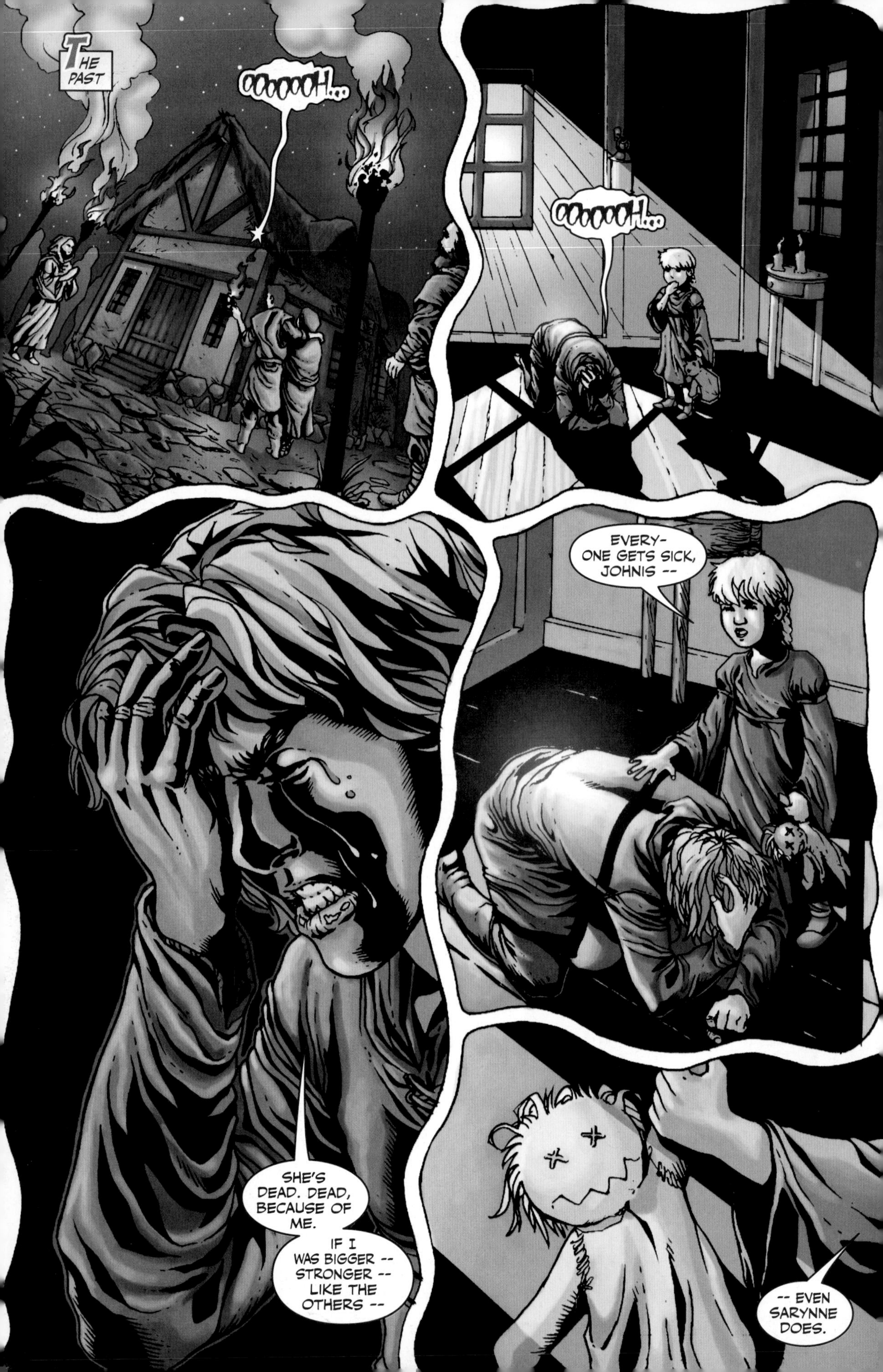
THE PAST
OOOOOOH...
OOOOOOH...
EVERY-ONE GETS SICK, JOHNIS --
SHE'S DEAD. DEAD, BECAUSE OF ME.
IF I WAS BIGGER -- STRONGER -- LIKE THE OTHERS --
-- EVEN SARYNNE DOES.

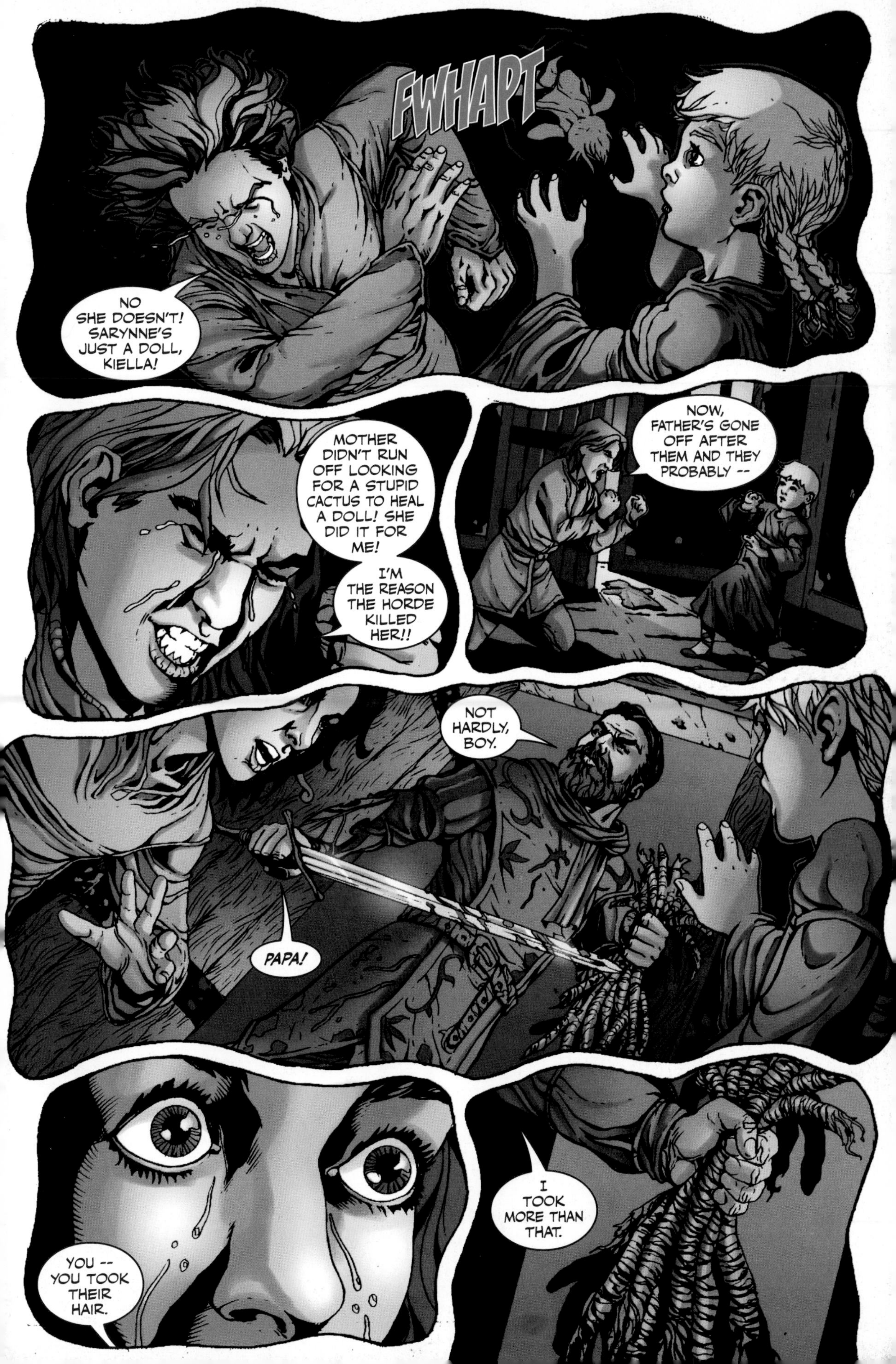
FWHAPT
NO SHE DOESN'T! SARYNNE'S JUST A DOLL, KIELLA!
MOTHER DIDN'T RUN OFF LOOKING FOR A STUPID CACTUS TO HEAL A DOLL! SHE DID IT FOR ME!
I'M THE REASON THE HORDE KILLED HER!!
NOW, FATHER'S GONE OFF AFTER THEM AND THEY PROBABLY --
NOT HARDLY, BOY.
PAPA!
YOU -- YOU TOOK THEIR HAIR.
I TOOK MORE THAN THAT.

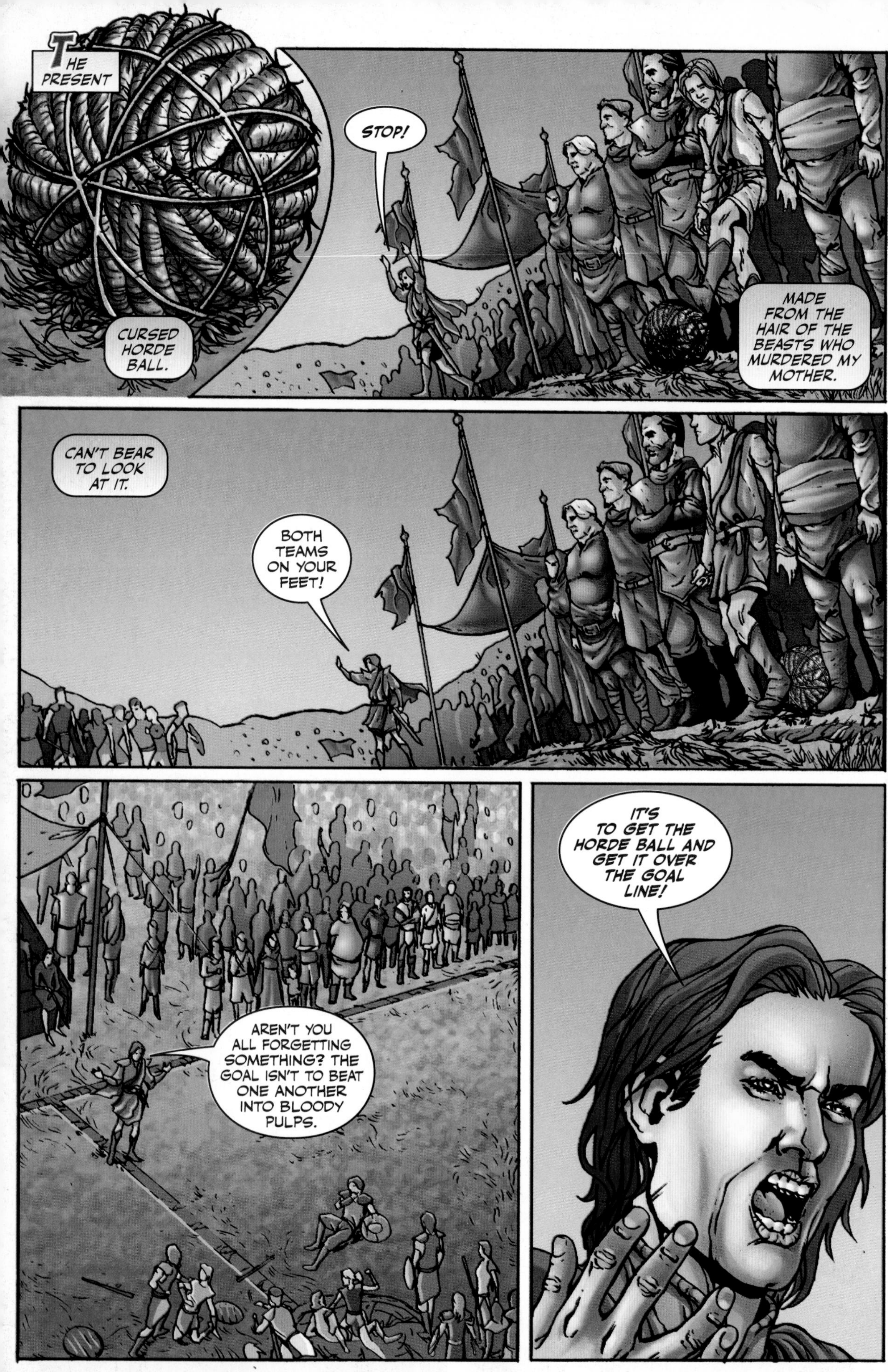
THE PRESENT
CURSED HORDE BALL.
STOP!
MADE FROM THE HAIR OF THE BEASTS WHO MURDERED MY MOTHER.
CAN'T BEAR TO LOOK AT IT.
BOTH TEAMS ON YOUR FEET!
AREN'T YOU ALL FORGETTING SOMETHING? THE GOAL ISN'T TO BEAT ONE ANOTHER INTO BLOODY PULPS.
IT'S TO GET THE HORDE BALL AND GET IT OVER THE GOAL LINE!

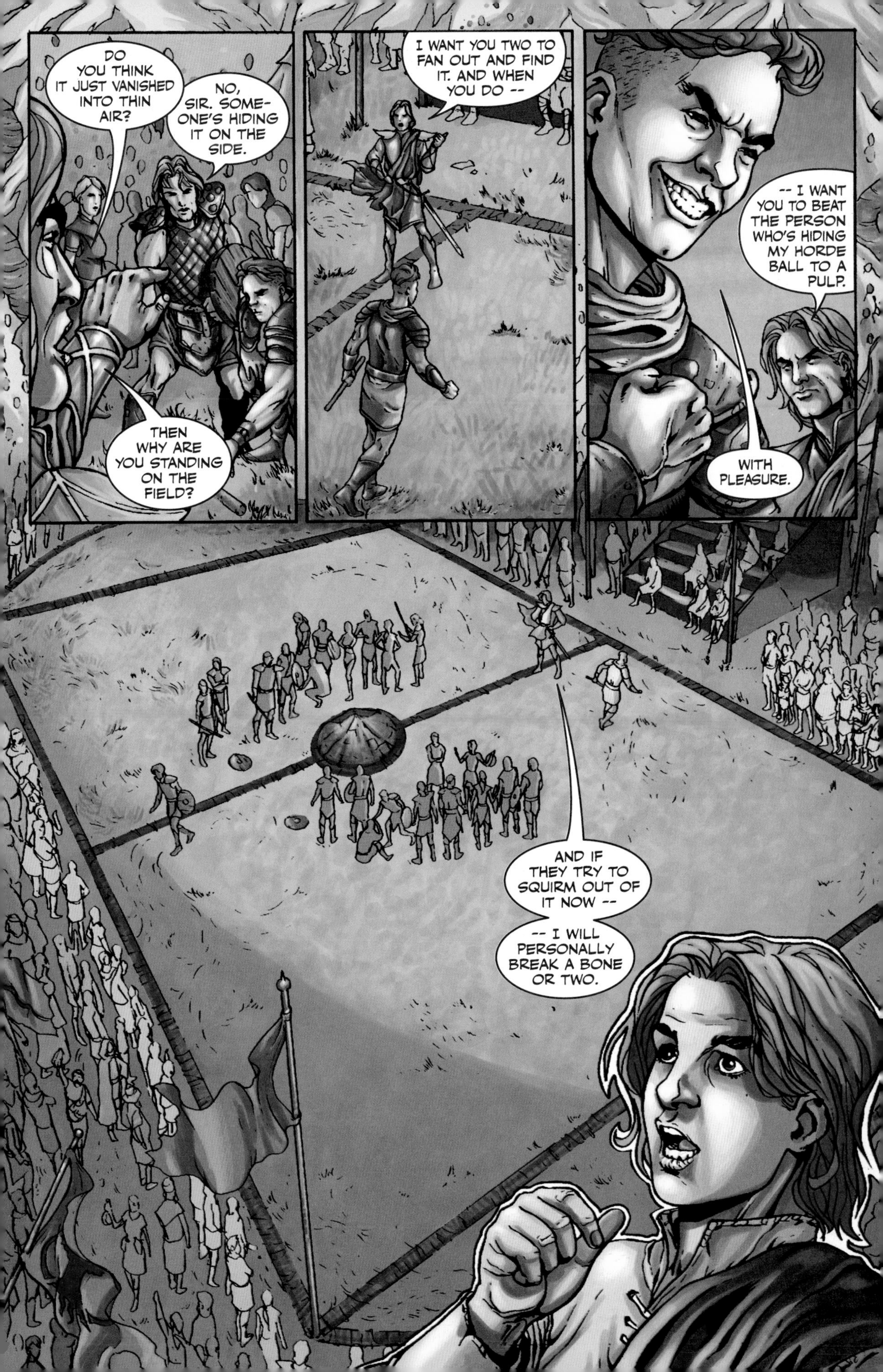
DO YOU THINK IT JUST VANISHED INTO THIN AIR?
NO, SIR. SOME-ONE'S HIDING IT ON THE SIDE.
THEN WHY ARE YOU STANDING ON THE FIELD?
I WANT YOU TWO TO FAN OUT AND FIND IT. AND WHEN YOU DO --
-- I WANT YOU TO BEAT THE PERSON WHO'S HIDING MY HORDE BALL TO A PULP.
WITH PLEASURE.
AND IF THEY TRY TO SQUIRM OUT OF IT NOW --
-- I WILL PERSONALLY BREAK A BONE OR TWO.

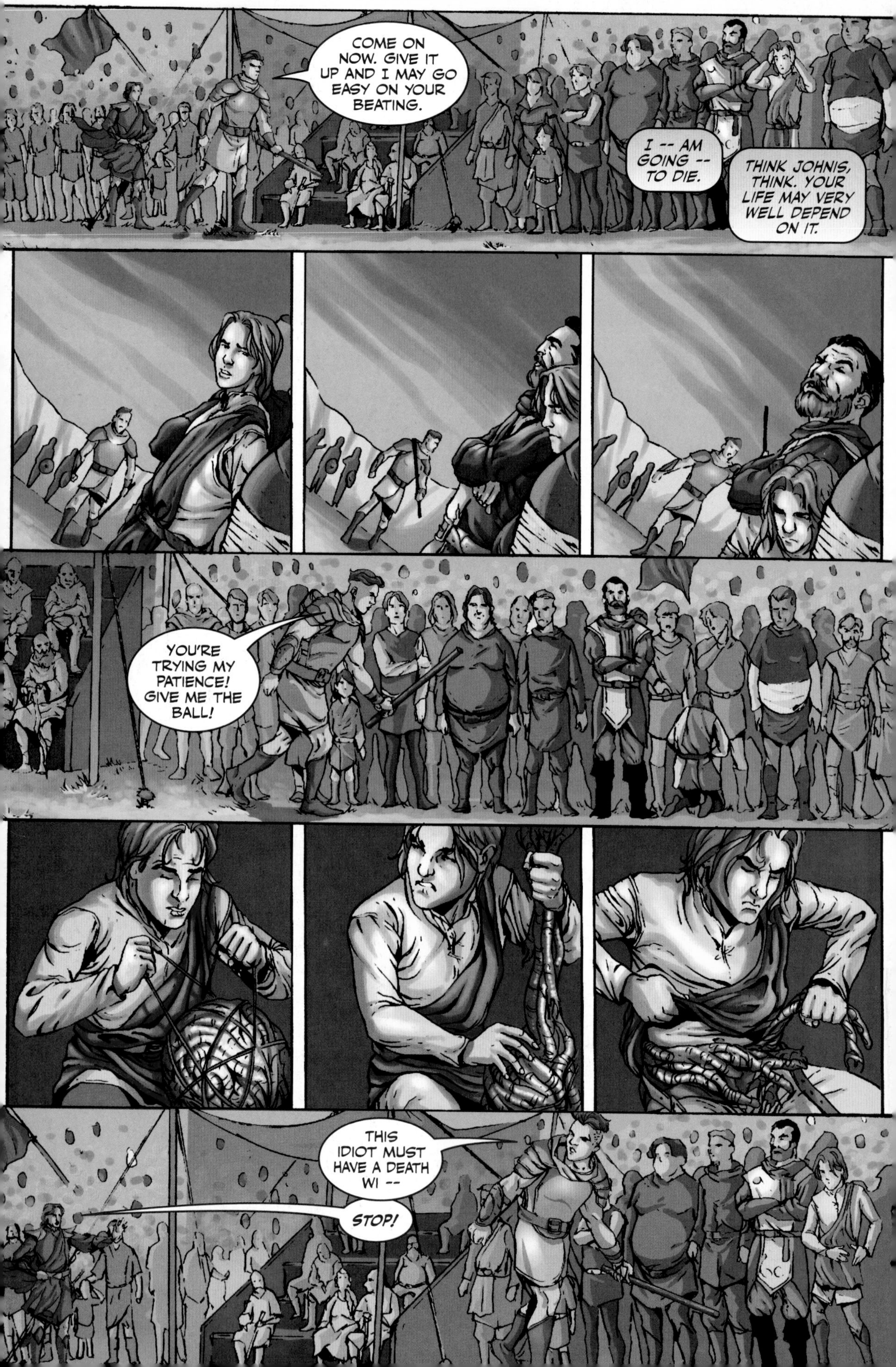
COME ON NOW. GIVE IT UP AND I MAY GO EASY ON YOUR BEATING.
I -- AM GOING -- TO DIE.
THINK JOHNIS, THINK. YOUR LIFE MAY VERY WELL DEPEND ON IT.
YOU'RE TRYING MY PATIENCE! GIVE ME THE BALL!
THIS IDIOT MUST HAVE A DEATH WI --
STOP!

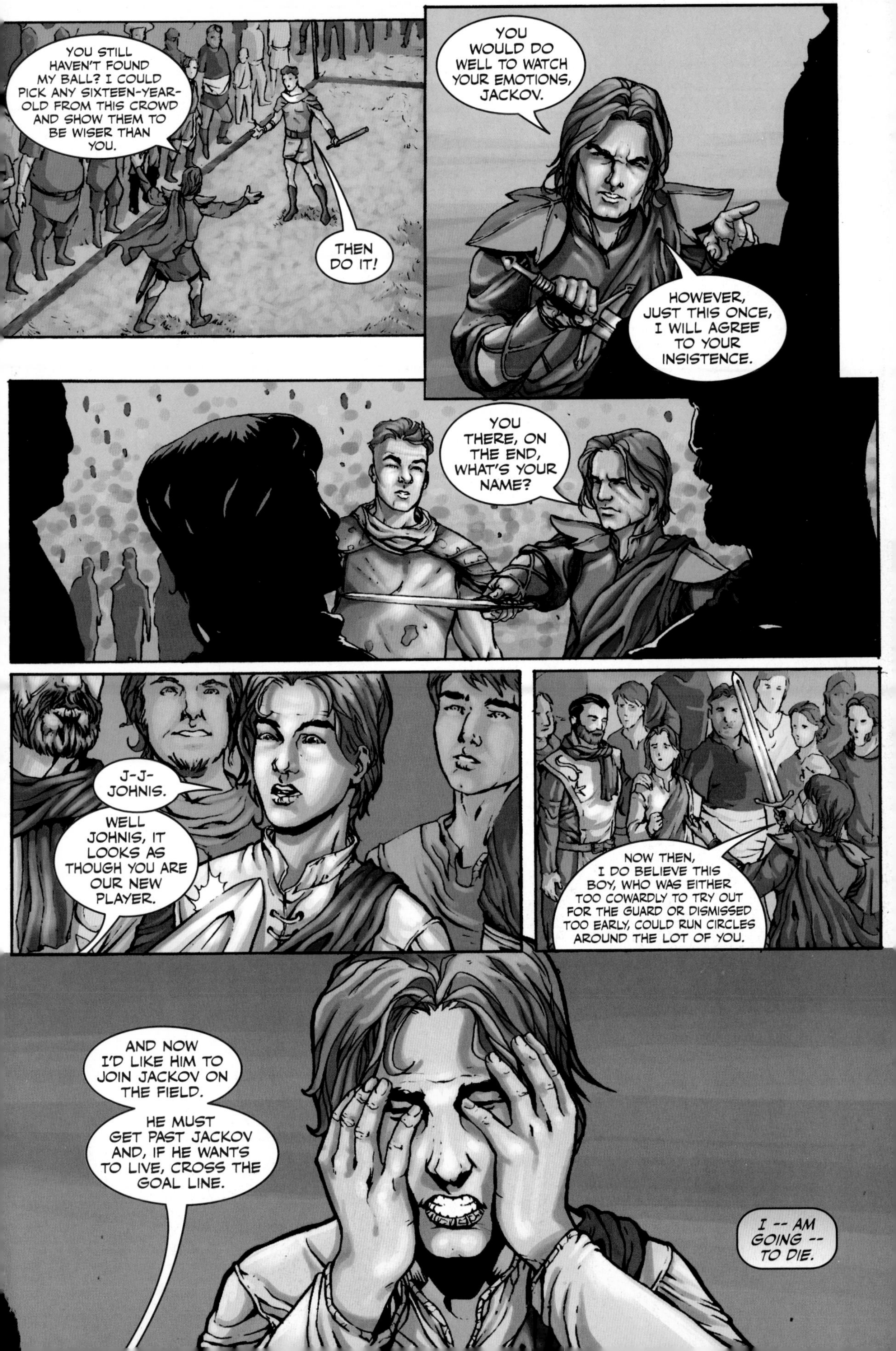
YOU STILL HAVEN'T FOUND MY BALL? I COULD PICK ANY SIXTEEN-YEAR-OLD FROM THIS CROWD AND SHOW THEM TO BE WISER THAN YOU.
THEN DO IT!
YOU WOULD DO WELL TO WATCH YOUR EMOTIONS, JACKOV.
HOWEVER, JUST THIS ONCE, I WILL AGREE TO YOUR INSISTENCE.
YOU THERE, ON THE END, WHAT'S YOUR NAME?
J-J-JOHNIS.
WELL JOHNIS, IT LOOKS AS THOUGH YOU ARE OUR NEW PLAYER.
NOW THEN, I DO BELIEVE THIS BOY, WHO WAS EITHER TOO COWARDLY TO TRY OUT FOR THE GUARD OR DISMISSED TOO EARLY, COULD RUN CIRCLES AROUND THE LOT OF YOU.
AND NOW I'D LIKE HIM TO JOIN JACKOV ON THE FIELD.
HE MUST GET PAST JACKOV AND, IF HE WANTS TO LIVE, CROSS THE GOAL LINE.
I -- AM GOING -- TO DIE.

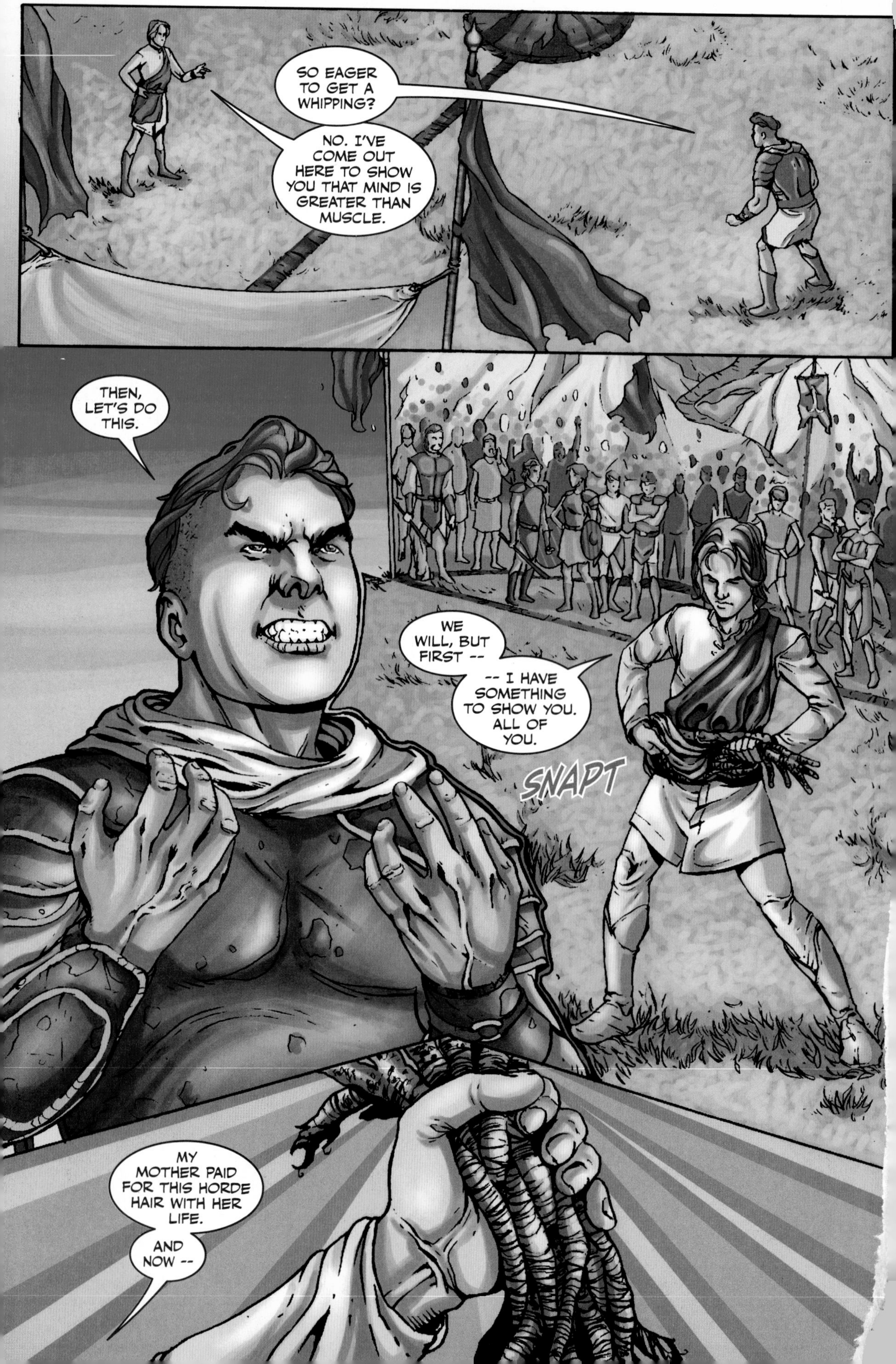
SO EAGER TO GET A WHIPPING?
NO. I'VE COME OUT HERE TO SHOW YOU THAT MIND IS GREATER THAN MUSCLE.
THEN, LET'S DO THIS.
WE WILL, BUT FIRST --
-- I HAVE SOMETHING TO SHOW YOU. ALL OF YOU.
SNAPT
MY MOTHER PAID FOR THIS HORDE HAIR WITH HER LIFE.
AND NOW --

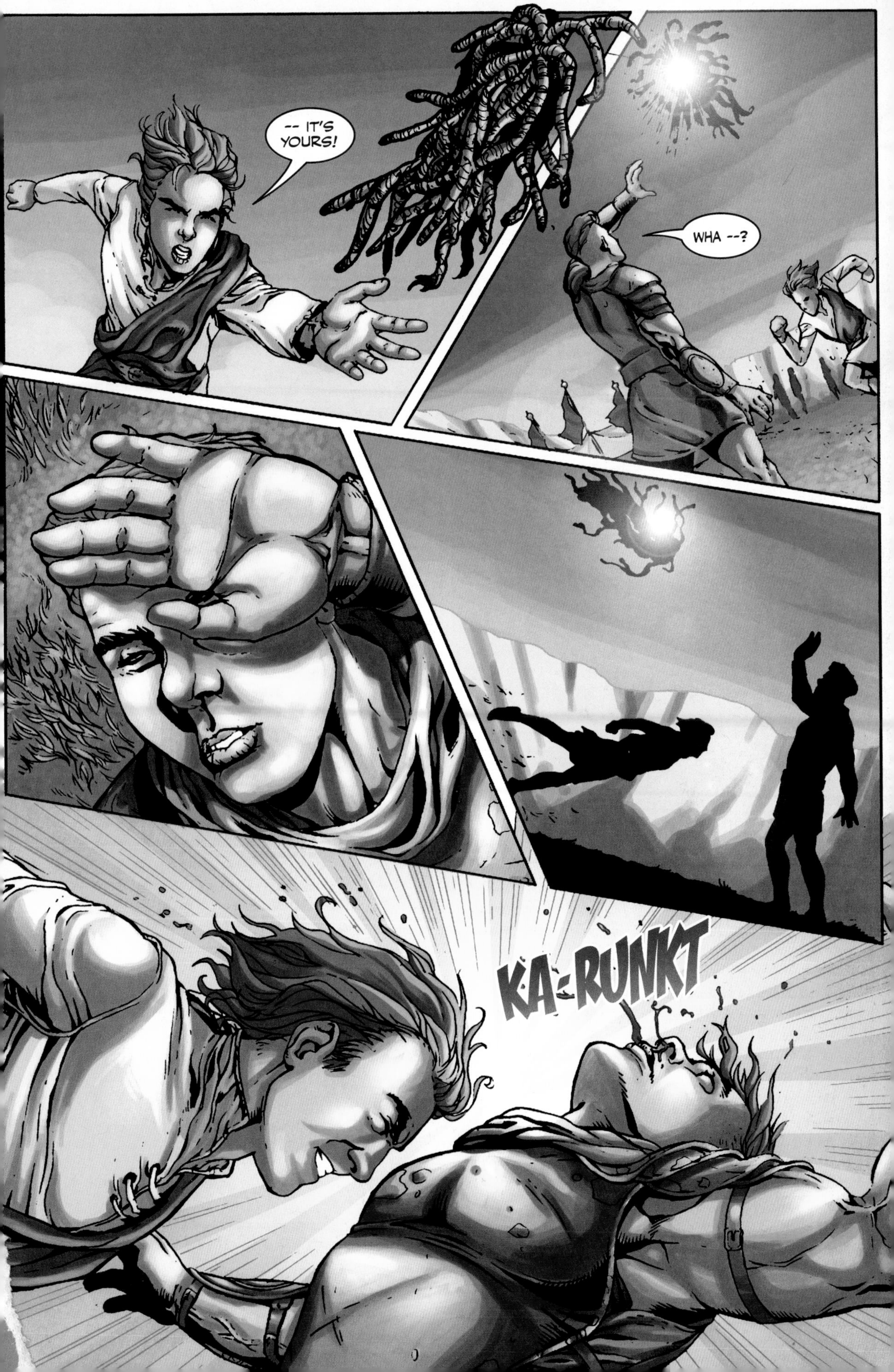
-- IT'S YOURS!
WHA --?
KA-RUNKT

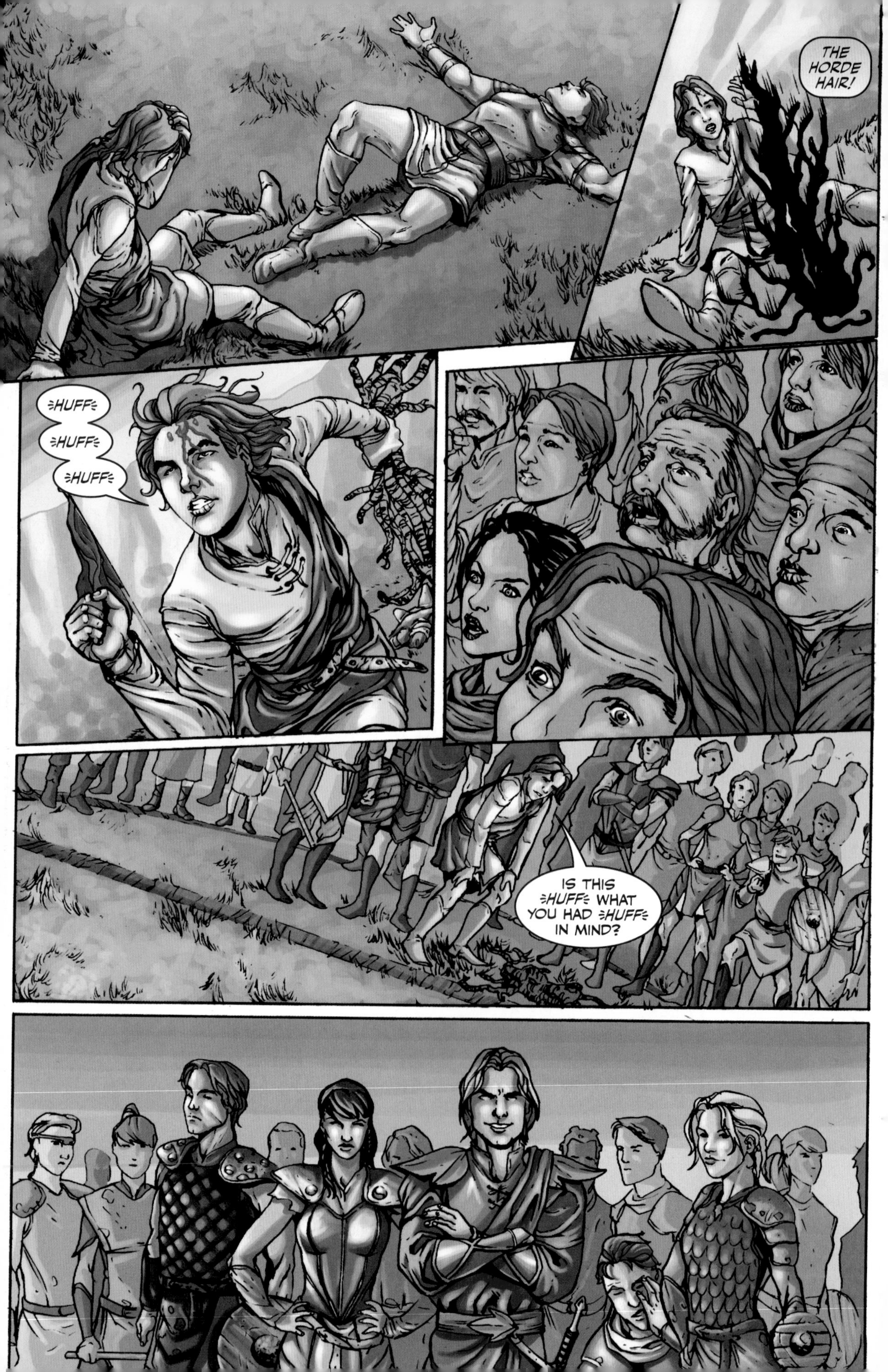
THE HORDE HAIR!
=HUFF=
=HUFF=
=HUFF=
IS THIS =HUFF= WHAT YOU HAD =HUFF= IN MIND?

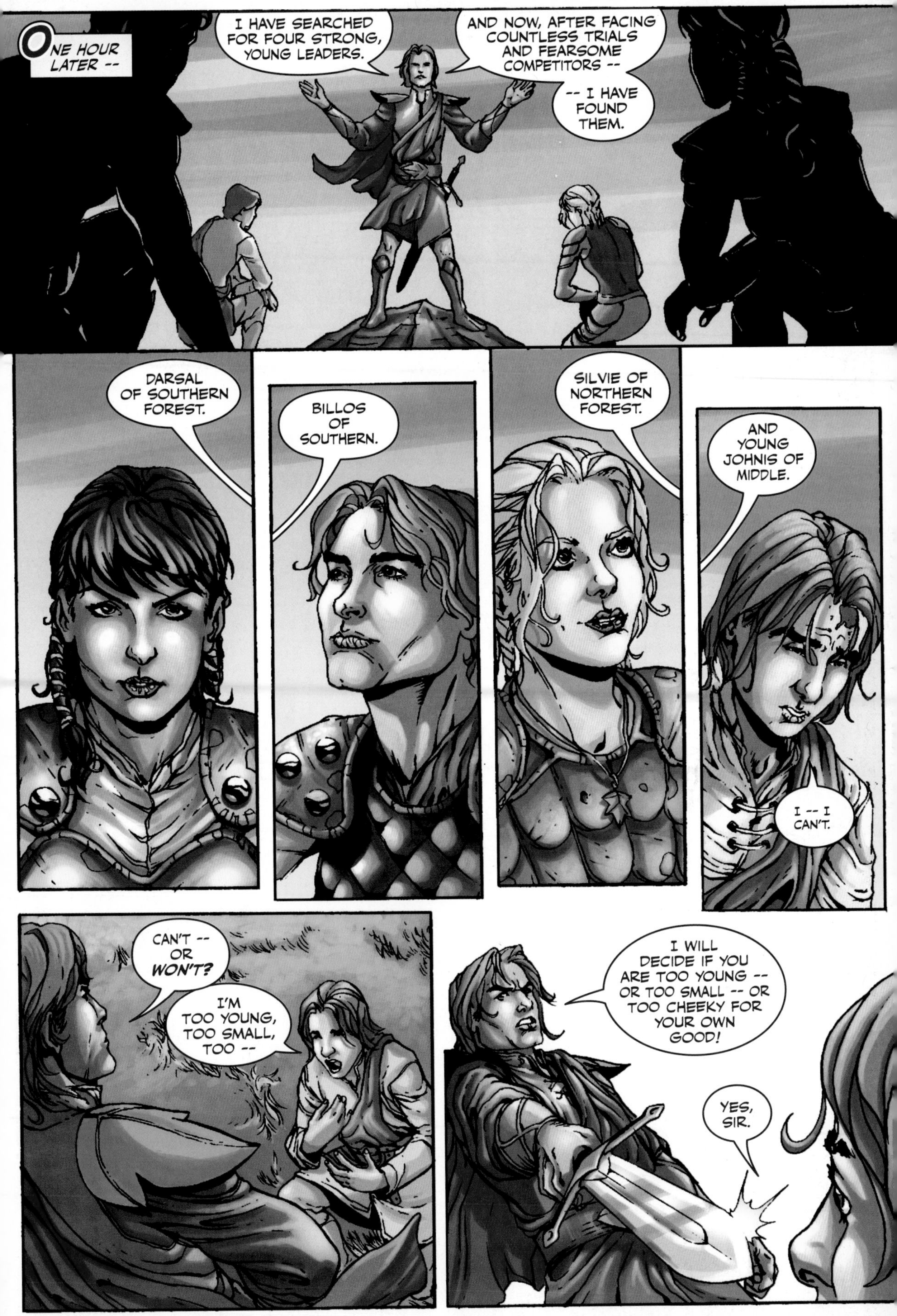
ONE HOUR LATER --
I HAVE SEARCHED FOR FOUR STRONG, YOUNG LEADERS.
AND NOW, AFTER FACING COUNTLESS TRIALS AND FEARSOME COMPETITORS --
-- I HAVE FOUND THEM.
DARSAL OF SOUTHERN FOREST.
BILLOS OF SOUTHERN.
SILVIE OF NORTHERN FOREST.
AND YOUNG JOHNIS OF MIDDLE.
I -- I CAN'T.
CAN'T -- OR *WON'T?*
I'M TOO YOUNG, TOO SMALL, TOO --
I WILL DECIDE IF YOU ARE TOO YOUNG -- OR TOO SMALL -- OR TOO CHEEKY FOR YOUR OWN GOOD!
YES, SIR.

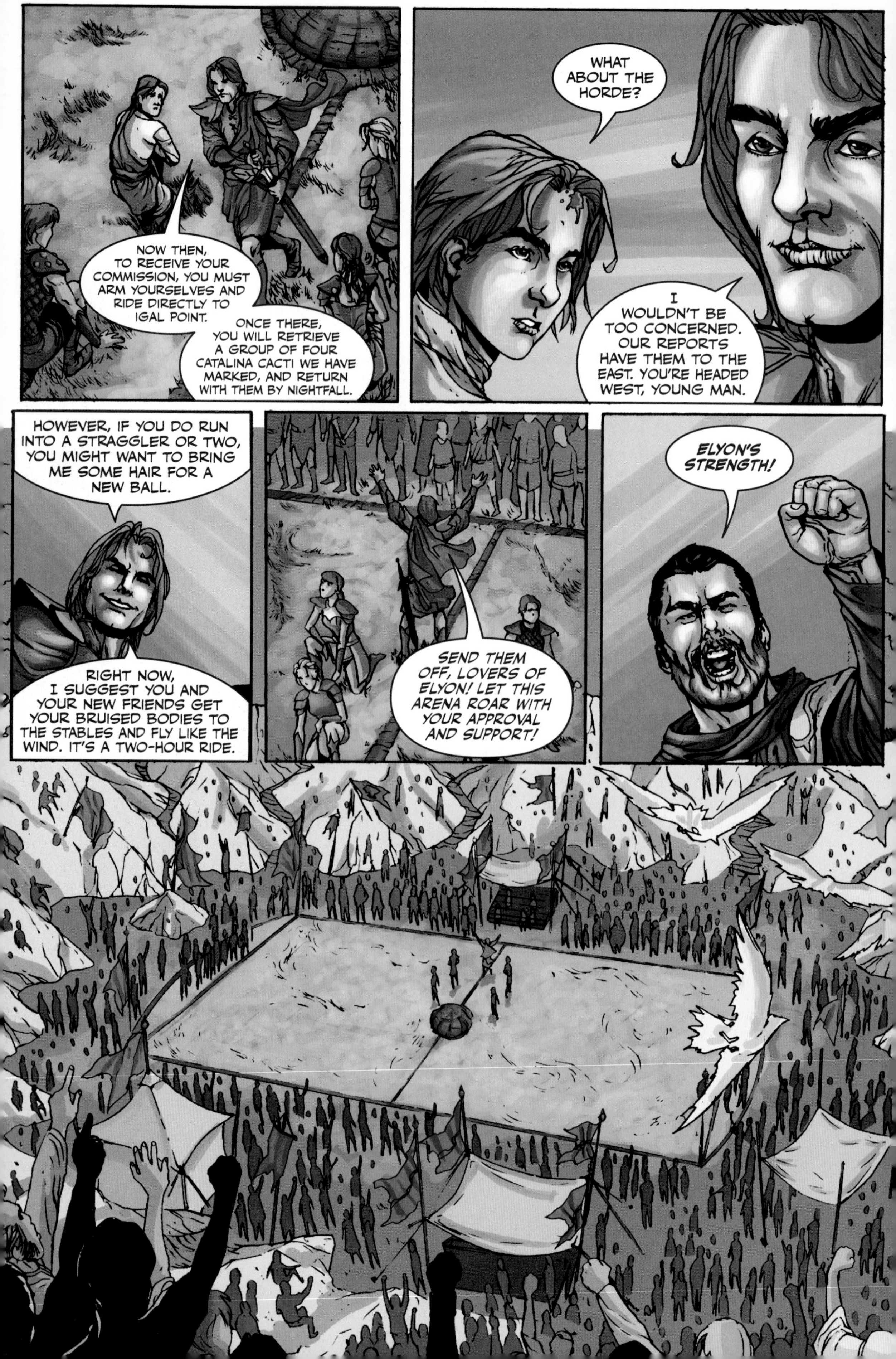
NOW THEN, TO RECEIVE YOUR COMMISSION, YOU MUST ARM YOURSELVES AND RIDE DIRECTLY TO IGAL POINT.
ONCE THERE, YOU WILL RETRIEVE A GROUP OF FOUR CATALINA CACTI WE HAVE MARKED, AND RETURN WITH THEM BY NIGHTFALL.
WHAT ABOUT THE HORDE?
I WOULDN'T BE TOO CONCERNED. OUR REPORTS HAVE THEM TO THE EAST. YOU'RE HEADED WEST, YOUNG MAN.
HOWEVER, IF YOU DO RUN INTO A STRAGGLER OR TWO, YOU MIGHT WANT TO BRING ME SOME HAIR FOR A NEW BALL.
RIGHT NOW, I SUGGEST YOU AND YOUR NEW FRIENDS GET YOUR BRUISED BODIES TO THE STABLES AND FLY LIKE THE WIND. IT'S A TWO-HOUR RIDE.
SEND THEM OFF, LOVERS OF ELYON! LET THIS ARENA ROAR WITH YOUR APPROVAL AND SUPPORT!
ELYON'S STRENGTH!

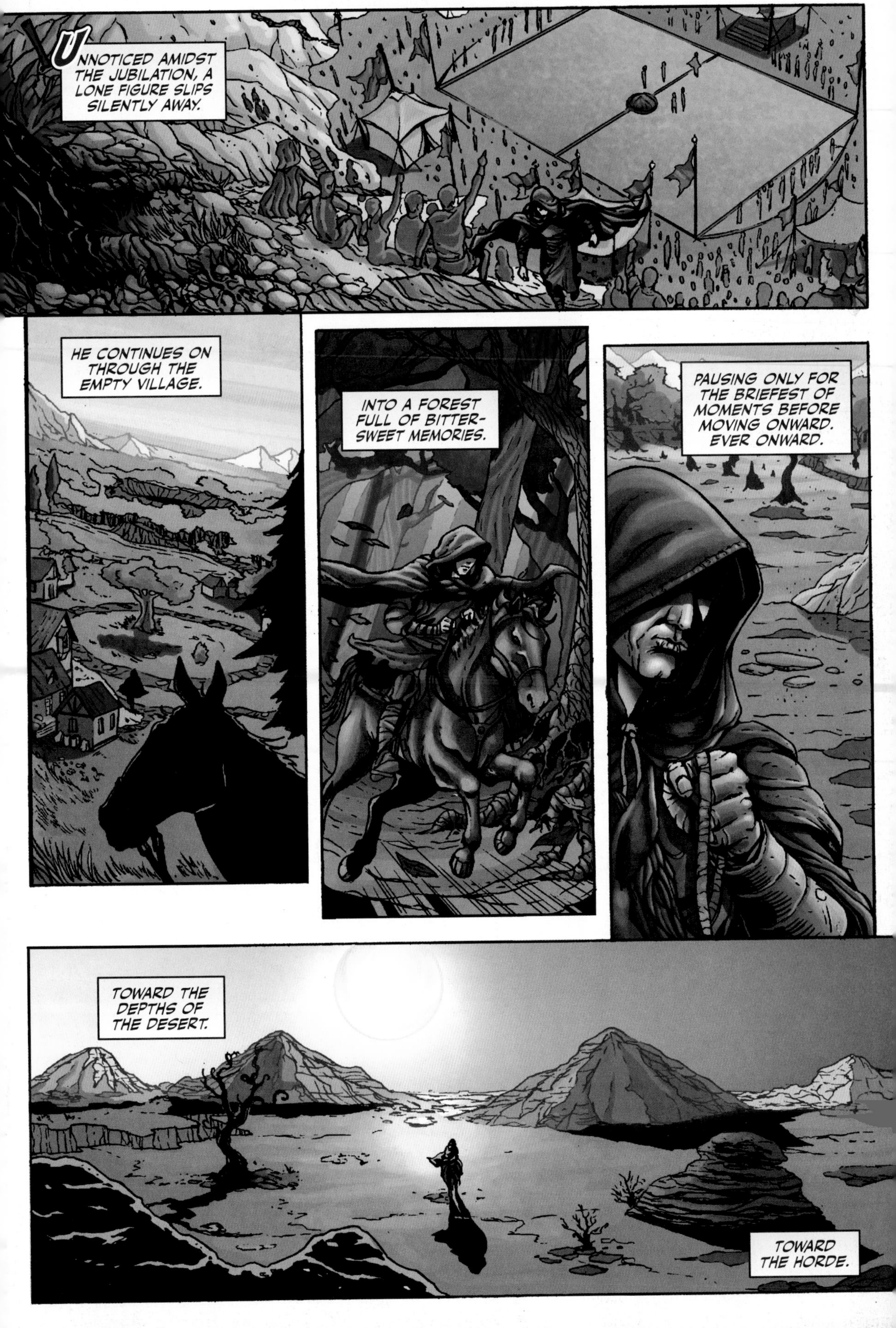
UNNOTICED AMIDST THE JUBILATION, A LONE FIGURE SLIPS SILENTLY AWAY.
HE CONTINUES ON THROUGH THE EMPTY VILLAGE.
INTO A FOREST FULL OF BITTER-SWEET MEMORIES.
PAUSING ONLY FOR THE BRIEFEST OF MOMENTS BEFORE MOVING ONWARD. EVER ONWARD.
TOWARD THE DEPTHS OF THE DESERT.
TOWARD THE HORDE.

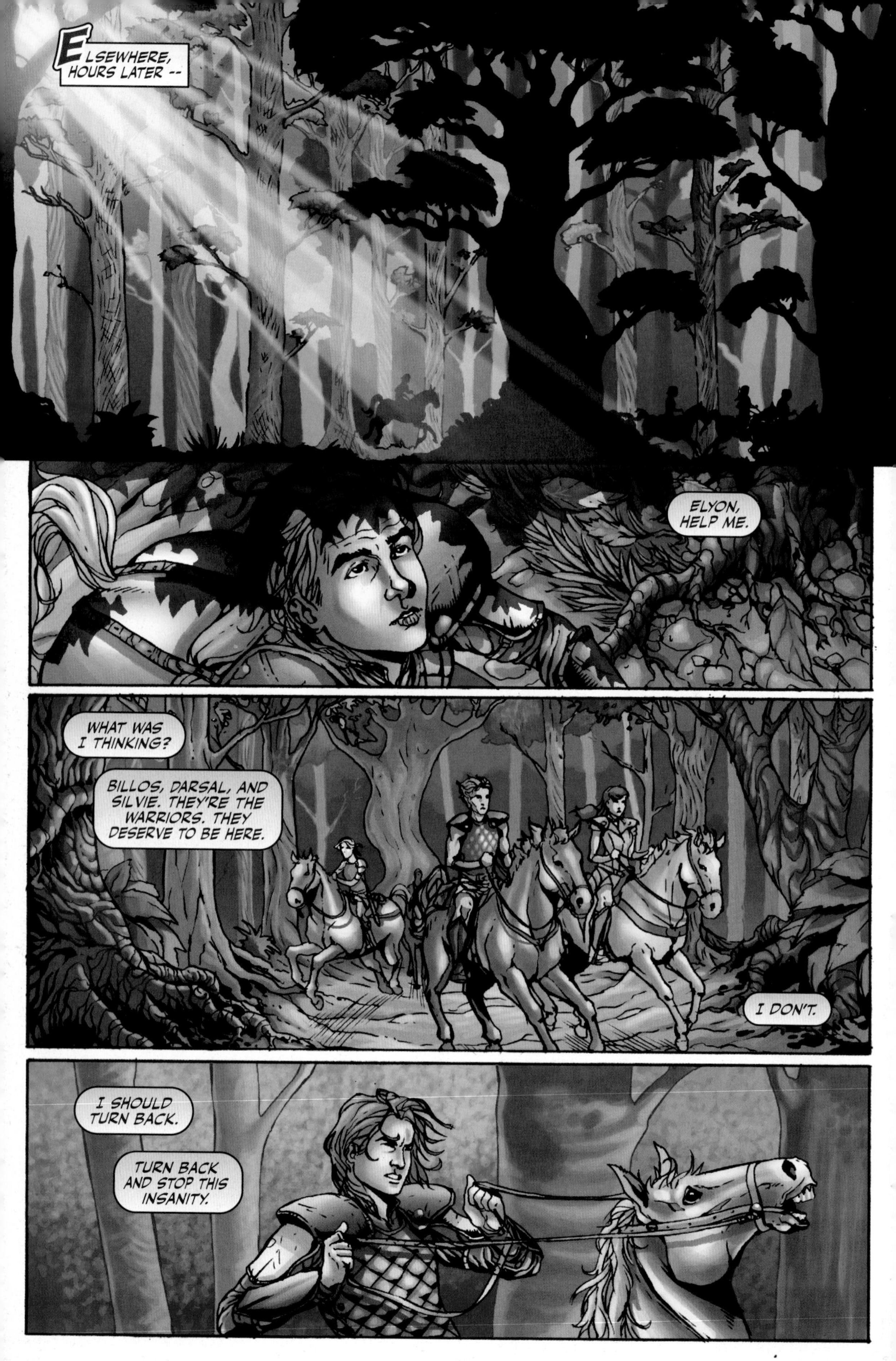
ELSEWHERE, HOURS LATER --
ELYON, HELP ME.
WHAT WAS I THINKING?
BILLOS, DARSAL, AND SILVIE. THEY'RE THE WARRIORS. THEY DESERVE TO BE HERE.
I DON'T.
I SHOULD TURN BACK.
TURN BACK AND STOP THIS INSANITY.

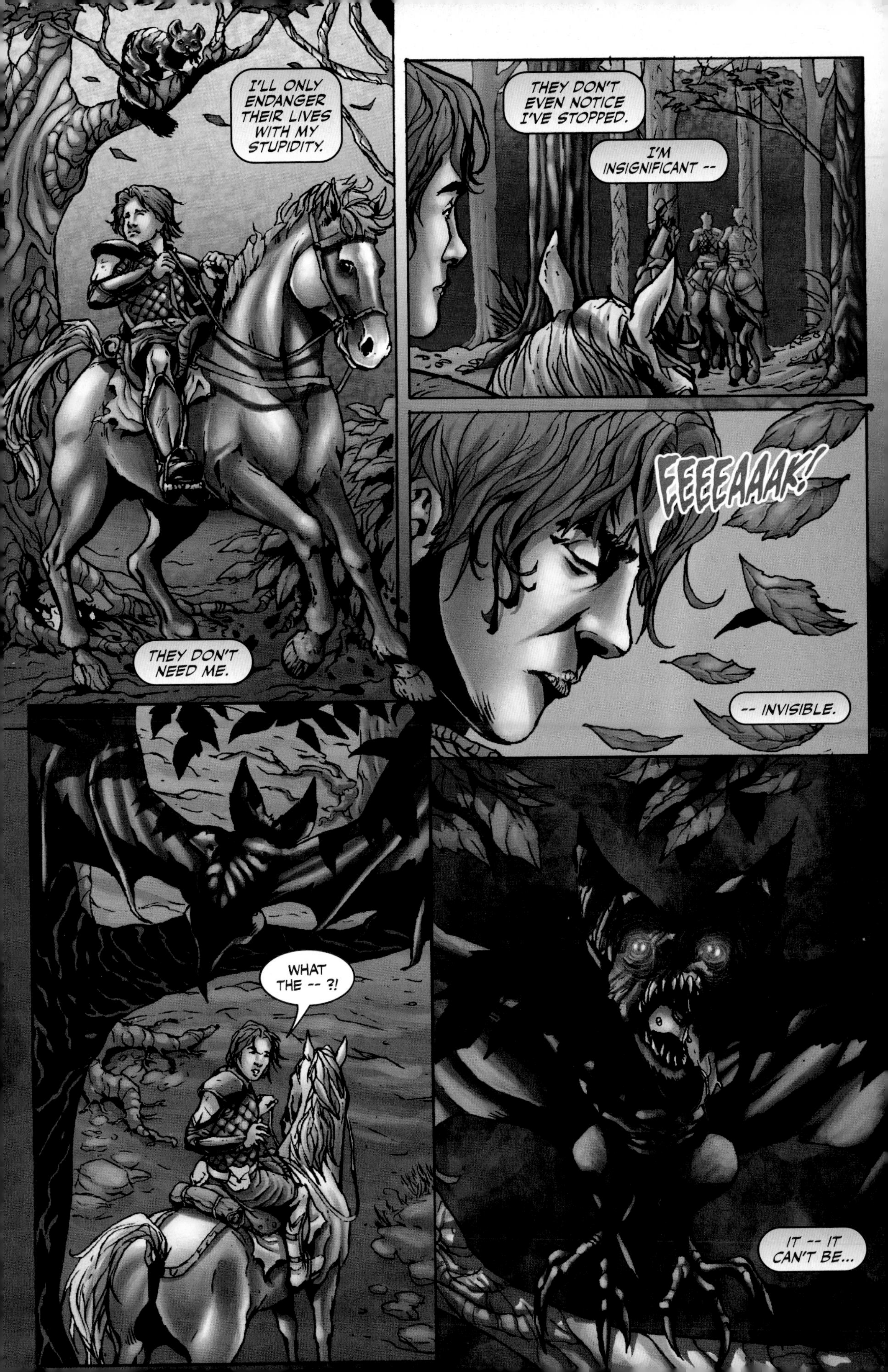
I'LL ONLY ENDANGER THEIR LIVES WITH MY STUPIDITY.
THEY DON'T NEED ME.
THEY DON'T EVEN NOTICE I'VE STOPPED.
I'M INSIGNIFICANT --
EEEEAAAK!
-- INVISIBLE.
WHAT THE -- ?!
IT -- IT CAN'T BE...

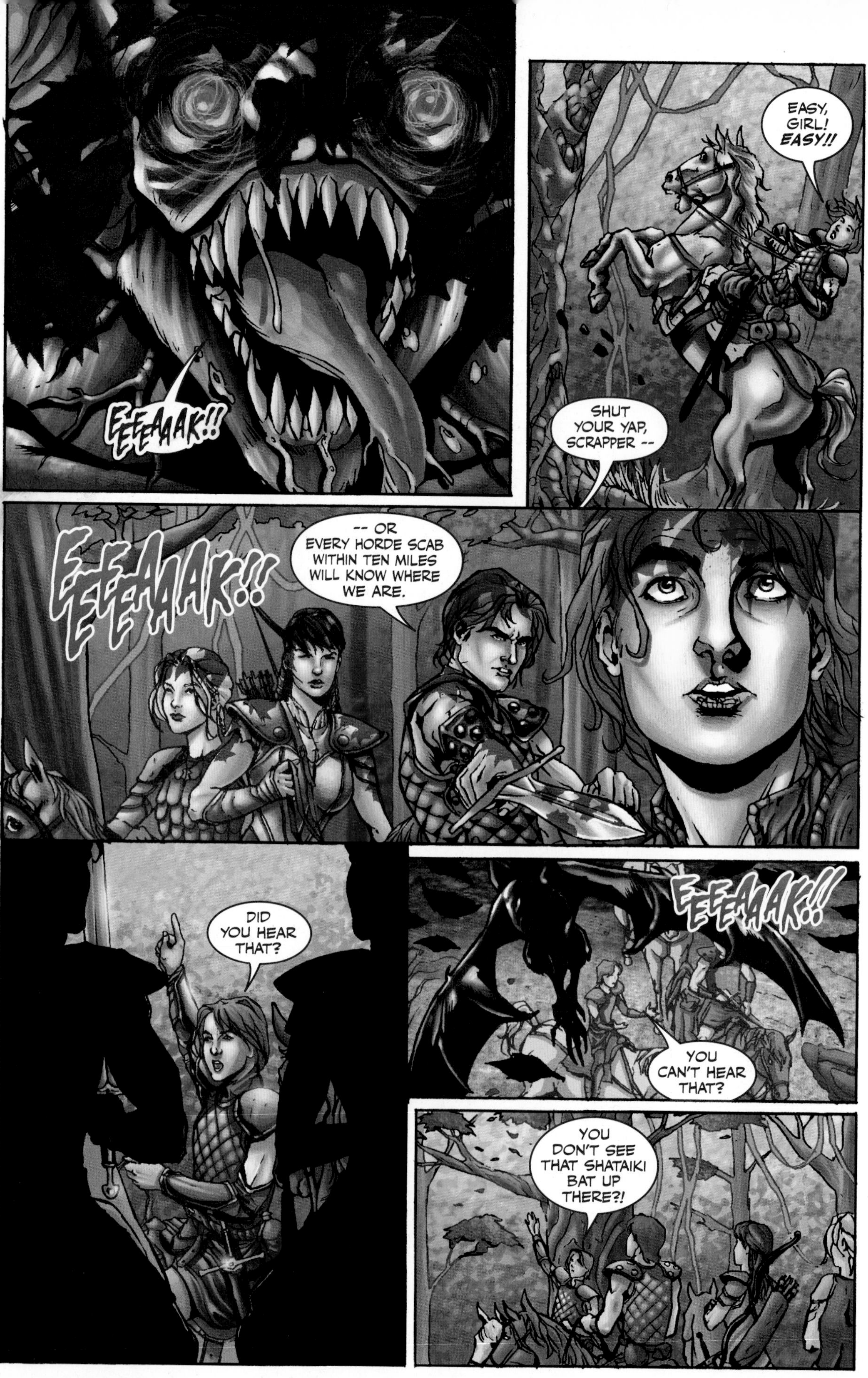
EEEEAAAK!!
EASY, GIRL! EASY!!
SHUT YOUR YAP, SCRAPPER --
EEEEAAAK!!
-- OR EVERY HORDE SCAB WITHIN TEN MILES WILL KNOW WHERE WE ARE.
DID YOU HEAR THAT?
EEEEAAAK!!
YOU CAN'T HEAR THAT?
YOU DON'T SEE THAT SHATAIKI BAT UP THERE?!

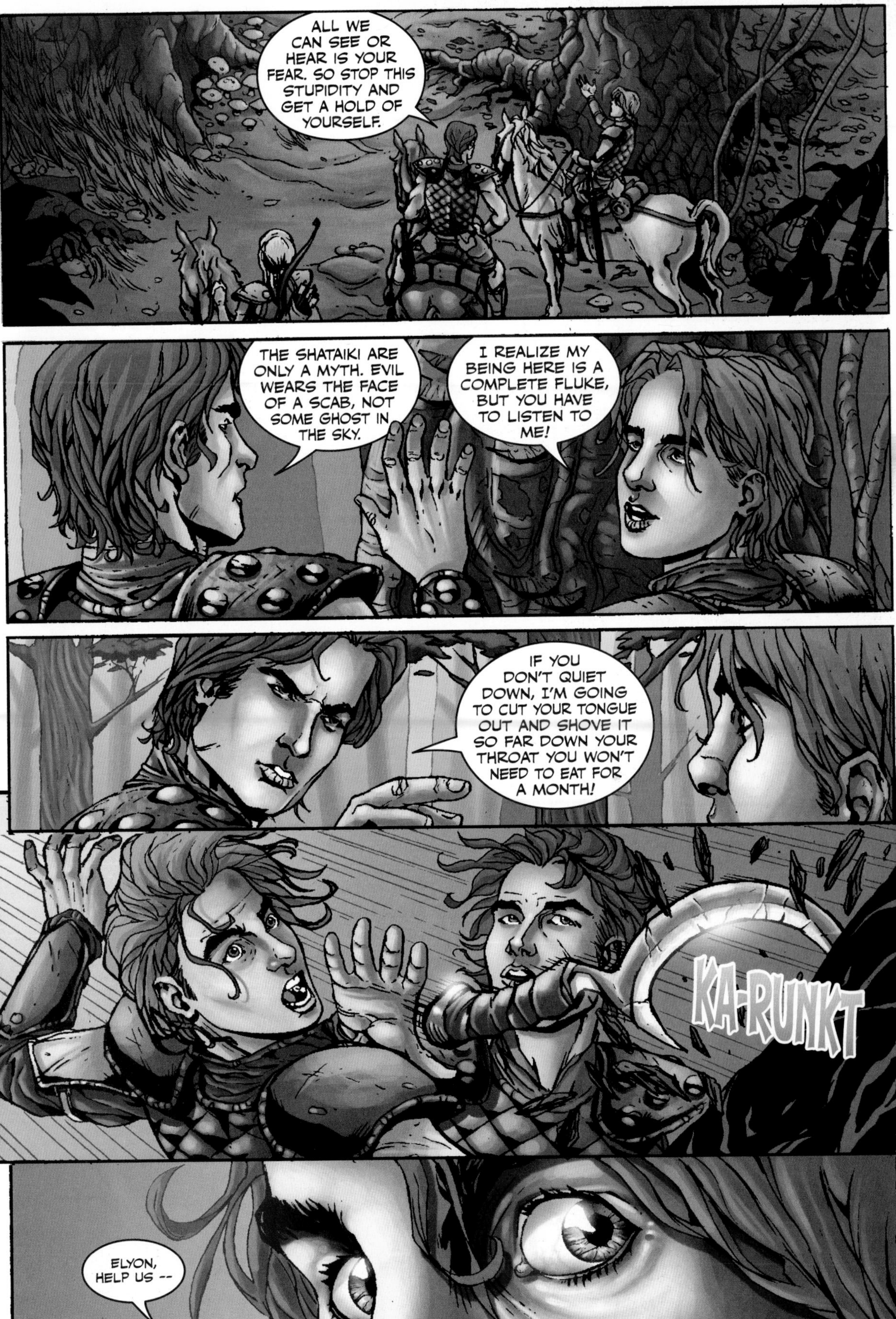
ALL WE CAN SEE OR HEAR IS YOUR FEAR. SO STOP THIS STUPIDITY AND GET A HOLD OF YOURSELF.
THE SHATAIKI ARE ONLY A MYTH. EVIL WEARS THE FACE OF A SCAB, NOT SOME GHOST IN THE SKY.
I REALIZE MY BEING HERE IS A COMPLETE FLUKE, BUT YOU HAVE TO LISTEN TO ME!
IF YOU DON'T QUIET DOWN, I'M GOING TO CUT YOUR TONGUE OUT AND SHOVE IT SO FAR DOWN YOUR THROAT YOU WON'T NEED TO EAT FOR A MONTH!
KA-RUNKT
ELYON, HELP US --

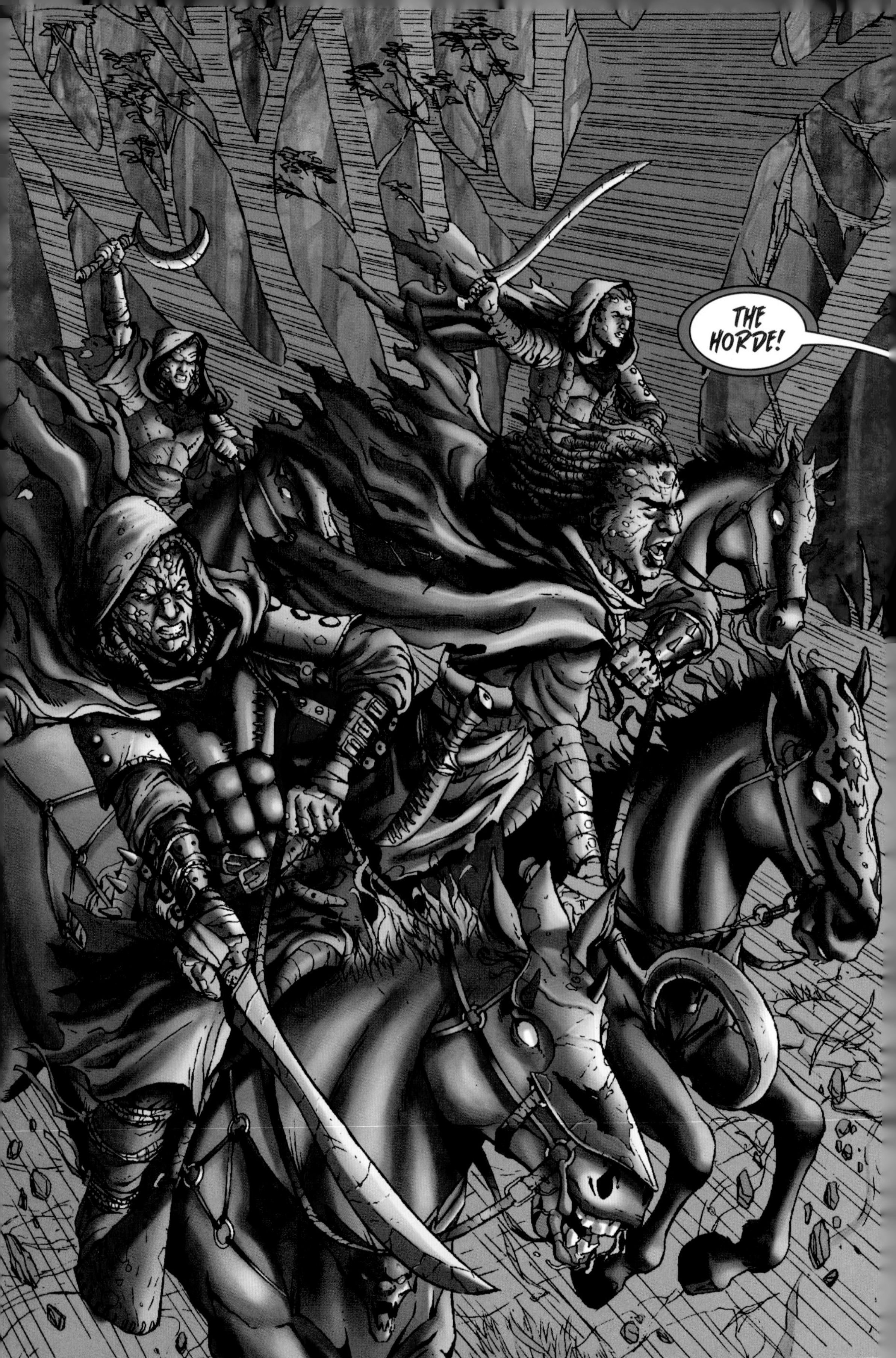
THE HORDE!

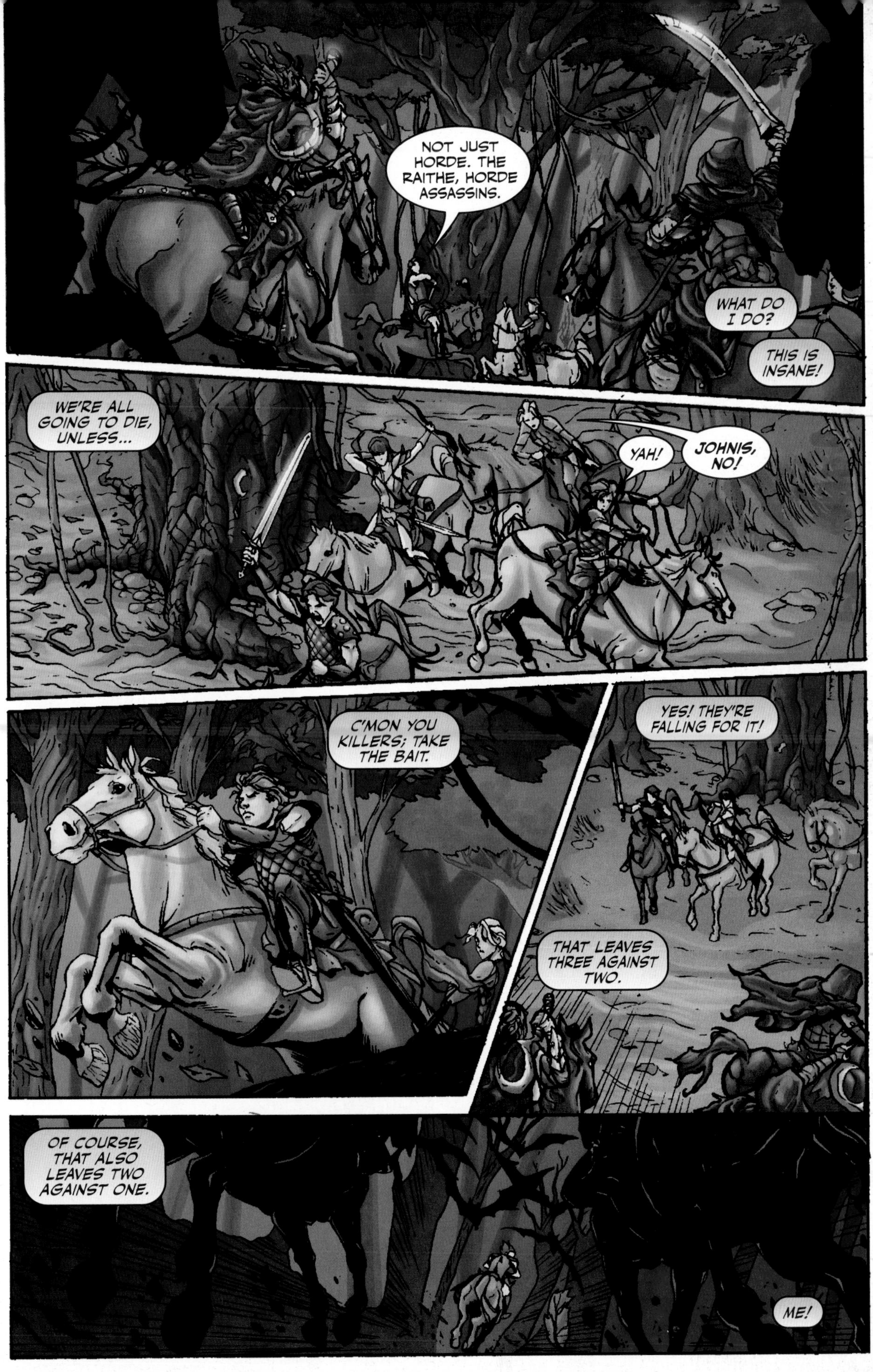
NOT JUST HORDE. THE RAITHE, HORDE ASSASSINS.
WHAT DO I DO?
THIS IS INSANE!
WE'RE ALL GOING TO DIE, UNLESS...
YAH!
JOHNIS, NO!
C'MON YOU KILLERS; TAKE THE BAIT.
YES! THEY'RE FALLING FOR IT!
THAT LEAVES THREE AGAINST TWO.
OF COURSE, THAT ALSO LEAVES TWO AGAINST ONE.
ME!

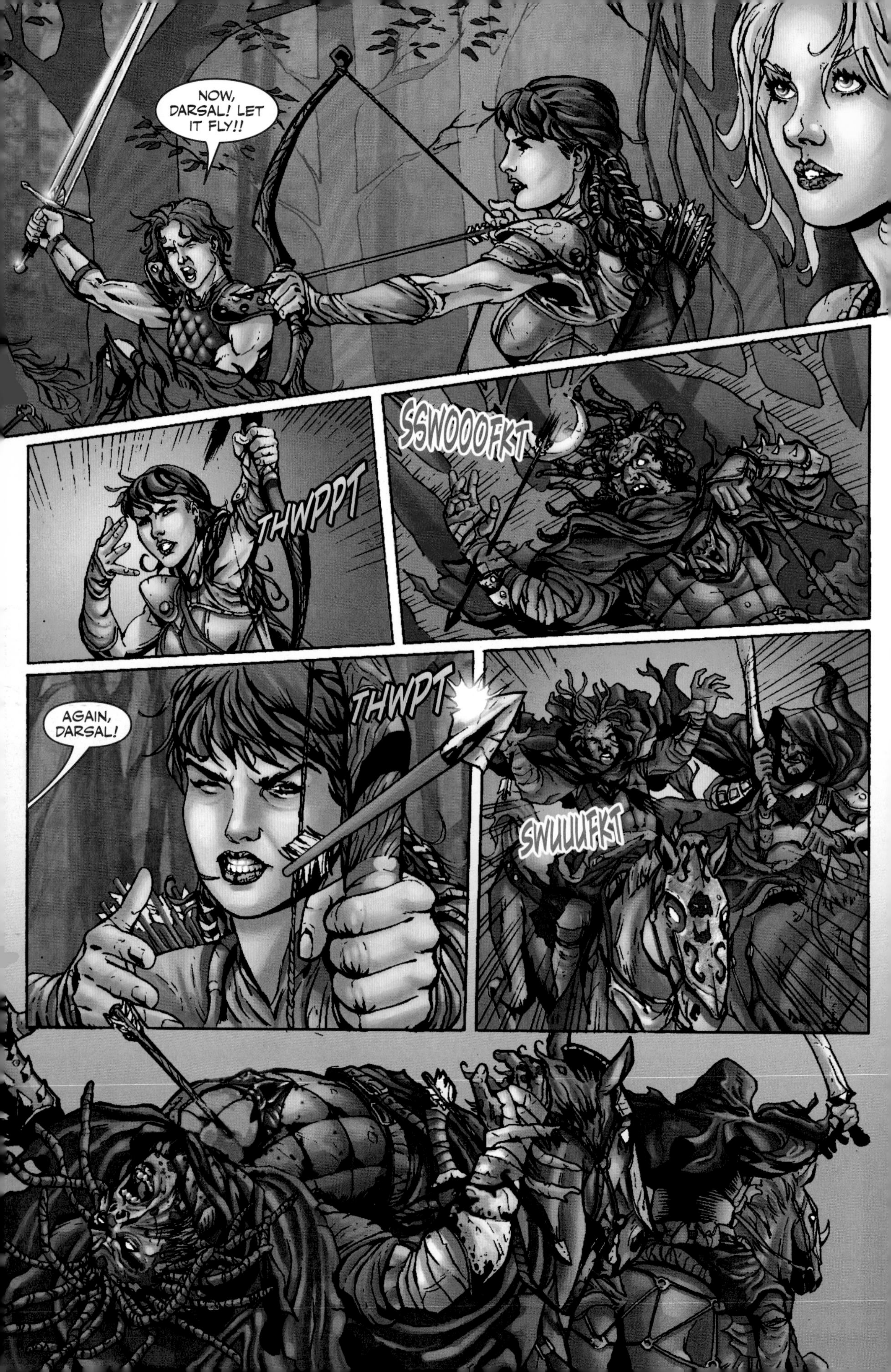
NOW, DARSAL! LET IT FLY!!
THWPPT
SSWOOOFKT
AGAIN, DARSAL!
THWPT
SWUUUFKT

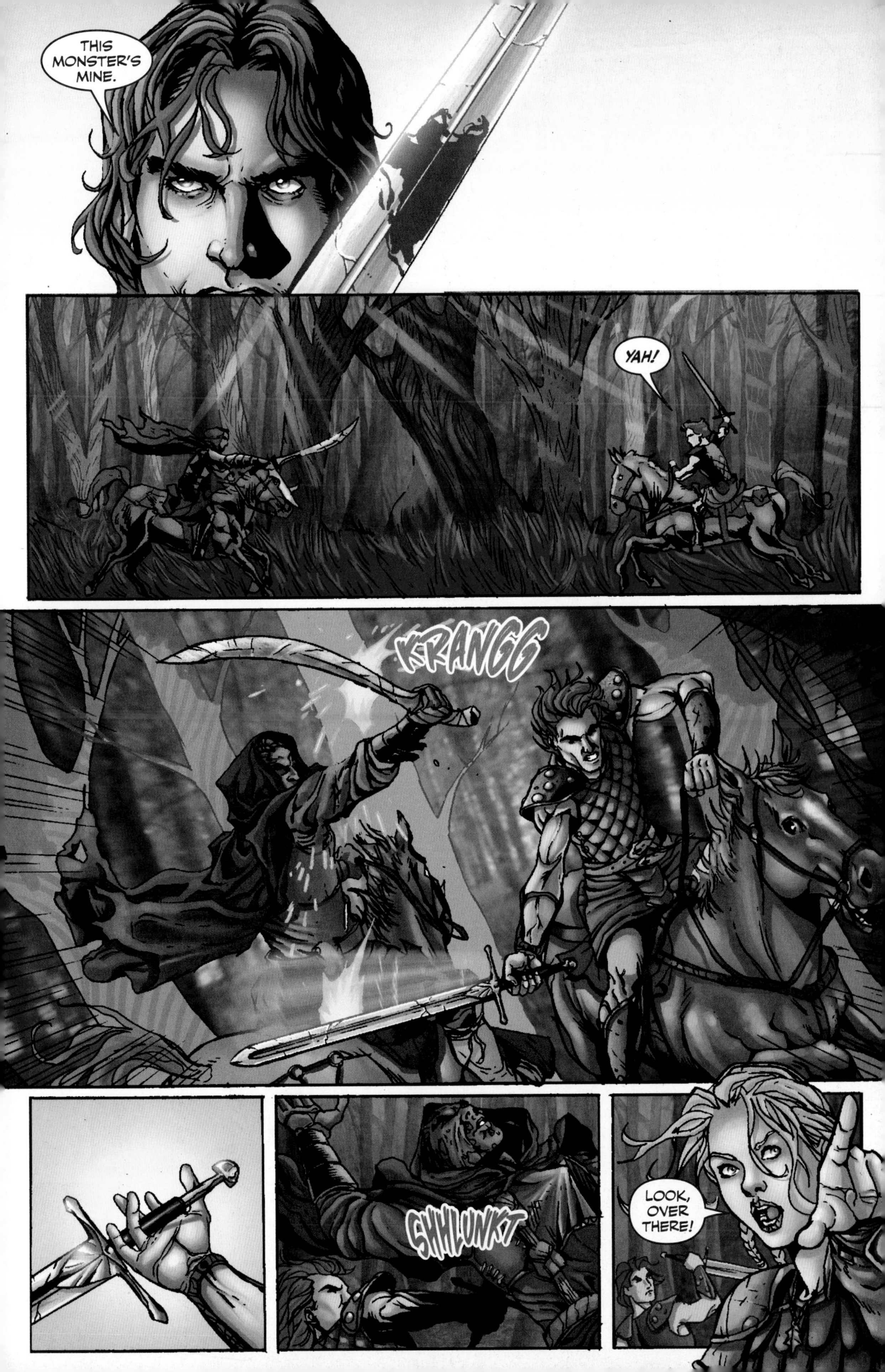
THIS MONSTER'S MINE.
YAH!
KRANGG
SHHLUNKT
LOOK, OVER THERE!

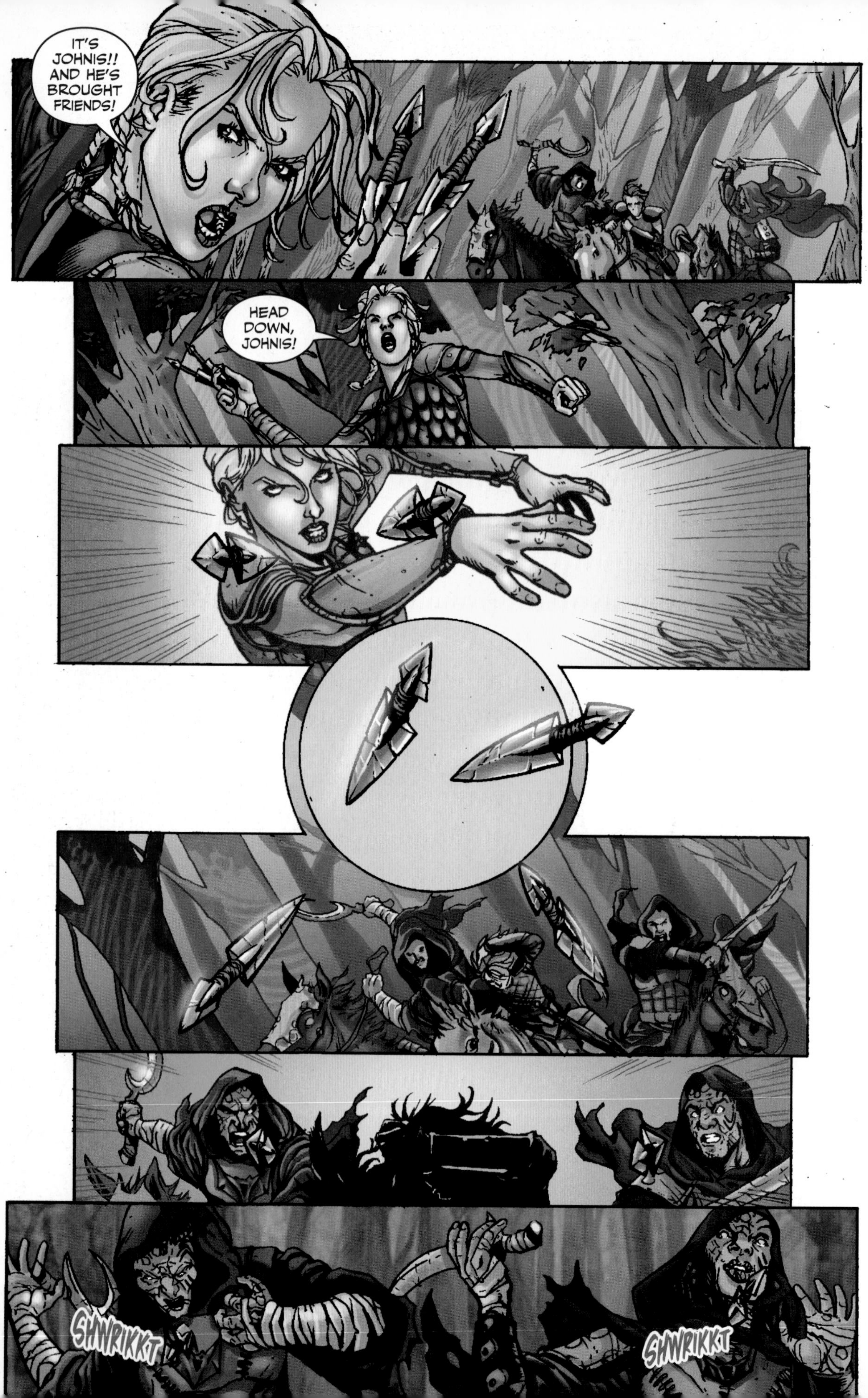
IT'S JOHNIS!! AND HE'S BROUGHT FRIENDS!
HEAD DOWN, JOHNIS!
SHWRIKKT
SHWRIKKT

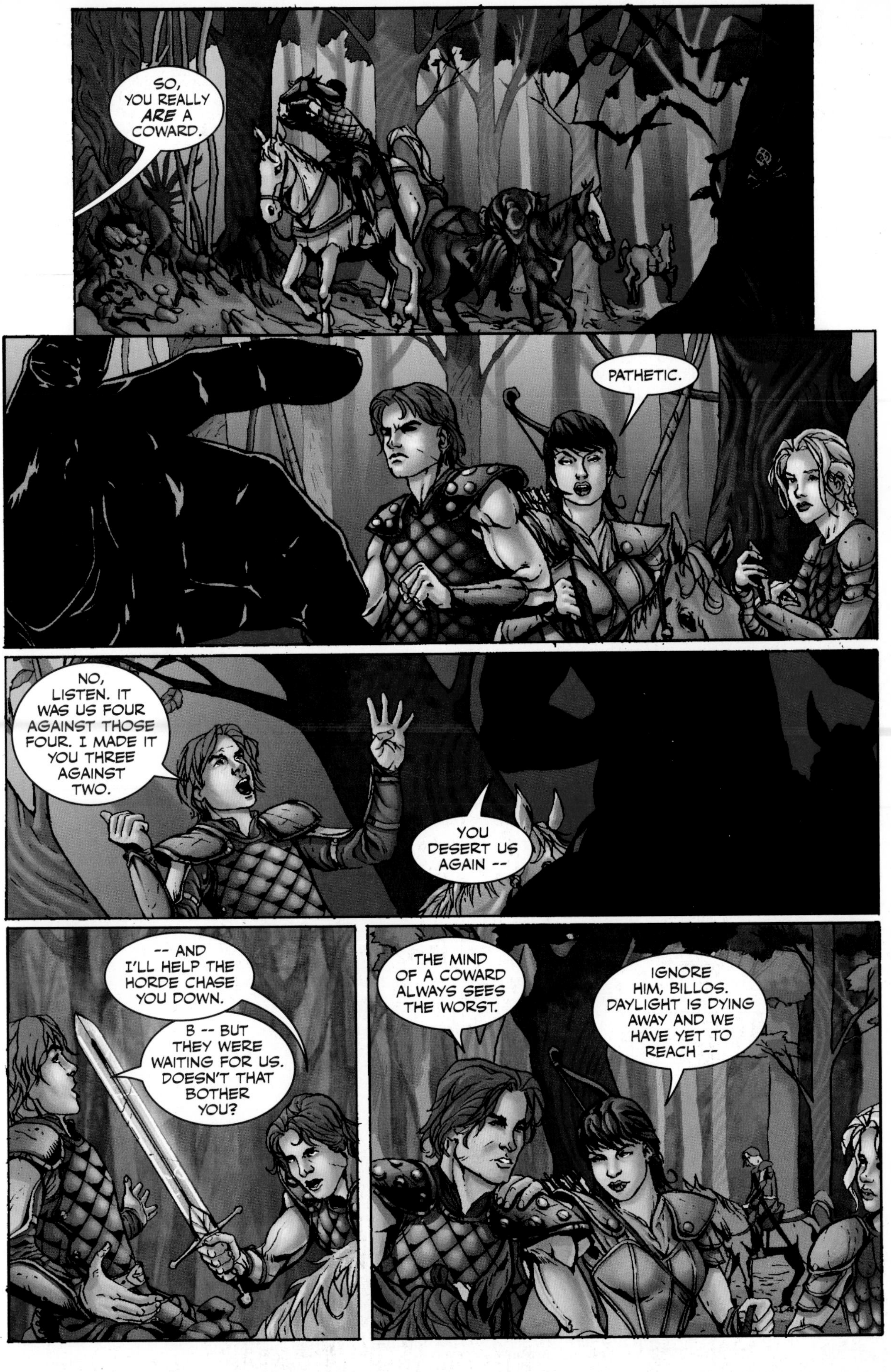
SO, YOU REALLY *ARE* A COWARD.
PATHETIC.
NO, LISTEN. IT WAS US FOUR AGAINST THOSE FOUR. I MADE IT YOU THREE AGAINST TWO.
YOU DESERT US AGAIN --
-- AND I'LL HELP THE HORDE CHASE YOU DOWN.
B -- BUT THEY WERE WAITING FOR US. DOESN'T THAT BOTHER YOU?
THE MIND OF A COWARD ALWAYS SEES THE WORST.
IGNORE HIM, BILLOS. DAYLIGHT IS DYING AWAY AND WE HAVE YET TO REACH --

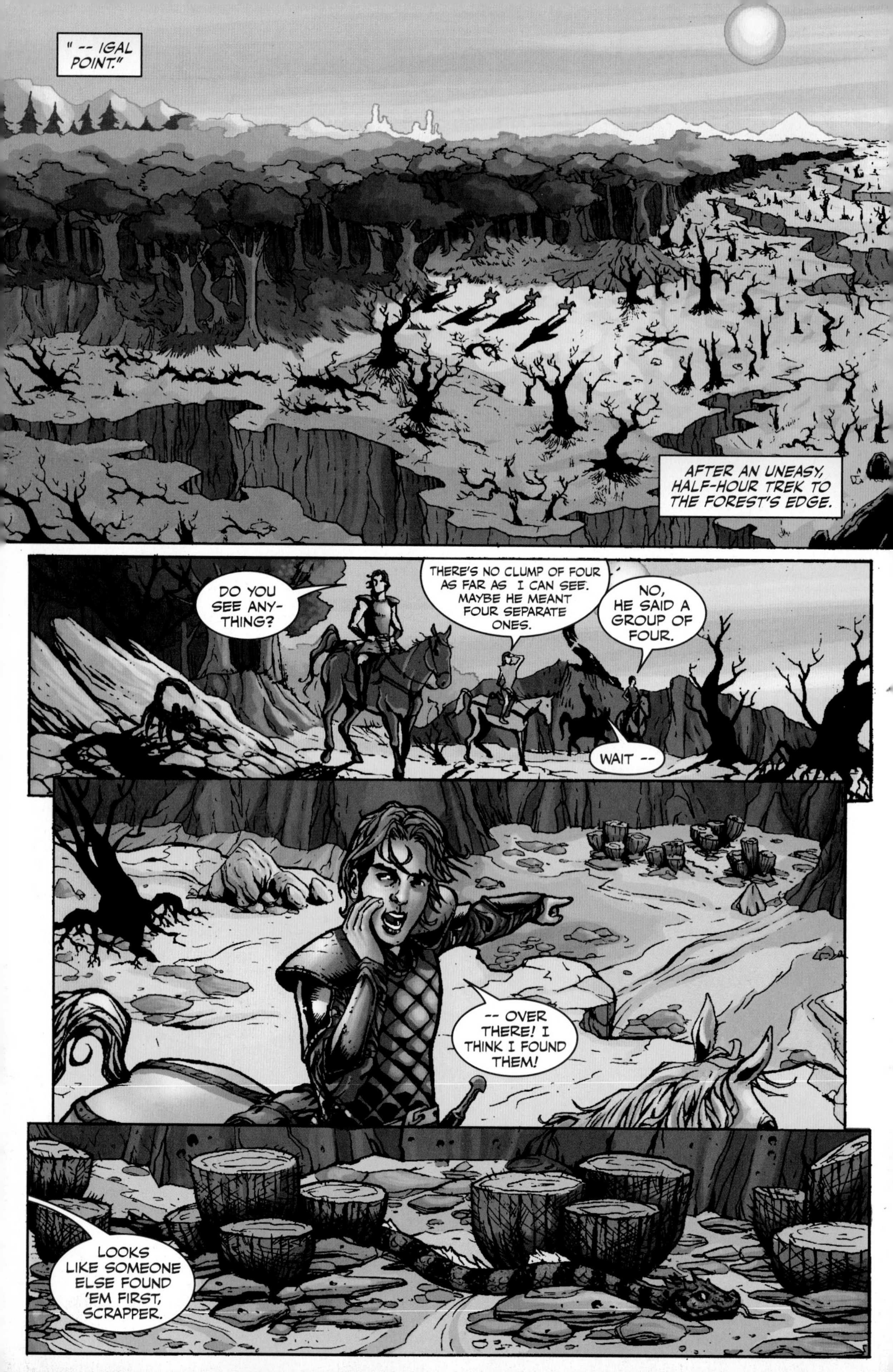
" -- IGAL POINT."
AFTER AN UNEASY, HALF-HOUR TREK TO THE FOREST'S EDGE.
DO YOU SEE ANY-THING?
THERE'S NO CLUMP OF FOUR AS FAR AS I CAN SEE. MAYBE HE MEANT FOUR SEPARATE ONES.
NO, HE SAID A GROUP OF FOUR.
WAIT --
-- OVER THERE! I THINK I FOUND THEM!
LOOKS LIKE SOMEONE ELSE FOUND 'EM FIRST, SCRAPPER.

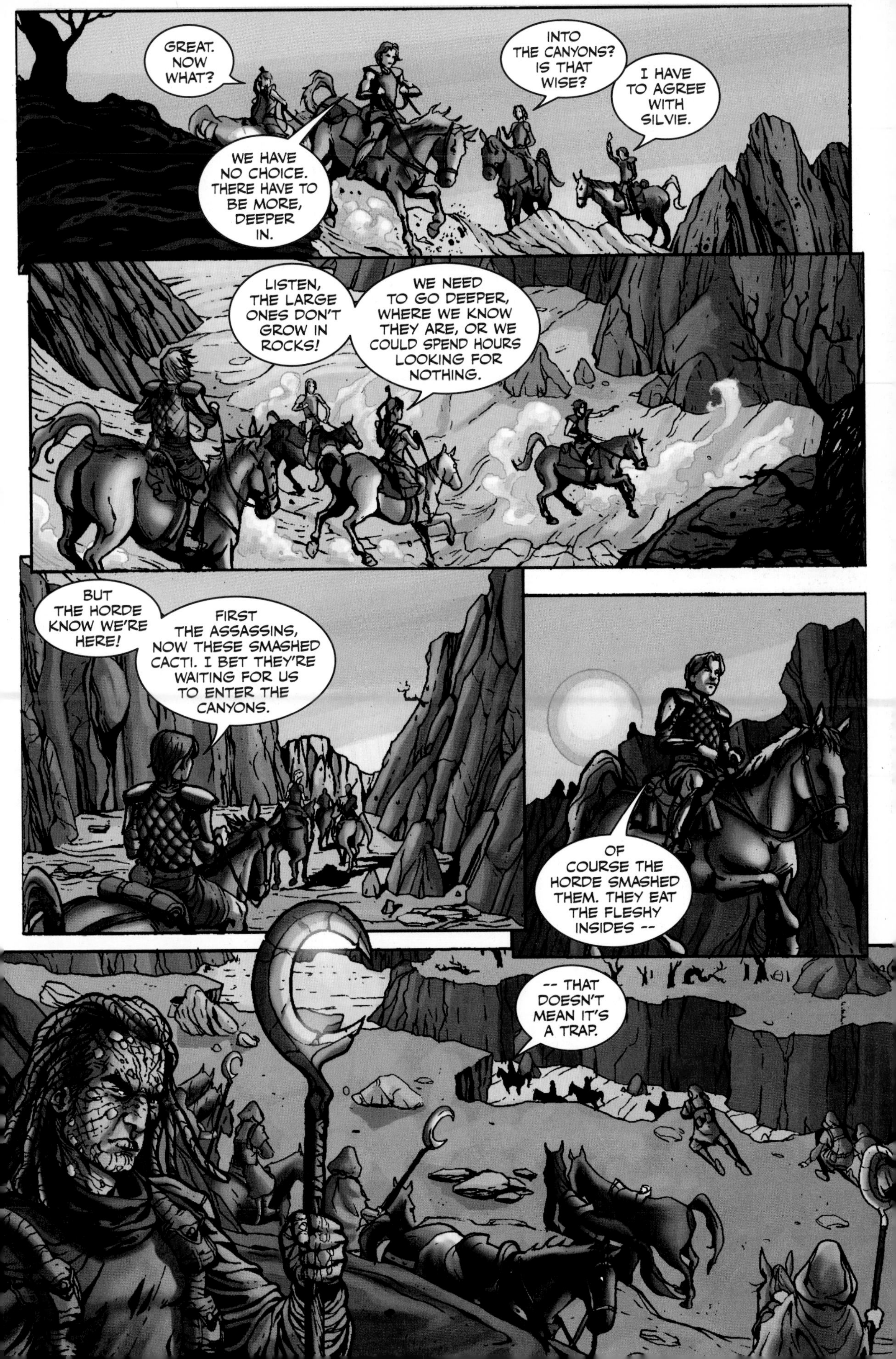
GREAT. NOW WHAT?
WE HAVE NO CHOICE. THERE HAVE TO BE MORE, DEEPER IN.
INTO THE CANYONS? IS THAT WISE?
I HAVE TO AGREE WITH SILVIE.
LISTEN, THE LARGE ONES DON'T GROW IN ROCKS!
WE NEED TO GO DEEPER, WHERE WE KNOW THEY ARE, OR WE COULD SPEND HOURS LOOKING FOR NOTHING.
BUT THE HORDE KNOW WE'RE HERE!
FIRST THE ASSASSINS, NOW THESE SMASHED CACTI. I BET THEY'RE WAITING FOR US TO ENTER THE CANYONS.
OF COURSE THE HORDE SMASHED THEM. THEY EAT THE FLESHY INSIDES --
-- THAT DOESN'T MEAN IT'S A TRAP.

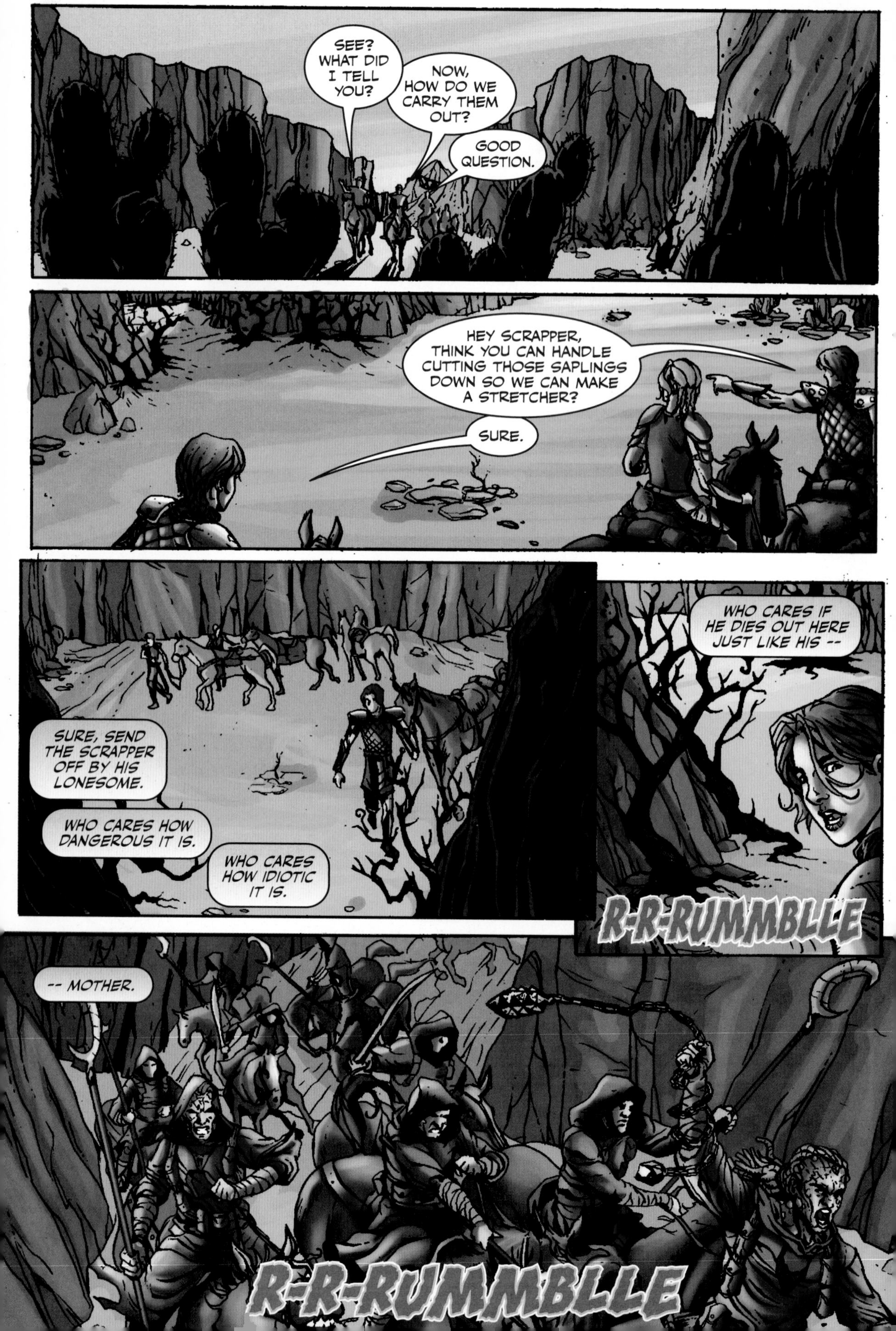
SEE? WHAT DID I TELL YOU?
NOW, HOW DO WE CARRY THEM OUT?
GOOD QUESTION.
HEY SCRAPPER, THINK YOU CAN HANDLE CUTTING THOSE SAPLINGS DOWN SO WE CAN MAKE A STRETCHER?
SURE.
SURE, SEND THE SCRAPPER OFF BY HIS LONESOME.
WHO CARES HOW DANGEROUS IT IS.
WHO CARES HOW IDIOTIC IT IS.
WHO CARES IF HE DIES OUT HERE JUST LIKE HIS --
R-R-RUMMBLLE
-- MOTHER.
R-R-RUMMBLLE

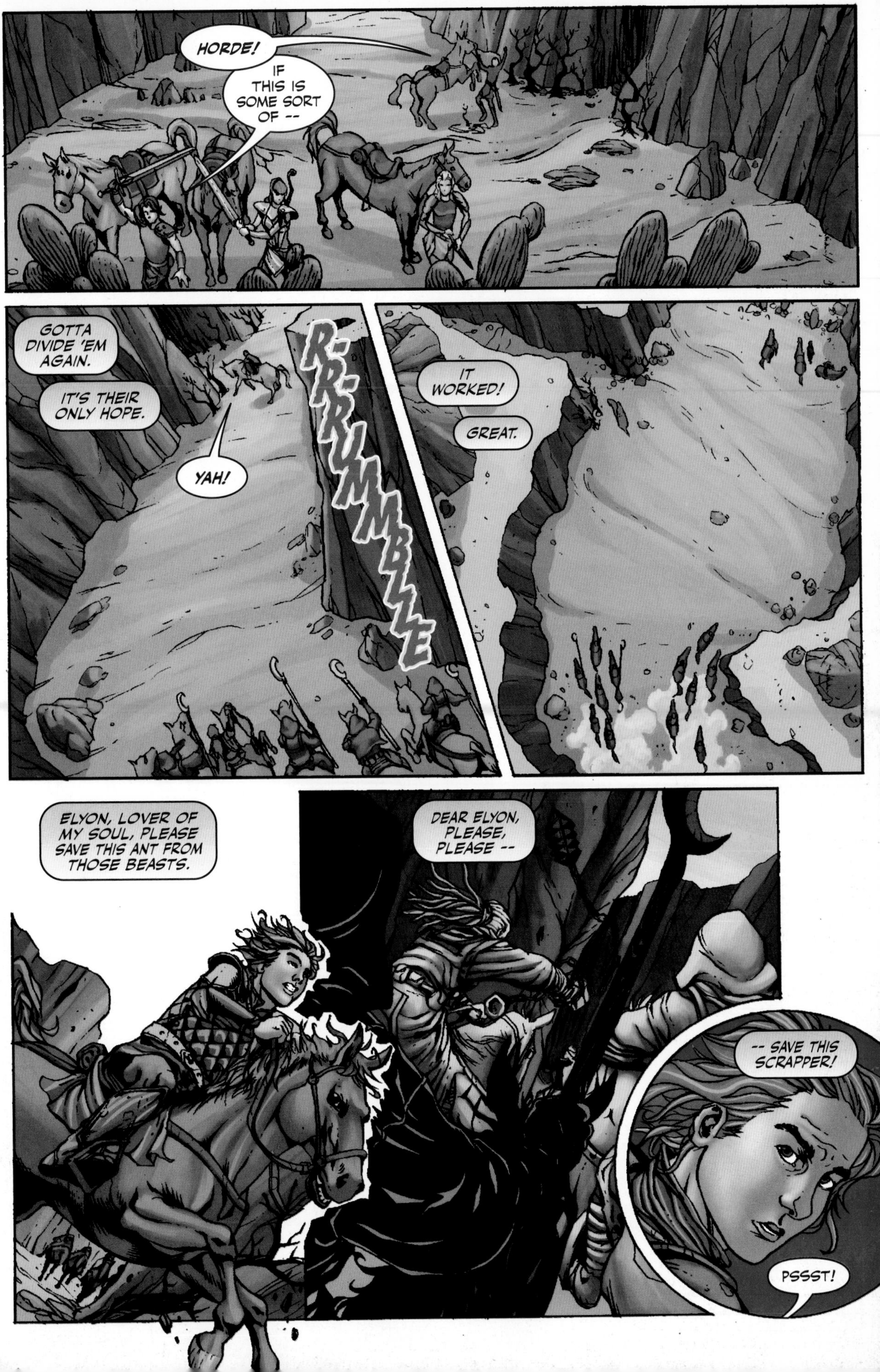
HORDE!
IF THIS IS SOME SORT OF --
GOTTA DIVIDE 'EM AGAIN.
IT'S THEIR ONLY HOPE.
YAH!
R-R-RUMMBLLE
IT WORKED!
GREAT.
ELYON, LOVER OF MY SOUL, PLEASE SAVE THIS ANT FROM THOSE BEASTS.
DEAR ELYON, PLEASE, PLEASE --
-- SAVE THIS SCRAPPER!
PSSST!

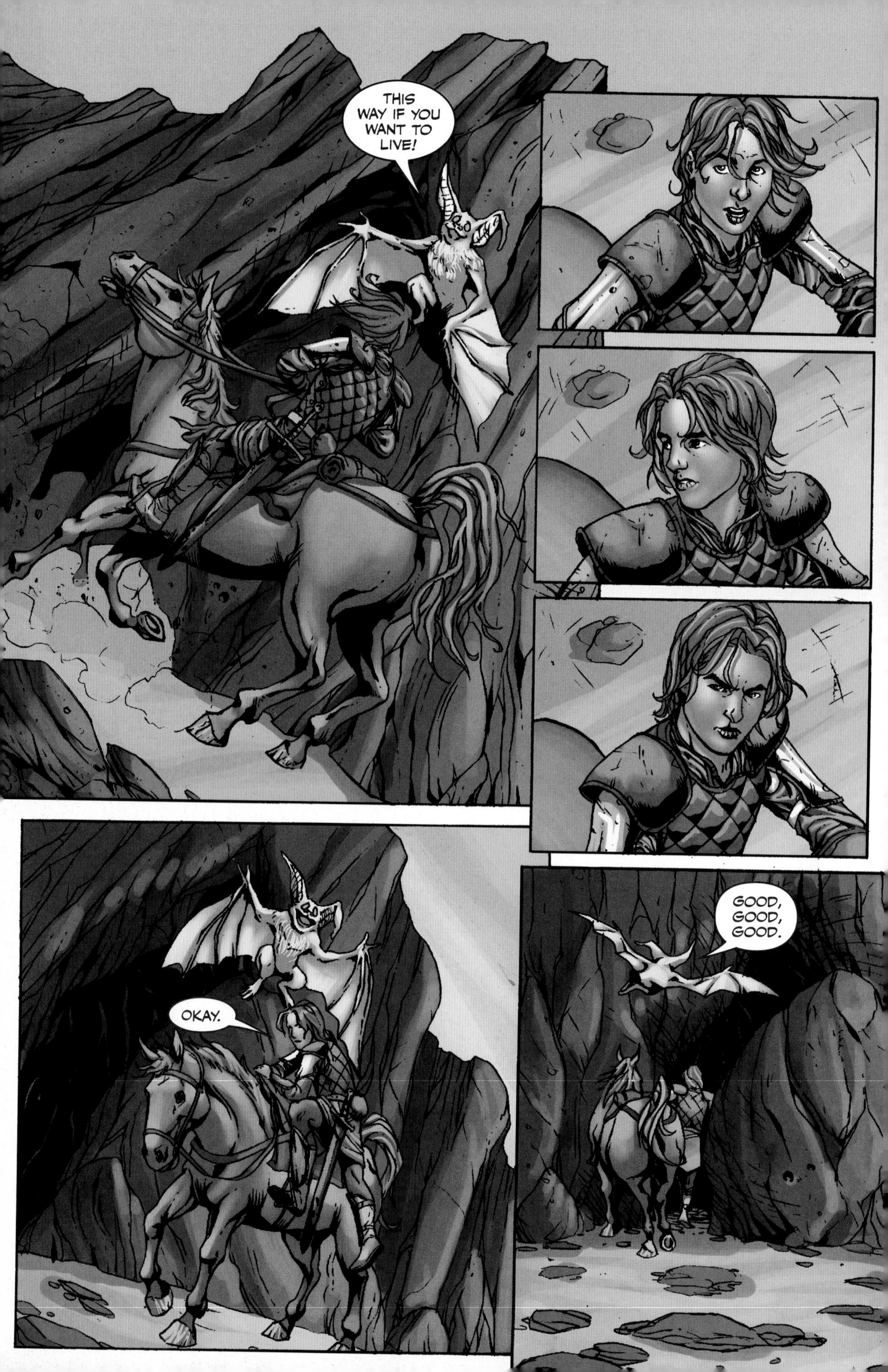
THIS WAY IF YOU WANT TO LIVE!
OKAY.
GOOD, GOOD, GOOD.

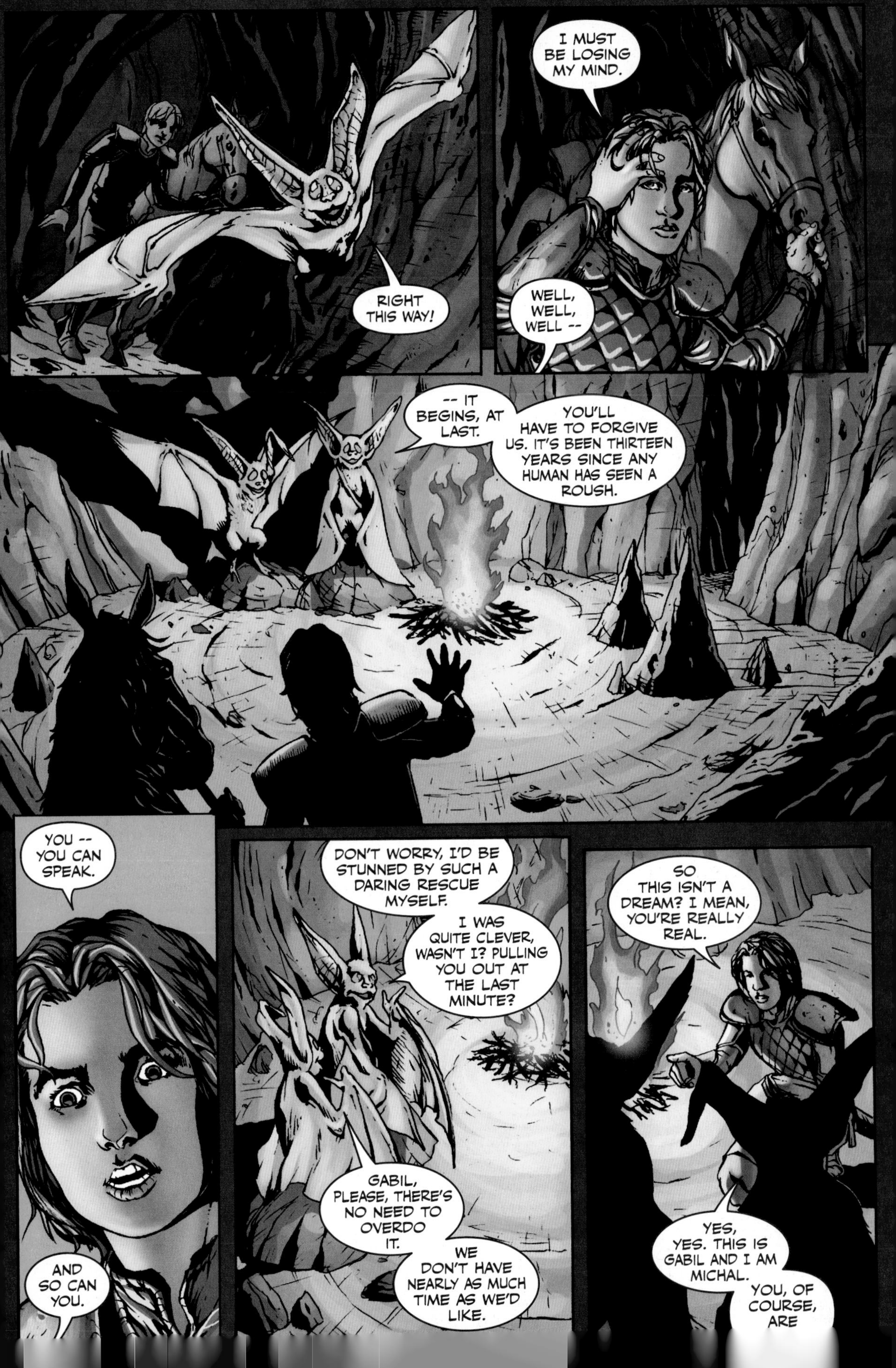
RIGHT THIS WAY!
I MUST BE LOSING MY MIND.
WELL, WELL, WELL --
-- IT BEGINS, AT LAST.
YOU'LL HAVE TO FORGIVE US. IT'S BEEN THIRTEEN YEARS SINCE ANY HUMAN HAS SEEN A ROUSH.
YOU -- YOU CAN SPEAK.
AND SO CAN YOU.
DON'T WORRY, I'D BE STUNNED BY SUCH A DARING RESCUE MYSELF.
I WAS QUITE CLEVER, WASN'T I? PULLING YOU OUT AT THE LAST MINUTE?
GABIL, PLEASE, THERE'S NO NEED TO OVERDO IT.
WE DON'T HAVE NEARLY AS MUCH TIME AS WE'D LIKE.
SO THIS ISN'T A DREAM? I MEAN, YOU'RE REALLY REAL.
YES, YES. THIS IS GABIL AND I AM MICHAL.
YOU, OF COURSE, ARE

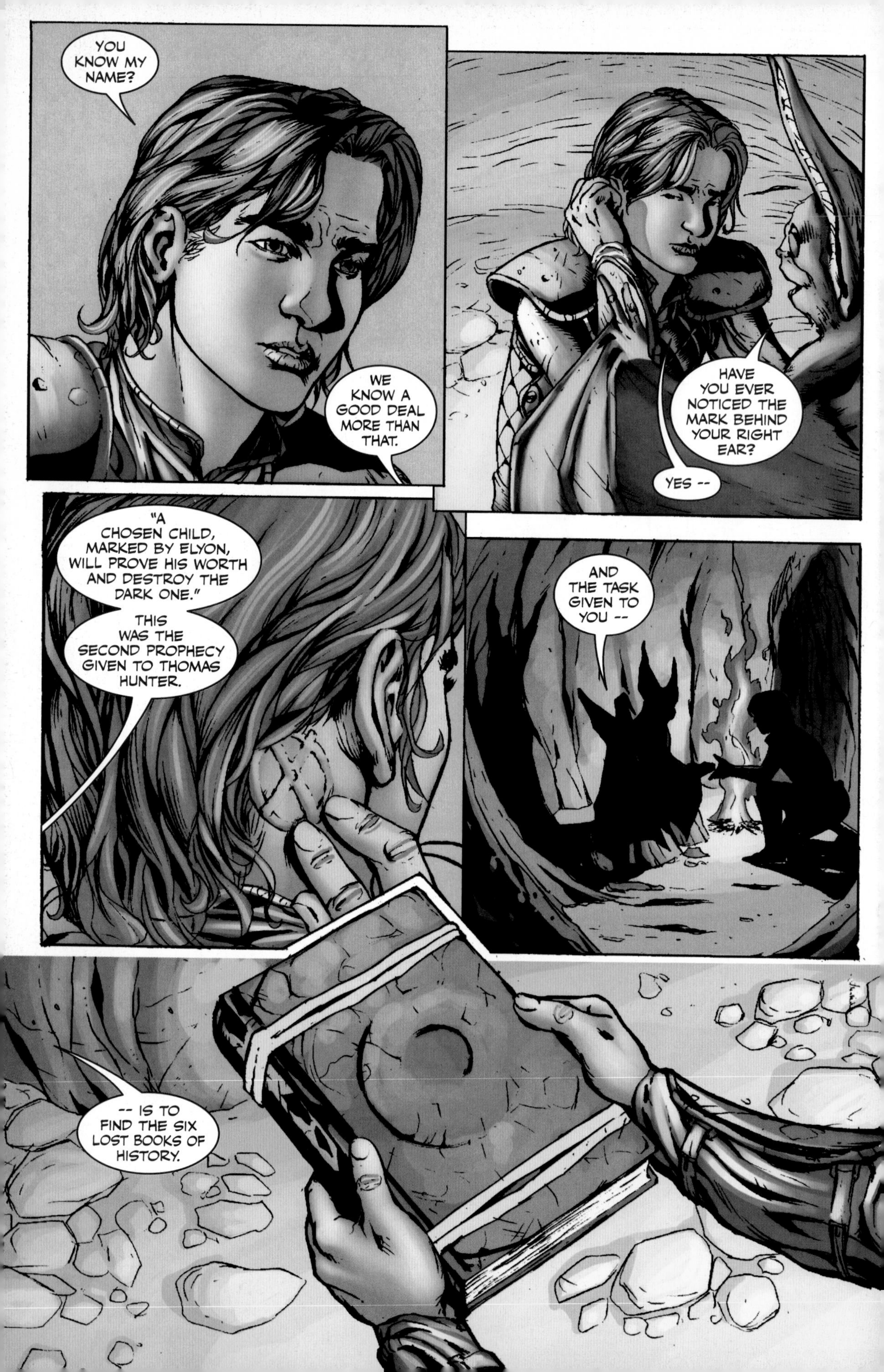
YOU KNOW MY NAME?
WE KNOW A GOOD DEAL MORE THAN THAT.
HAVE YOU EVER NOTICED THE MARK BEHIND YOUR RIGHT EAR?
YES --
"A CHOSEN CHILD, MARKED BY ELYON, WILL PROVE HIS WORTH AND DESTROY THE DARK ONE."
THIS WAS THE SECOND PROPHECY GIVEN TO THOMAS HUNTER.
AND THE TASK GIVEN TO YOU --
-- IS TO FIND THE SIX LOST BOOKS OF HISTORY.

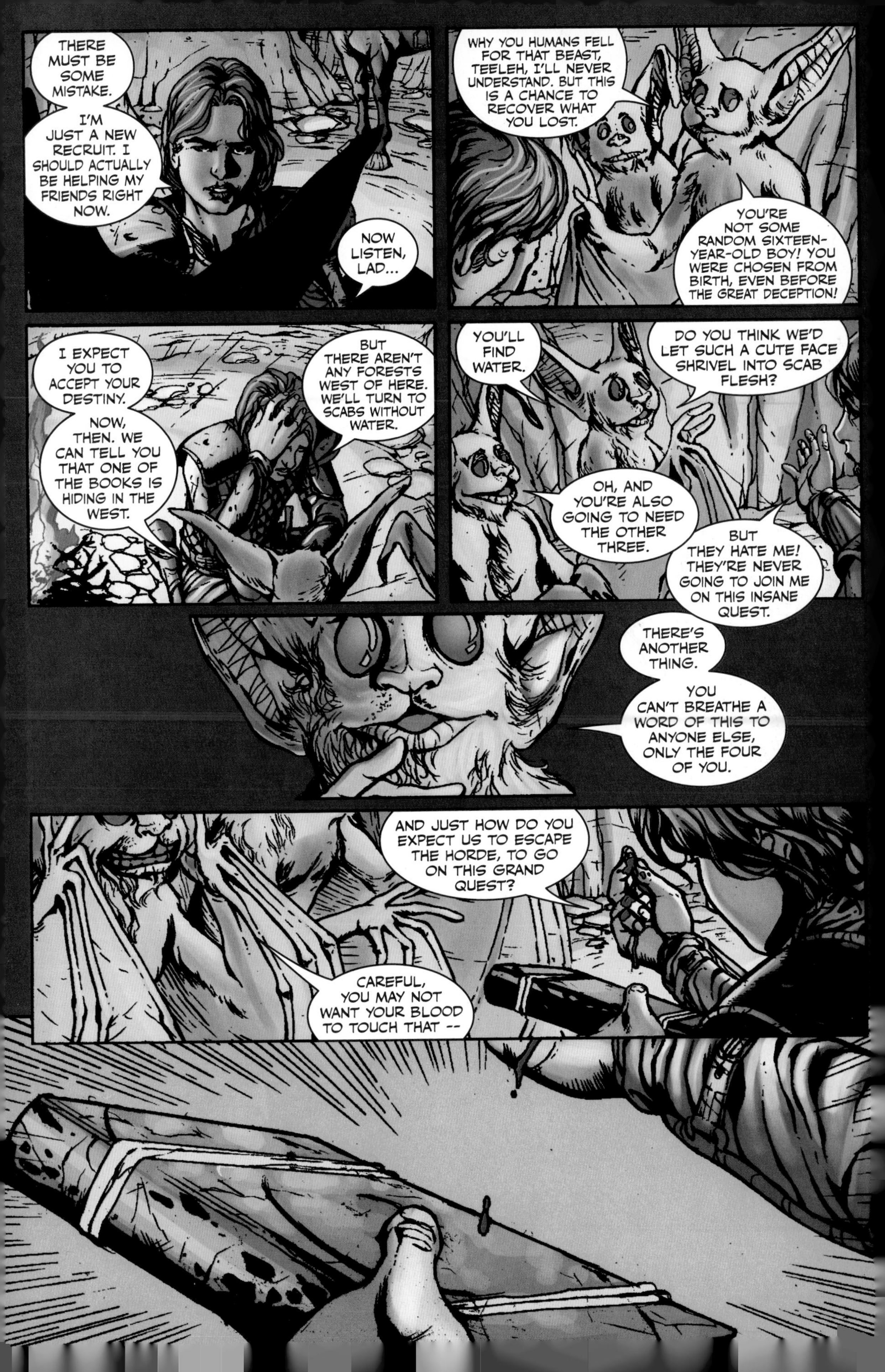
THERE MUST BE SOME MISTAKE.
I'M JUST A NEW RECRUIT. I SHOULD ACTUALLY BE HELPING MY FRIENDS RIGHT NOW.
NOW LISTEN, LAD...
WHY YOU HUMANS FELL FOR THAT BEAST, TEELEH, I'LL NEVER UNDERSTAND. BUT THIS IS A CHANCE TO RECOVER WHAT YOU LOST.
YOU'RE NOT SOME RANDOM SIXTEEN-YEAR-OLD BOY! YOU WERE CHOSEN FROM BIRTH, EVEN BEFORE THE GREAT DECEPTION!
I EXPECT YOU TO ACCEPT YOUR DESTINY.
NOW, THEN. WE CAN TELL YOU THAT ONE OF THE BOOKS IS HIDING IN THE WEST.
BUT THERE AREN'T ANY FORESTS WEST OF HERE. WE'LL TURN TO SCABS WITHOUT WATER.
YOU'LL FIND WATER.
DO YOU THINK WE'D LET SUCH A CUTE FACE SHRIVEL INTO SCAB FLESH?
OH, AND YOU'RE ALSO GOING TO NEED THE OTHER THREE.
BUT THEY HATE ME! THEY'RE NEVER GOING TO JOIN ME ON THIS INSANE QUEST.
THERE'S ANOTHER THING.
YOU CAN'T BREATHE A WORD OF THIS TO ANYONE ELSE, ONLY THE FOUR OF YOU.
AND JUST HOW DO YOU EXPECT US TO ESCAPE THE HORDE, TO GO ON THIS GRAND QUEST?
CAREFUL, YOU MAY NOT WANT YOUR BLOOD TO TOUCH THAT --

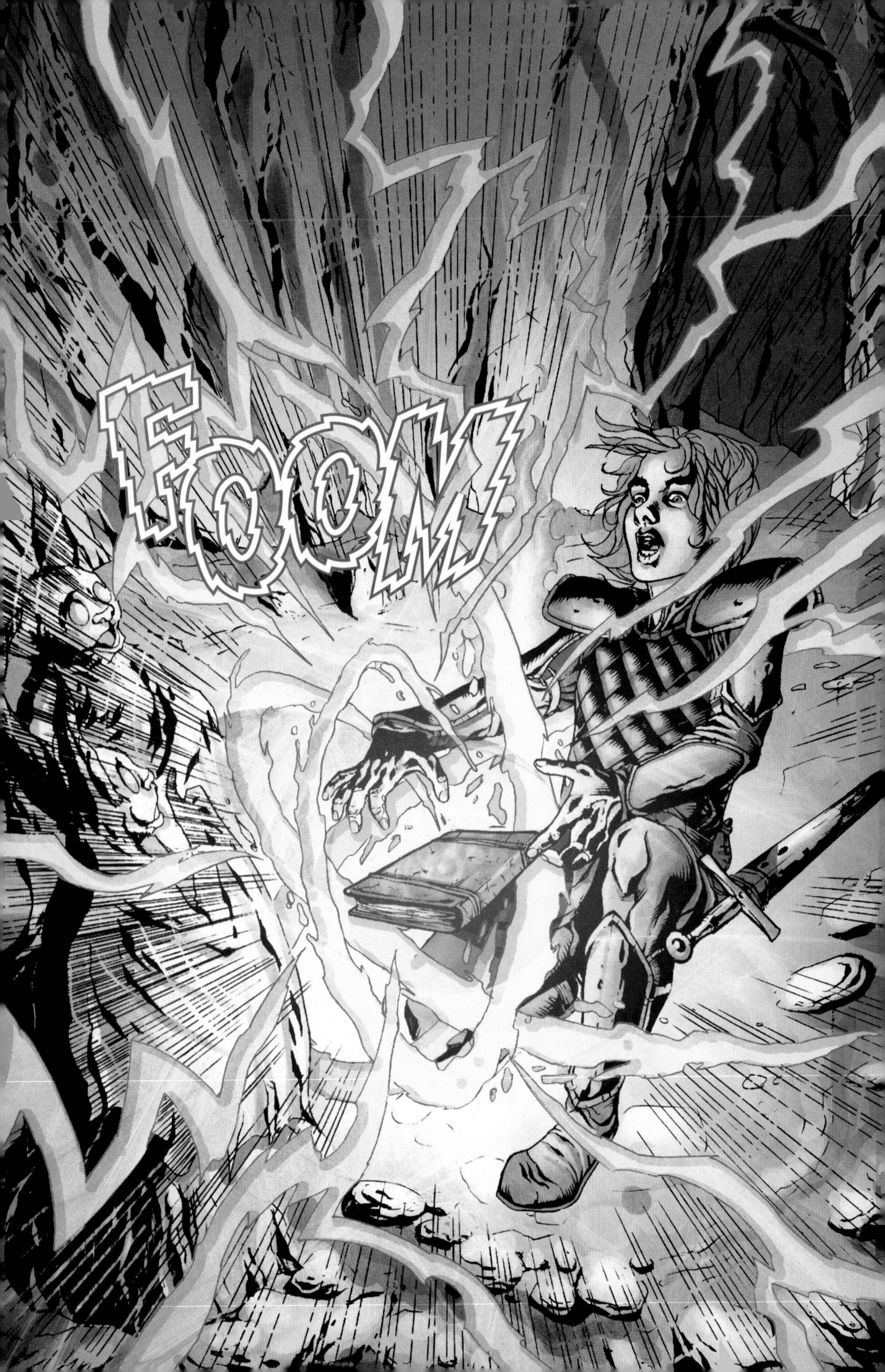
FOOM

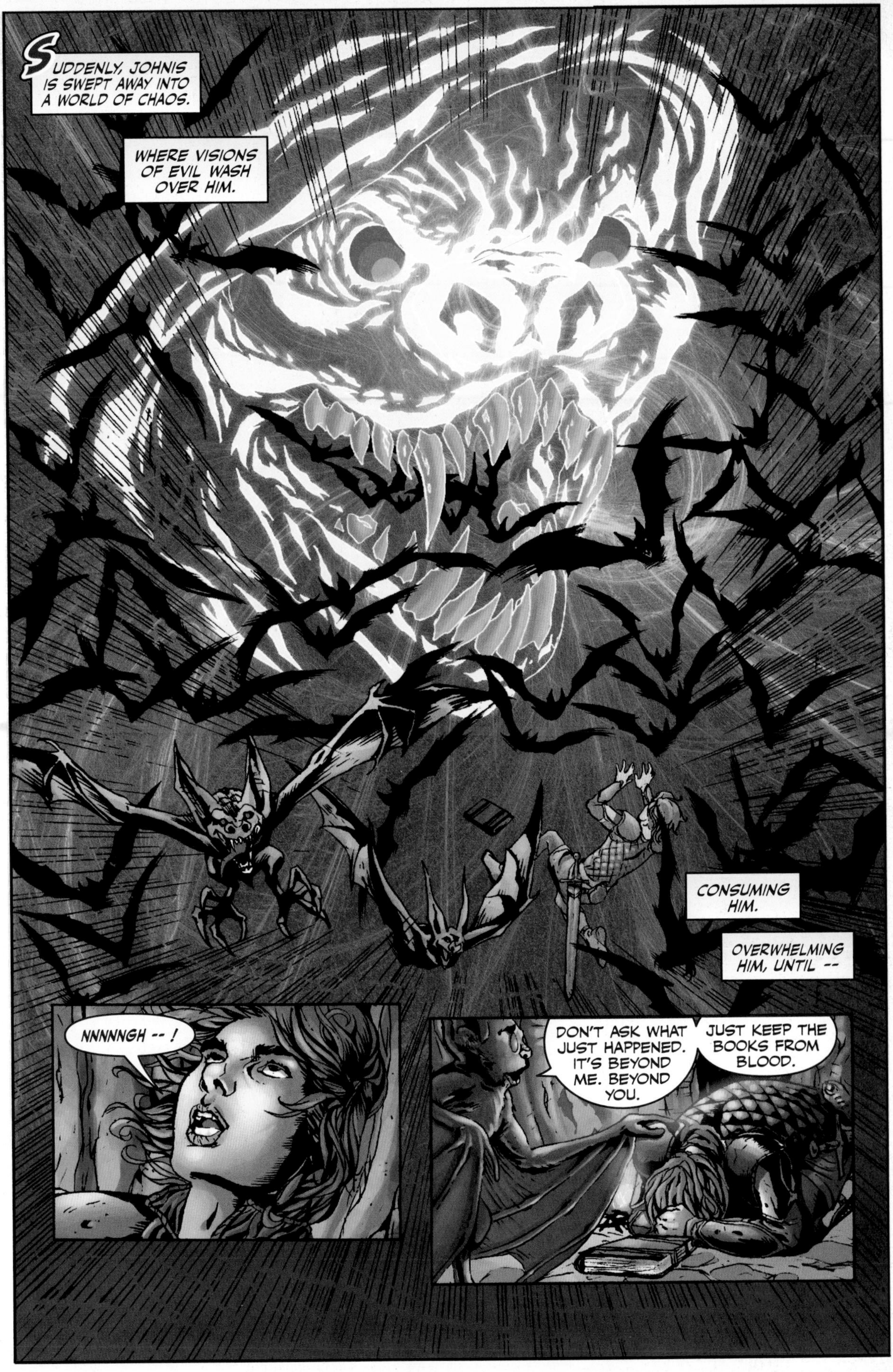
SUDDENLY, JOHNIS IS SWEPT AWAY INTO A WORLD OF CHAOS.
WHERE VISIONS OF EVIL WASH OVER HIM.
CONSUMING HIM.
OVERWHELMING HIM, UNTIL --
NNNNNGH -- !
DON'T ASK WHAT JUST HAPPENED. IT'S BEYOND ME. BEYOND YOU.
JUST KEEP THE BOOKS FROM BLOOD.

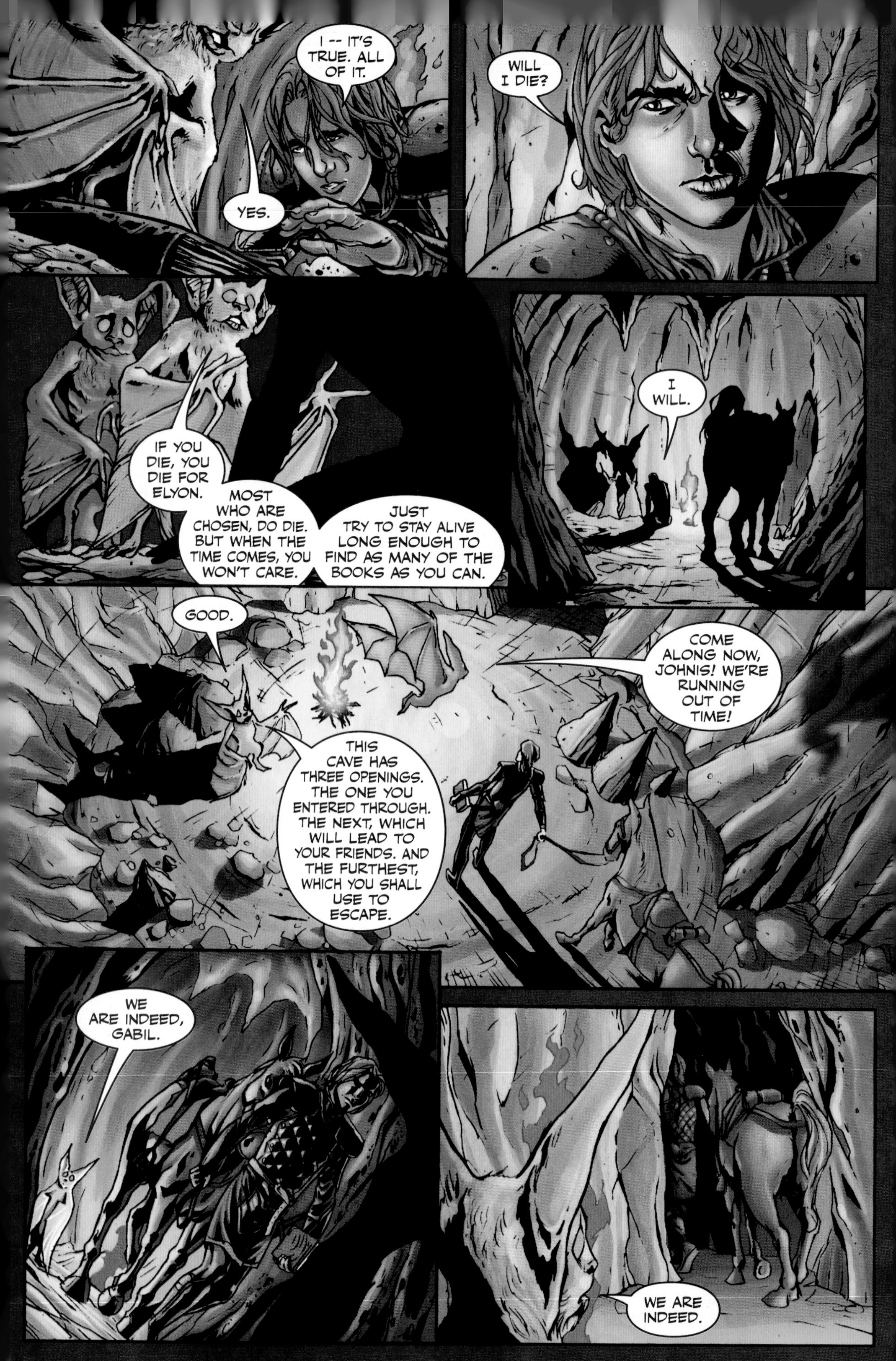
I -- IT'S TRUE. ALL OF IT.
YES.
WILL I DIE?
IF YOU DIE, YOU DIE FOR ELYON.
MOST WHO ARE CHOSEN, DO DIE. BUT WHEN THE TIME COMES, YOU WON'T CARE.
JUST TRY TO STAY ALIVE LONG ENOUGH TO FIND AS MANY OF THE BOOKS AS YOU CAN.
I WILL.
GOOD.
THIS CAVE HAS THREE OPENINGS. THE ONE YOU ENTERED THROUGH. THE NEXT, WHICH WILL LEAD TO YOUR FRIENDS. AND THE FURTHEST, WHICH YOU SHALL USE TO ESCAPE.
COME ALONG NOW, JOHNIS! WE'RE RUNNING OUT OF TIME!
WE ARE INDEED, GABIL.
WE ARE INDEED.

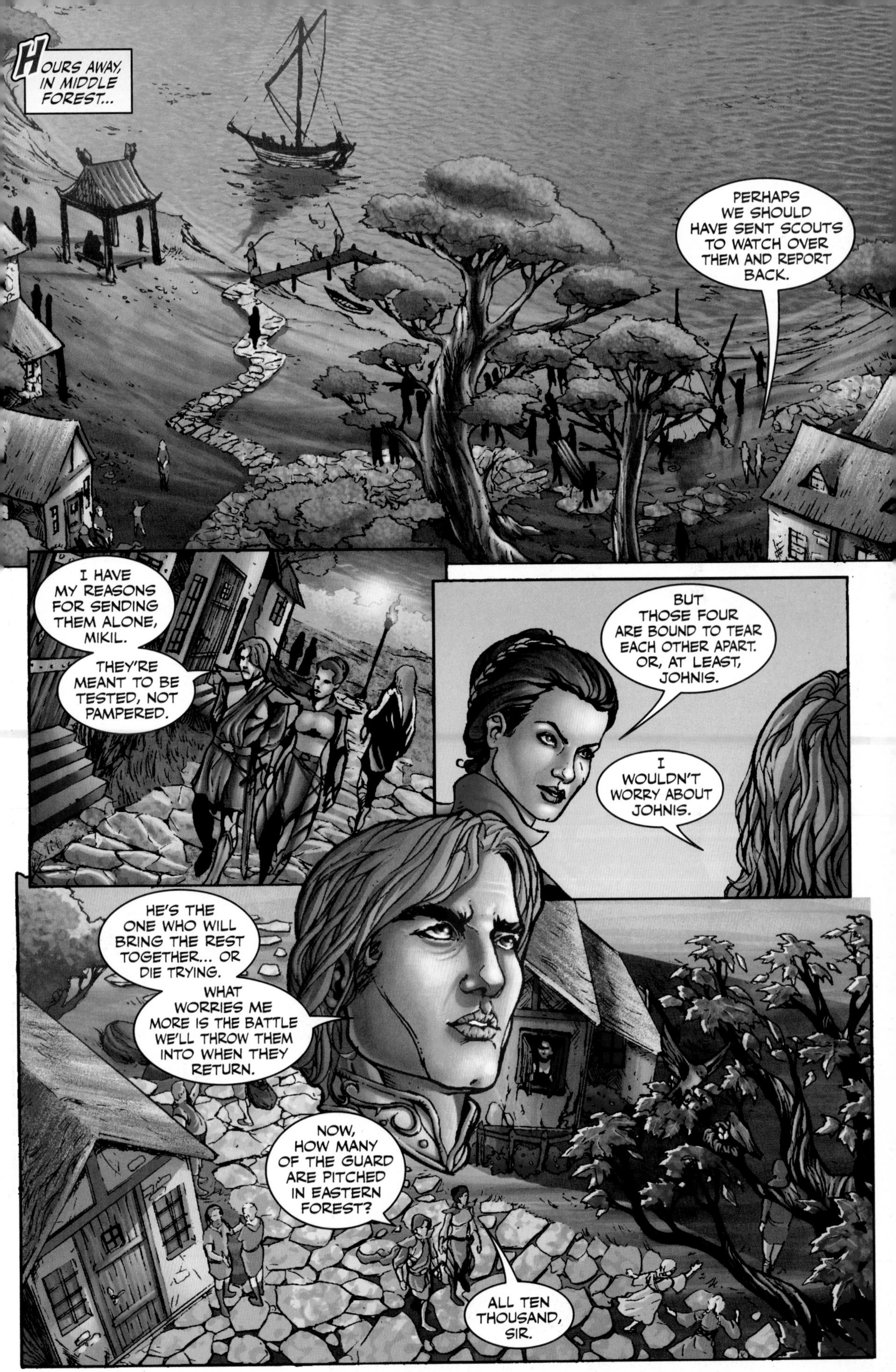
HOURS AWAY, IN MIDDLE FOREST...
PERHAPS WE SHOULD HAVE SENT SCOUTS TO WATCH OVER THEM AND REPORT BACK.
I HAVE MY REASONS FOR SENDING THEM ALONE, MIKIL.
THEY'RE MEANT TO BE TESTED, NOT PAMPERED.
BUT THOSE FOUR ARE BOUND TO TEAR EACH OTHER APART. OR, AT LEAST, JOHNIS.
I WOULDN'T WORRY ABOUT JOHNIS.
HE'S THE ONE WHO WILL BRING THE REST TOGETHER... OR DIE TRYING.
WHAT WORRIES ME MORE IS THE BATTLE WE'LL THROW THEM INTO WHEN THEY RETURN.
NOW, HOW MANY OF THE GUARD ARE PITCHED IN EASTERN FOREST?
ALL TEN THOUSAND, SIR.

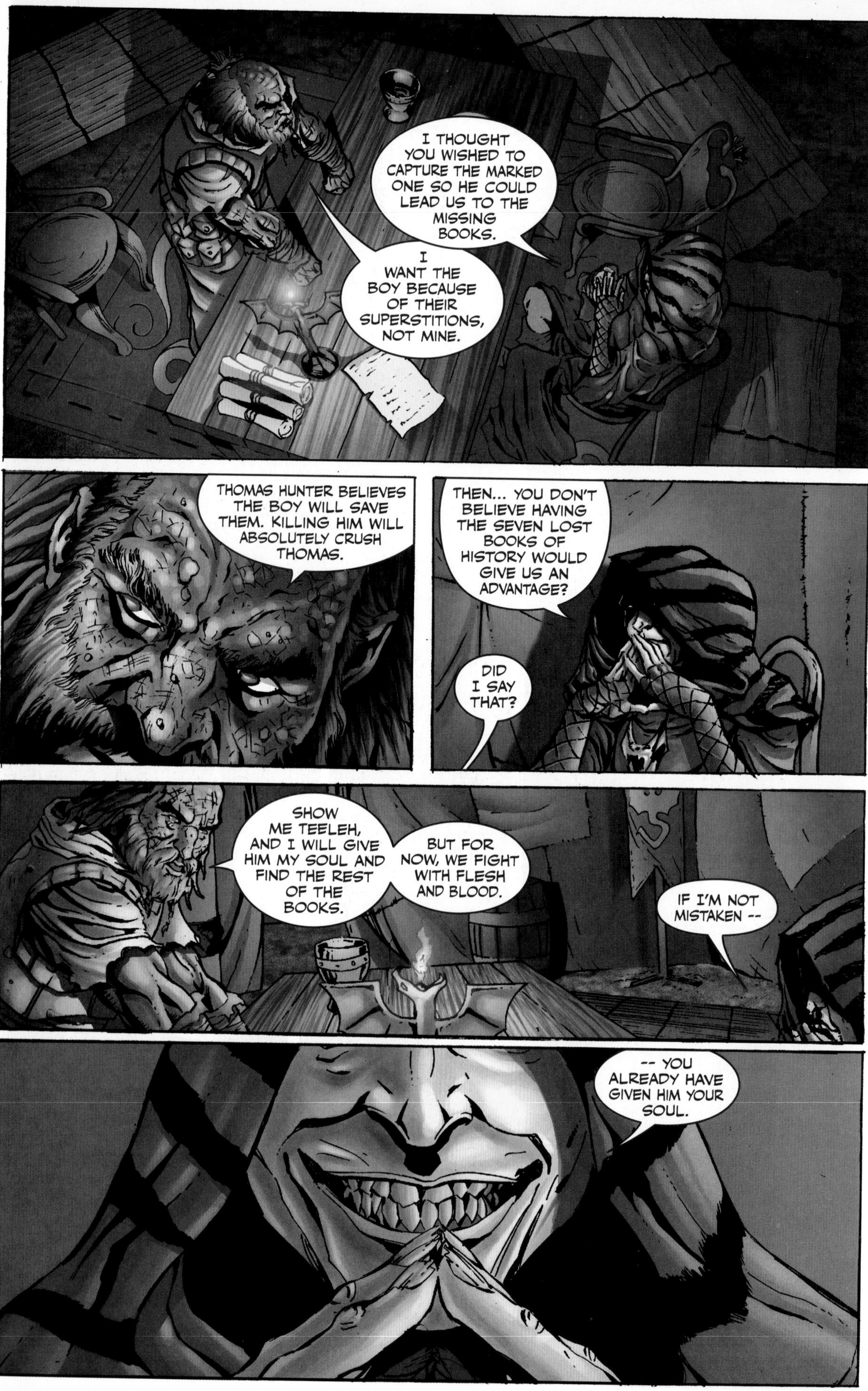
I THOUGHT YOU WISHED TO CAPTURE THE MARKED ONE SO HE COULD LEAD US TO THE MISSING BOOKS.
I WANT THE BOY BECAUSE OF THEIR SUPERSTITIONS, NOT MINE.
THOMAS HUNTER BELIEVES THE BOY WILL SAVE THEM. KILLING HIM WILL ABSOLUTELY CRUSH THOMAS.
THEN... YOU DON'T BELIEVE HAVING THE SEVEN LOST BOOKS OF HISTORY WOULD GIVE US AN ADVANTAGE?
DID I SAY THAT?
SHOW ME TEELEH, AND I WILL GIVE HIM MY SOUL AND FIND THE REST OF THE BOOKS.
BUT FOR NOW, WE FIGHT WITH FLESH AND BLOOD.
IF I'M NOT MISTAKEN --
-- YOU ALREADY HAVE GIVEN HIM YOUR SOUL.

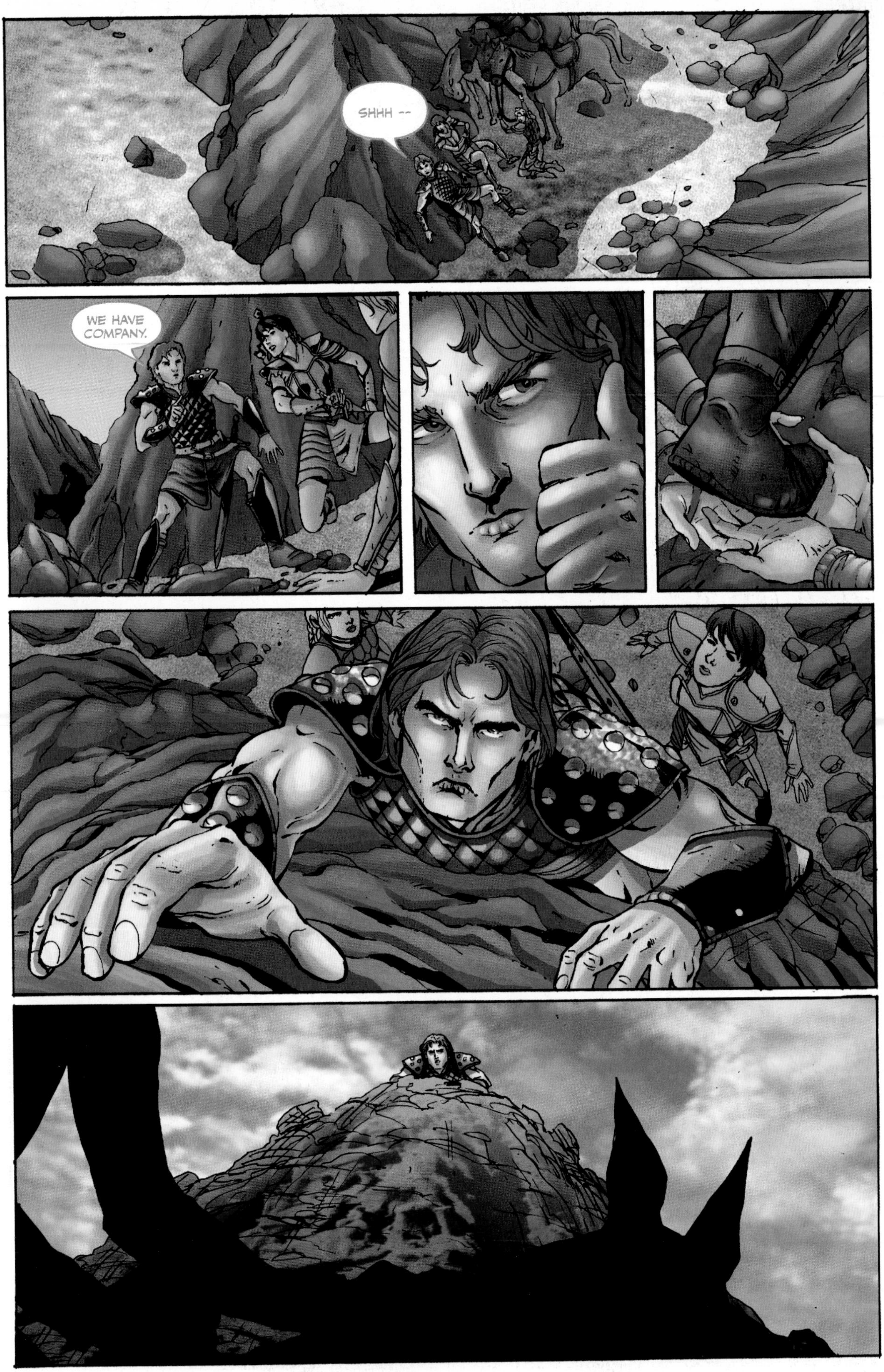
SHHH --
WE HAVE COMPANY.

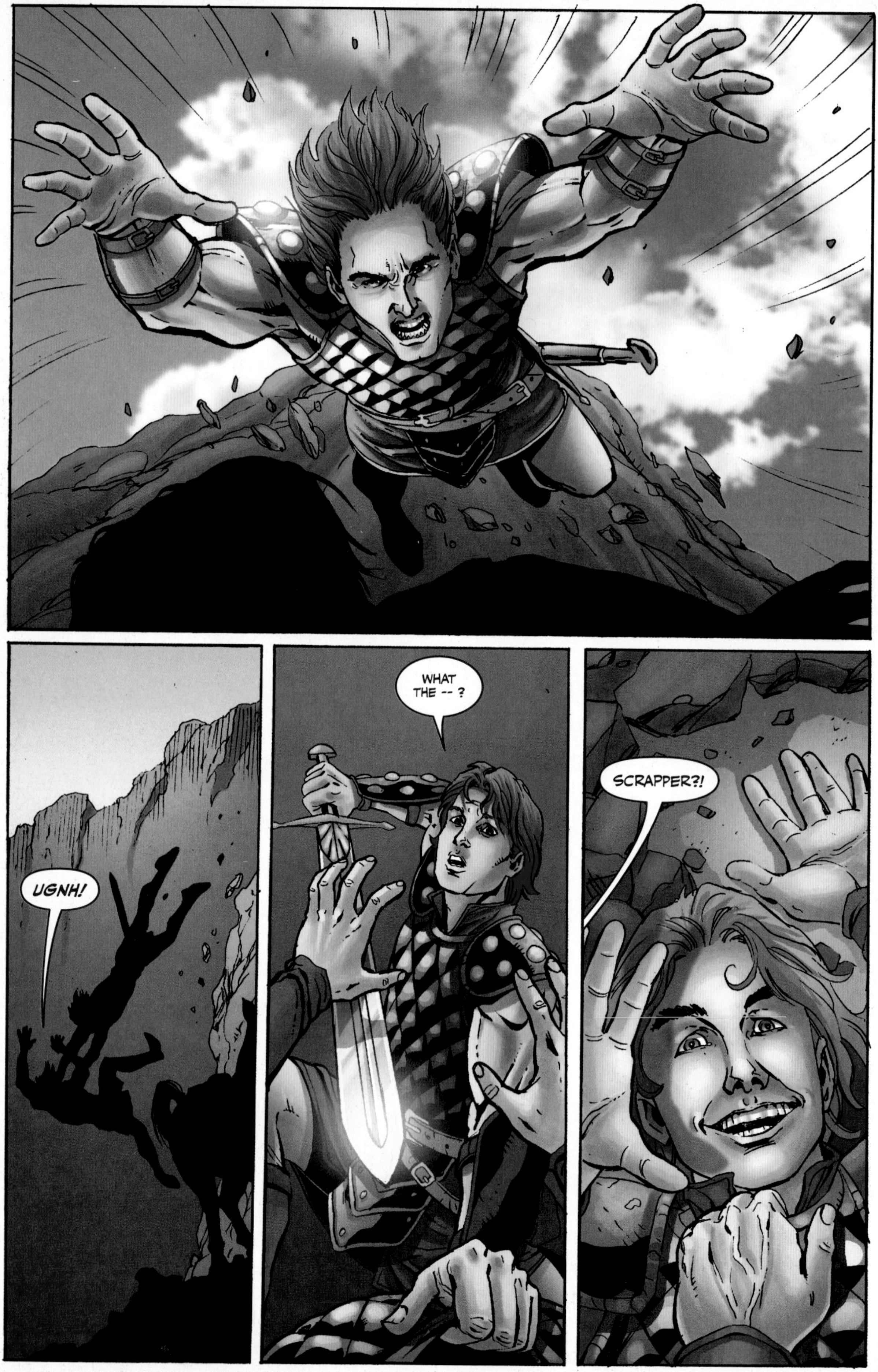
UGNH!
WHAT THE -- ?
SCRAPPER?!

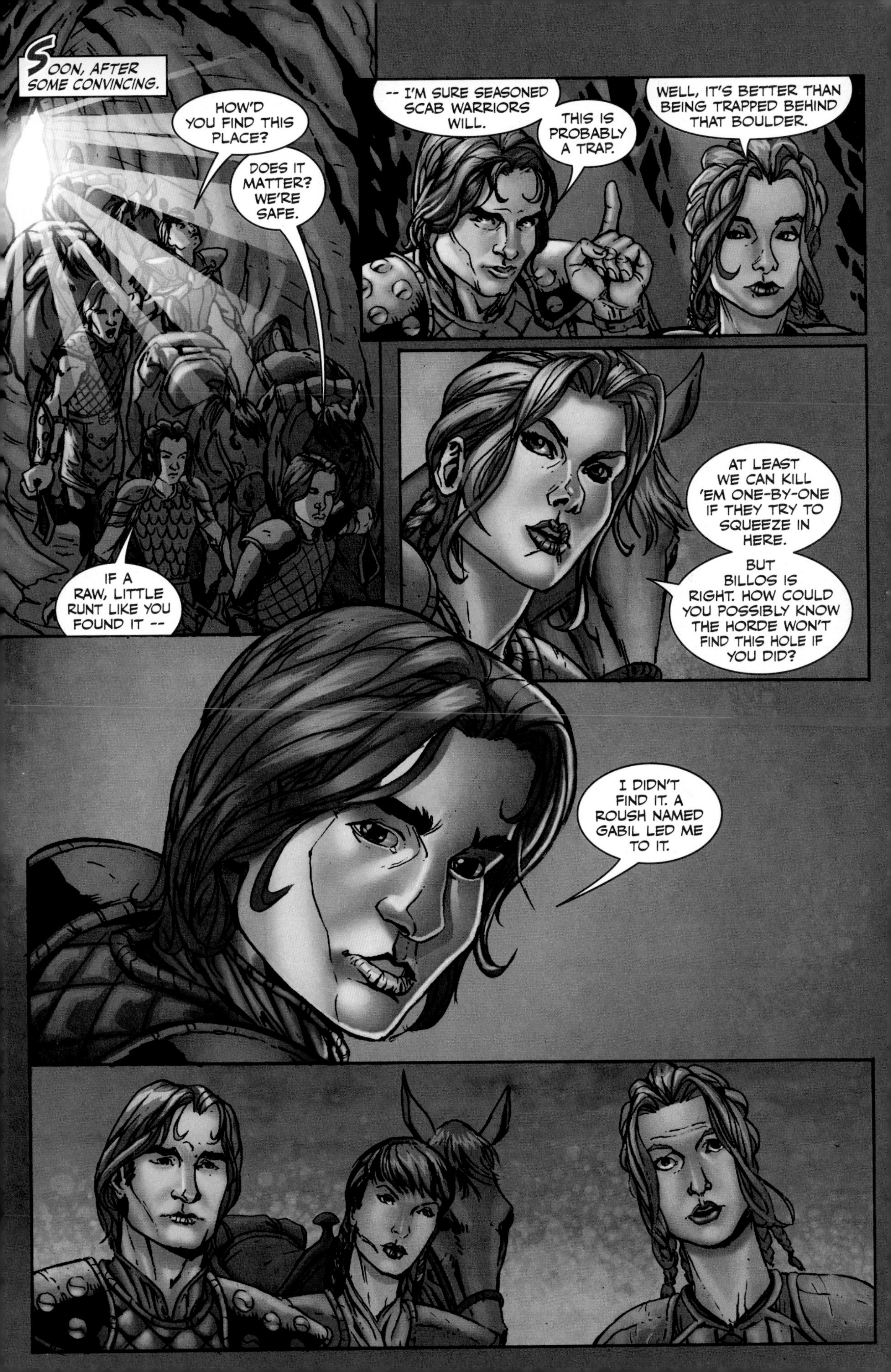
SOON, AFTER SOME CONVINCING.
HOW'D YOU FIND THIS PLACE?
DOES IT MATTER? WE'RE SAFE.
IF A RAW, LITTLE RUNT LIKE YOU FOUND IT --
-- I'M SURE SEASONED SCAB WARRIORS WILL.
THIS IS PROBABLY A TRAP.
WELL, IT'S BETTER THAN BEING TRAPPED BEHIND THAT BOULDER.
AT LEAST WE CAN KILL 'EM ONE-BY-ONE IF THEY TRY TO SQUEEZE IN HERE.
BUT BILLOS IS RIGHT. HOW COULD YOU POSSIBLY KNOW THE HORDE WON'T FIND THIS HOLE IF YOU DID?
I DIDN'T FIND IT. A ROUSH NAMED GABIL LED ME TO IT.

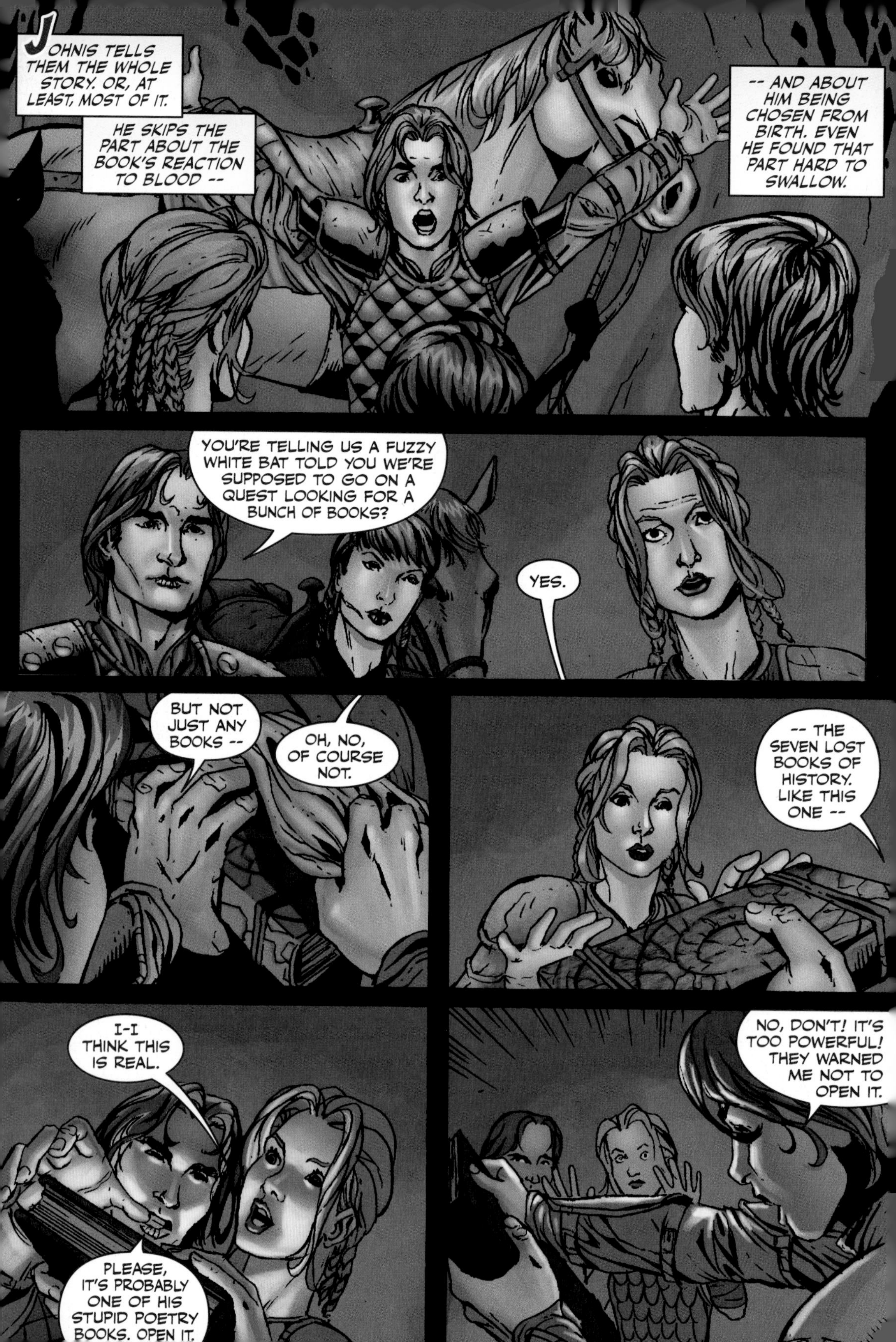
JOHNIS TELLS THEM THE WHOLE STORY. OR, AT LEAST, MOST OF IT.
HE SKIPS THE PART ABOUT THE BOOK'S REACTION TO BLOOD --
-- AND ABOUT HIM BEING CHOSEN FROM BIRTH. EVEN HE FOUND THAT PART HARD TO SWALLOW.
YOU'RE TELLING US A FUZZY WHITE BAT TOLD YOU WE'RE SUPPOSED TO GO ON A QUEST LOOKING FOR A BUNCH OF BOOKS?
YES.
BUT NOT JUST ANY BOOKS --
OH, NO, OF COURSE NOT.
-- THE SEVEN LOST BOOKS OF HISTORY. LIKE THIS ONE --
I-I THINK THIS IS REAL.
PLEASE, IT'S PROBABLY ONE OF HIS STUPID POETRY BOOKS. OPEN IT.
NO, DON'T! IT'S TOO POWERFUL! THEY WARNED ME NOT TO OPEN IT.

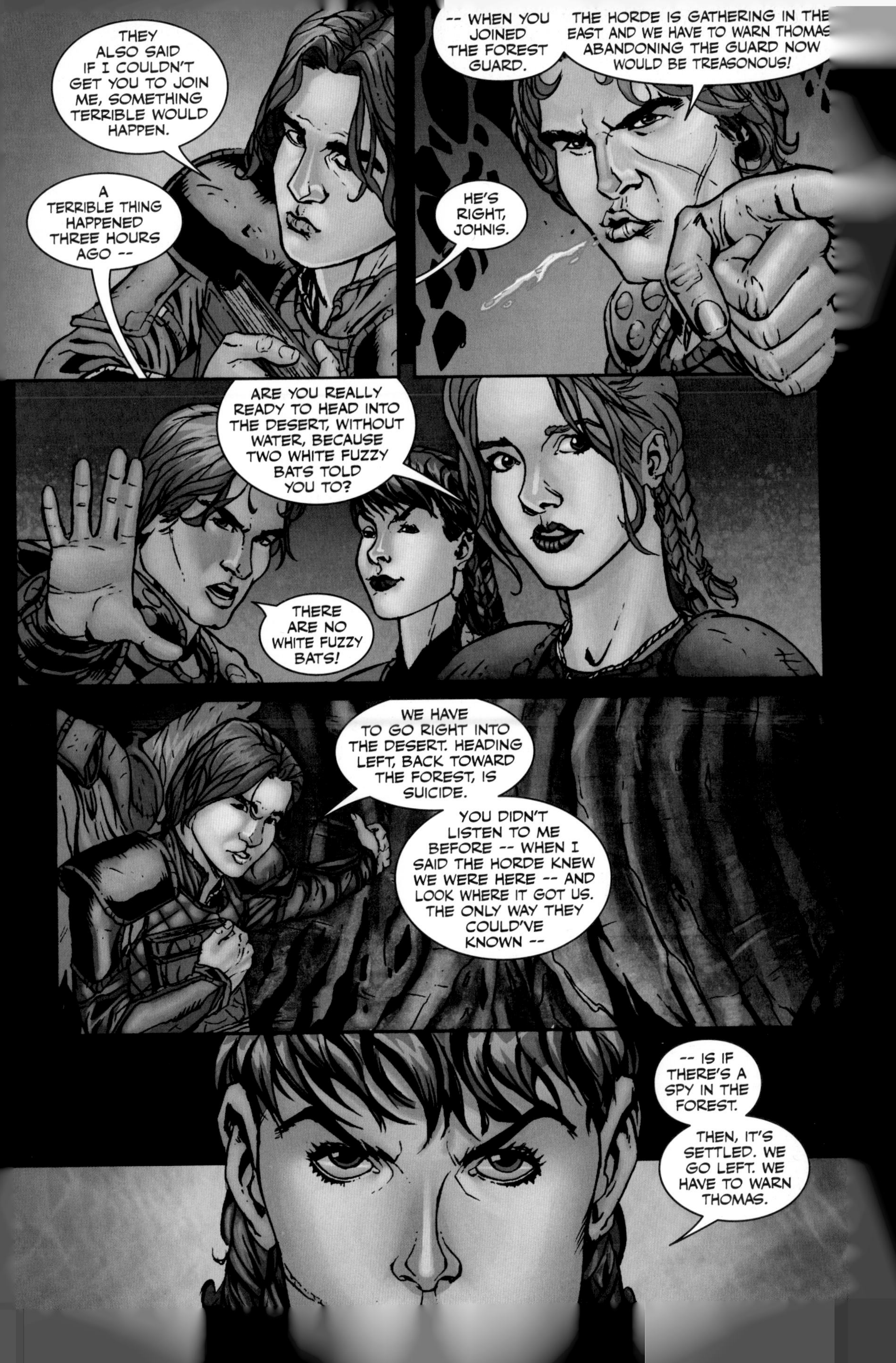
THEY ALSO SAID IF I COULDN'T GET YOU TO JOIN ME, SOMETHING TERRIBLE WOULD HAPPEN.
A TERRIBLE THING HAPPENED THREE HOURS AGO --
-- WHEN YOU JOINED THE FOREST GUARD.
THE HORDE IS GATHERING IN THE EAST AND WE HAVE TO WARN THOMAS. ABANDONING THE GUARD NOW WOULD BE TREASONOUS!
HE'S RIGHT, JOHNIS.
ARE YOU REALLY READY TO HEAD INTO THE DESERT, WITHOUT WATER, BECAUSE TWO WHITE FUZZY BATS TOLD YOU TO?
THERE ARE NO WHITE FUZZY BATS!
WE HAVE TO GO RIGHT INTO THE DESERT. HEADING LEFT, BACK TOWARD THE FOREST, IS SUICIDE.
YOU DIDN'T LISTEN TO ME BEFORE -- WHEN I SAID THE HORDE KNEW WE WERE HERE -- AND LOOK WHERE IT GOT US. THE ONLY WAY THEY COULD'VE KNOWN --
-- IS IF THERE'S A SPY IN THE FOREST.
THEN, IT'S SETTLED. WE GO LEFT. WE HAVE TO WARN THOMAS.

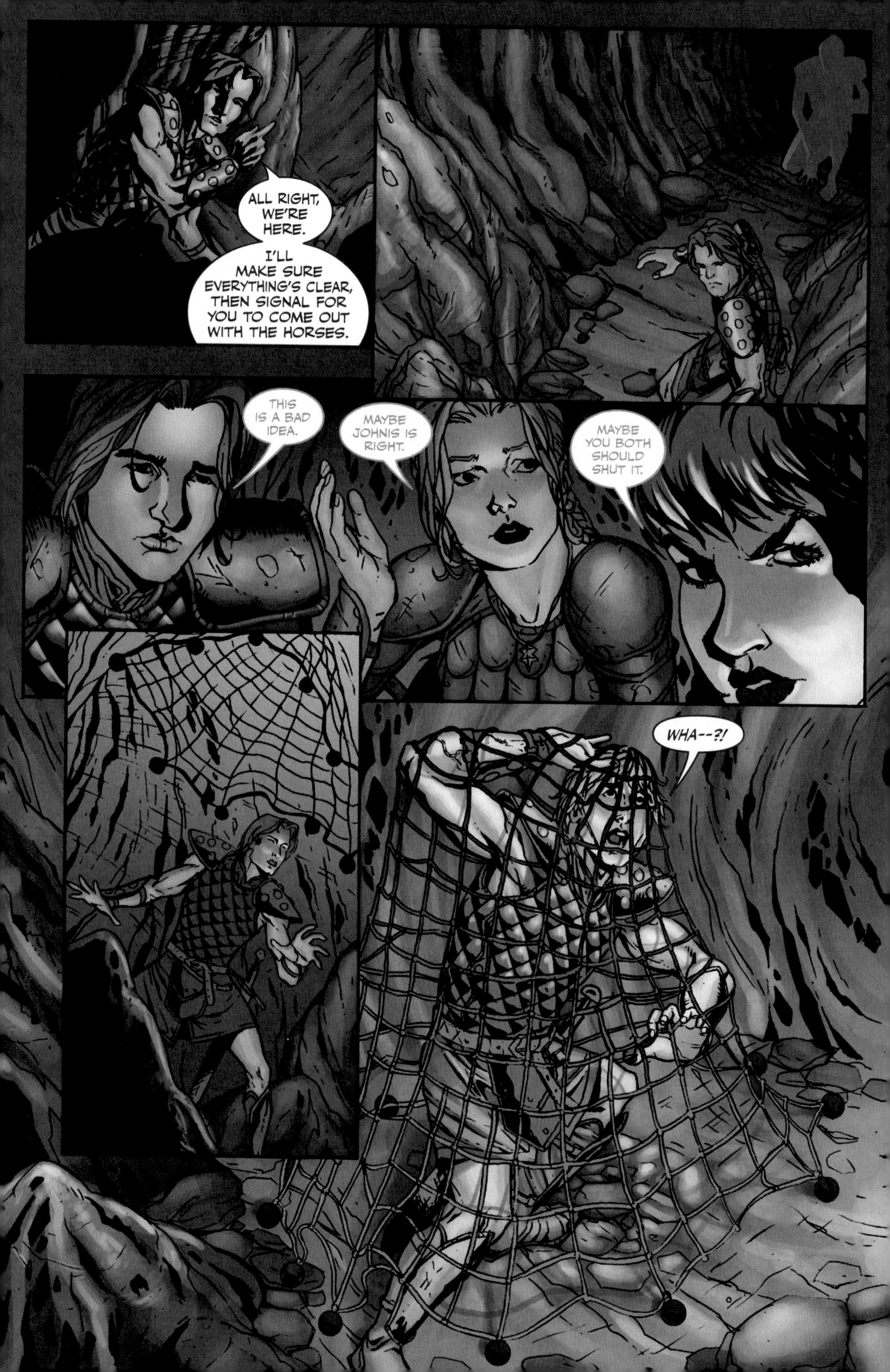
ALL RIGHT, WE'RE HERE.
I'LL MAKE SURE EVERYTHING'S CLEAR, THEN SIGNAL FOR YOU TO COME OUT WITH THE HORSES.
THIS IS A BAD IDEA.
MAYBE JOHNIS IS RIGHT.
MAYBE YOU BOTH SHOULD SHUT IT.
WHA--?!

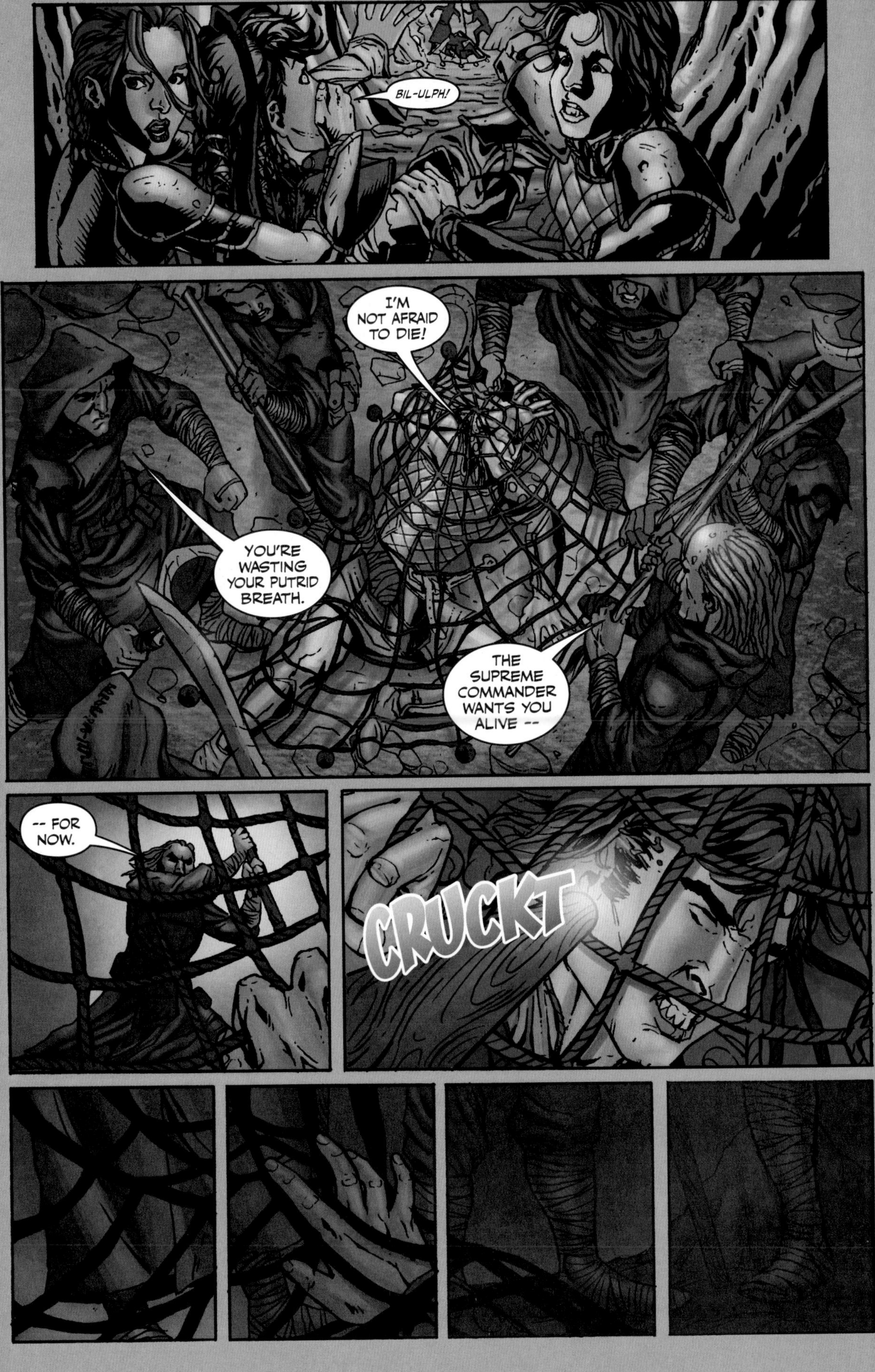
BIL-ULPH!
I'M NOT AFRAID TO DIE!
YOU'RE WASTING YOUR PUTRID BREATH.
THE SUPREME COMMANDER WANTS YOU ALIVE --
-- FOR NOW.
CRUCKT

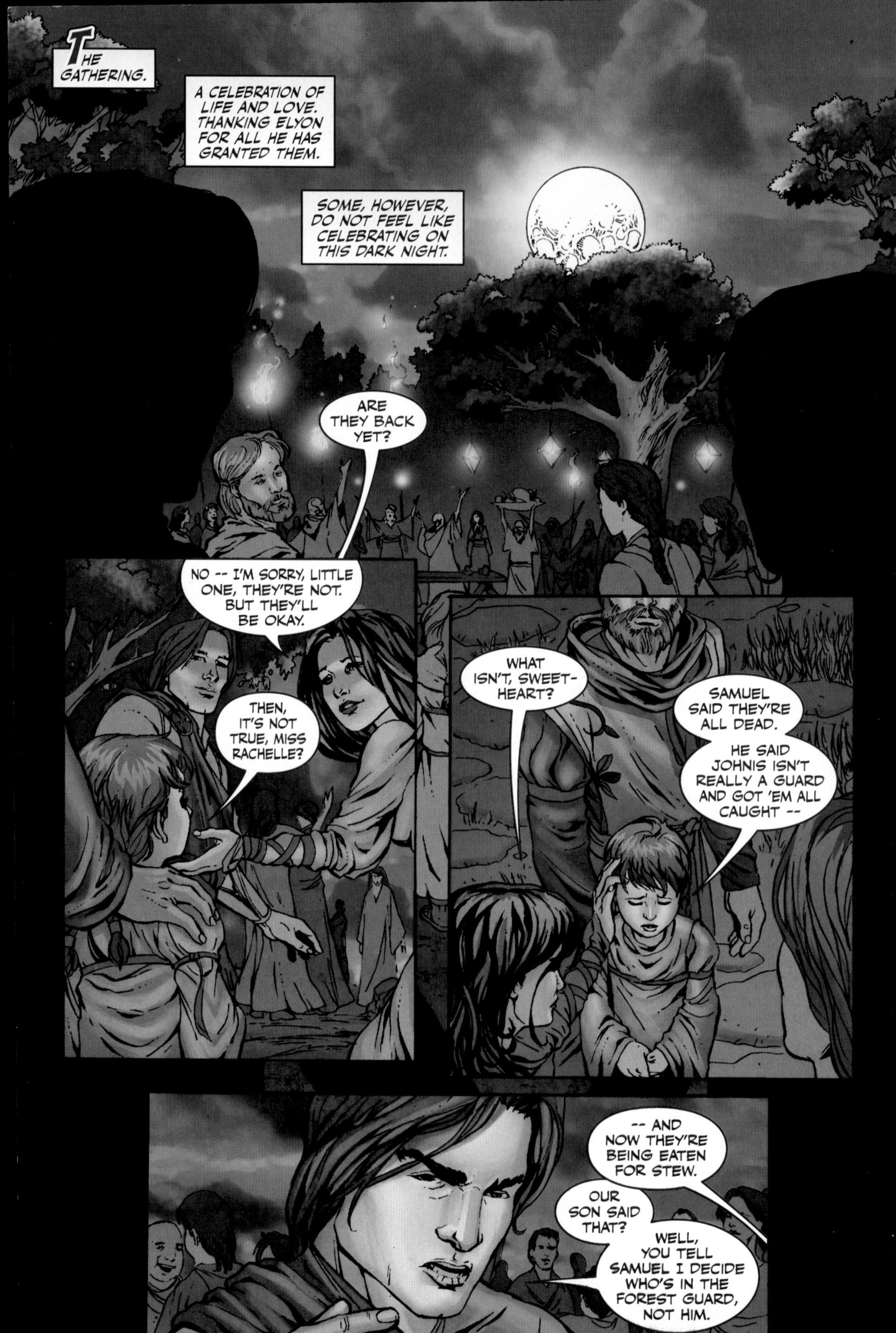
THE GATHERING.
A CELEBRATION OF LIFE AND LOVE. THANKING ELYON FOR ALL HE HAS GRANTED THEM.
SOME, HOWEVER, DO NOT FEEL LIKE CELEBRATING ON THIS DARK NIGHT.
ARE THEY BACK YET?
NO -- I'M SORRY, LITTLE ONE, THEY'RE NOT. BUT THEY'LL BE OKAY.
THEN, IT'S NOT TRUE, MISS RACHELLE?
WHAT ISN'T, SWEET-HEART?
SAMUEL SAID THEY'RE ALL DEAD.
HE SAID JOHNIS ISN'T REALLY A GUARD AND GOT 'EM ALL CAUGHT --
-- AND NOW THEY'RE BEING EATEN FOR STEW.
OUR SON SAID THAT?
WELL, YOU TELL SAMUEL I DECIDE WHO'S IN THE FOREST GUARD, NOT HIM.

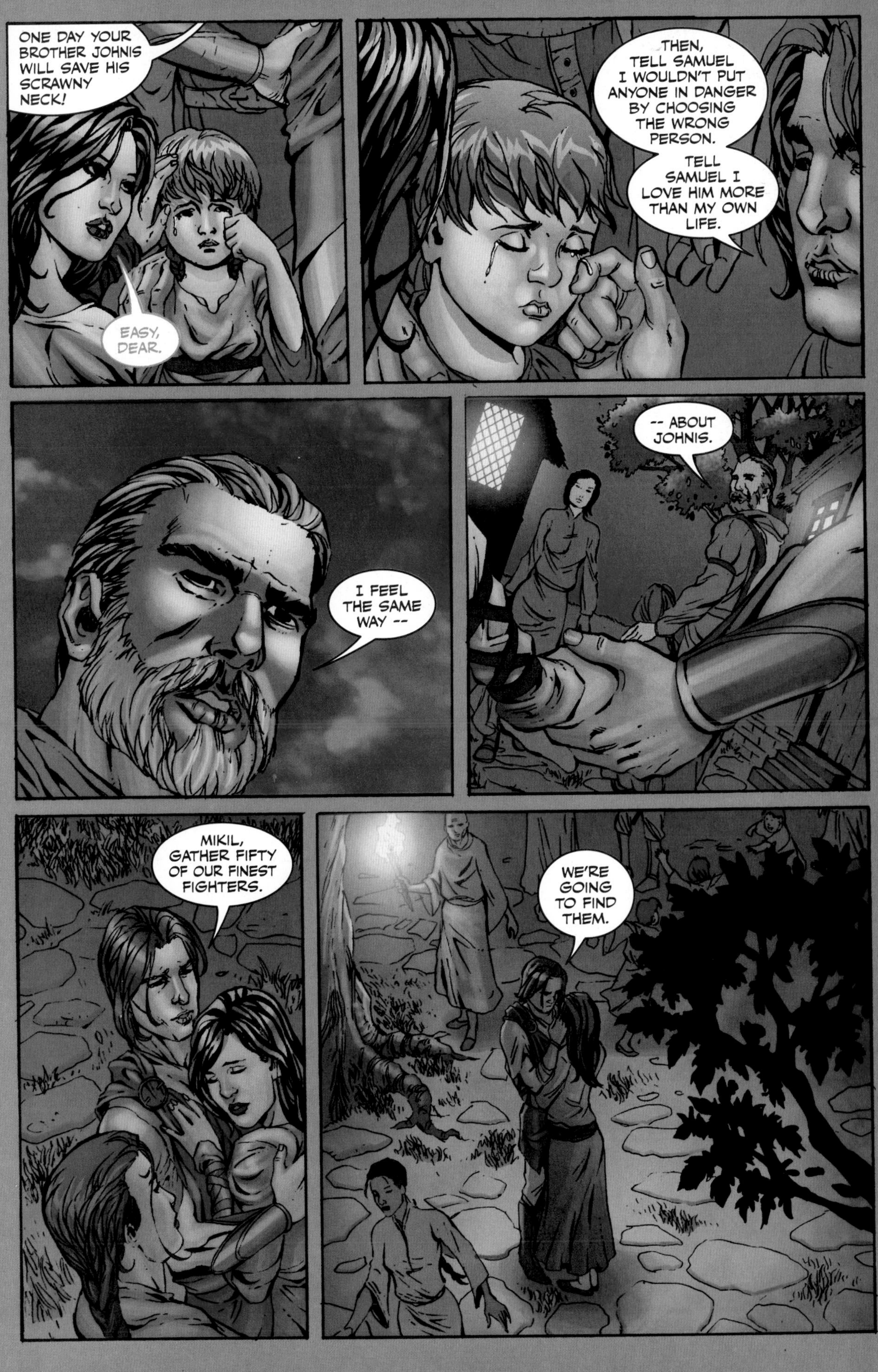
ONE DAY YOUR BROTHER JOHNIS WILL SAVE HIS SCRAWNY NECK!
EASY, DEAR.
THEN, TELL SAMUEL I WOULDN'T PUT ANYONE IN DANGER BY CHOOSING THE WRONG PERSON.
TELL SAMUEL I LOVE HIM MORE THAN MY OWN LIFE.
I FEEL THE SAME WAY --
-- ABOUT JOHNIS.
MIKIL, GATHER FIFTY OF OUR FINEST FIGHTERS.
WE'RE GOING TO FIND THEM.

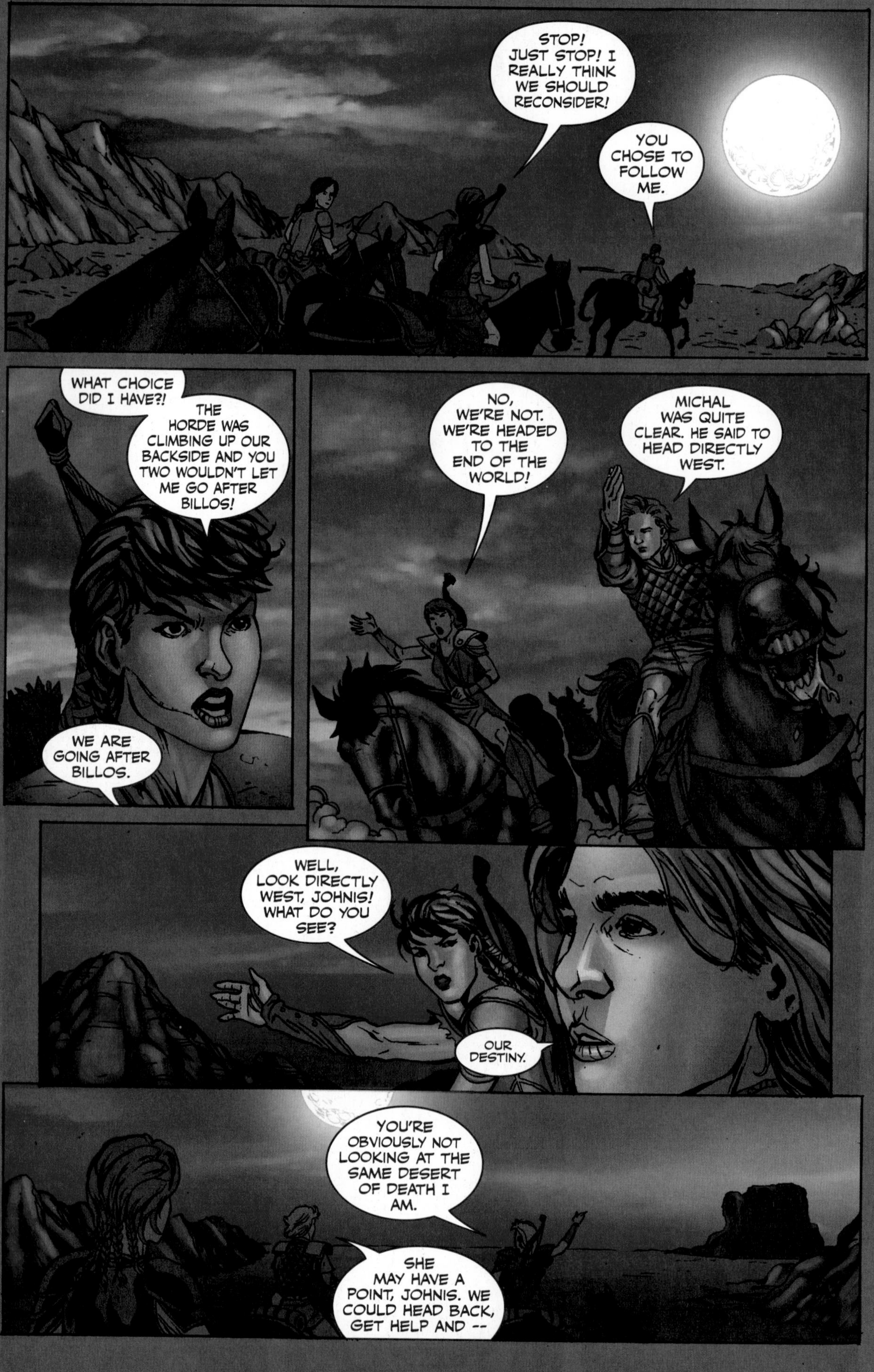
STOP! JUST STOP! I REALLY THINK WE SHOULD RECONSIDER!
YOU CHOSE TO FOLLOW ME.
WHAT CHOICE DID I HAVE?!
THE HORDE WAS CLIMBING UP OUR BACKSIDE AND YOU TWO WOULDN'T LET ME GO AFTER BILLOS!
WE ARE GOING AFTER BILLOS.
NO, WE'RE NOT. WE'RE HEADED TO THE END OF THE WORLD!
MICHAL WAS QUITE CLEAR. HE SAID TO HEAD DIRECTLY WEST.
WELL, LOOK DIRECTLY WEST, JOHNIS! WHAT DO YOU SEE?
OUR DESTINY.
YOU'RE OBVIOUSLY NOT LOOKING AT THE SAME DESERT OF DEATH I AM.
SHE MAY HAVE A POINT, JOHNIS. WE COULD HEAD BACK, GET HELP AND --

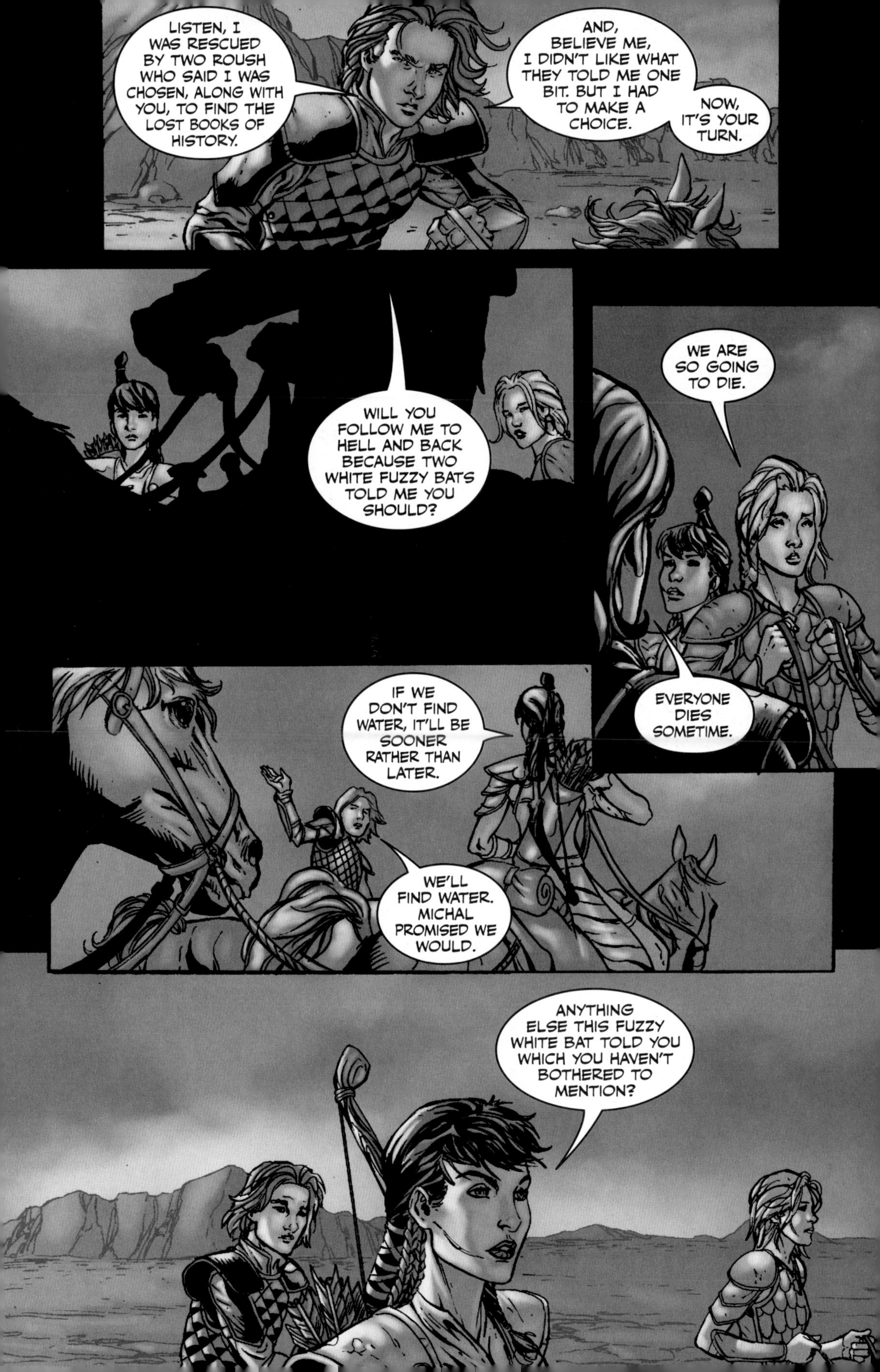
LISTEN, I WAS RESCUED BY TWO ROUSH WHO SAID I WAS CHOSEN, ALONG WITH YOU, TO FIND THE LOST BOOKS OF HISTORY.
AND, BELIEVE ME, I DIDN'T LIKE WHAT THEY TOLD ME ONE BIT. BUT I HAD TO MAKE A CHOICE.
NOW, IT'S YOUR TURN.
WILL YOU FOLLOW ME TO HELL AND BACK BECAUSE TWO WHITE FUZZY BATS TOLD ME YOU SHOULD?
WE ARE SO GOING TO DIE.
EVERYONE DIES SOMETIME.
IF WE DON'T FIND WATER, IT'LL BE SOONER RATHER THAN LATER.
WE'LL FIND WATER. MICHAL PROMISED WE WOULD.
ANYTHING ELSE THIS FUZZY WHITE BAT TOLD YOU WHICH YOU HAVEN'T BOTHERED TO MENTION?

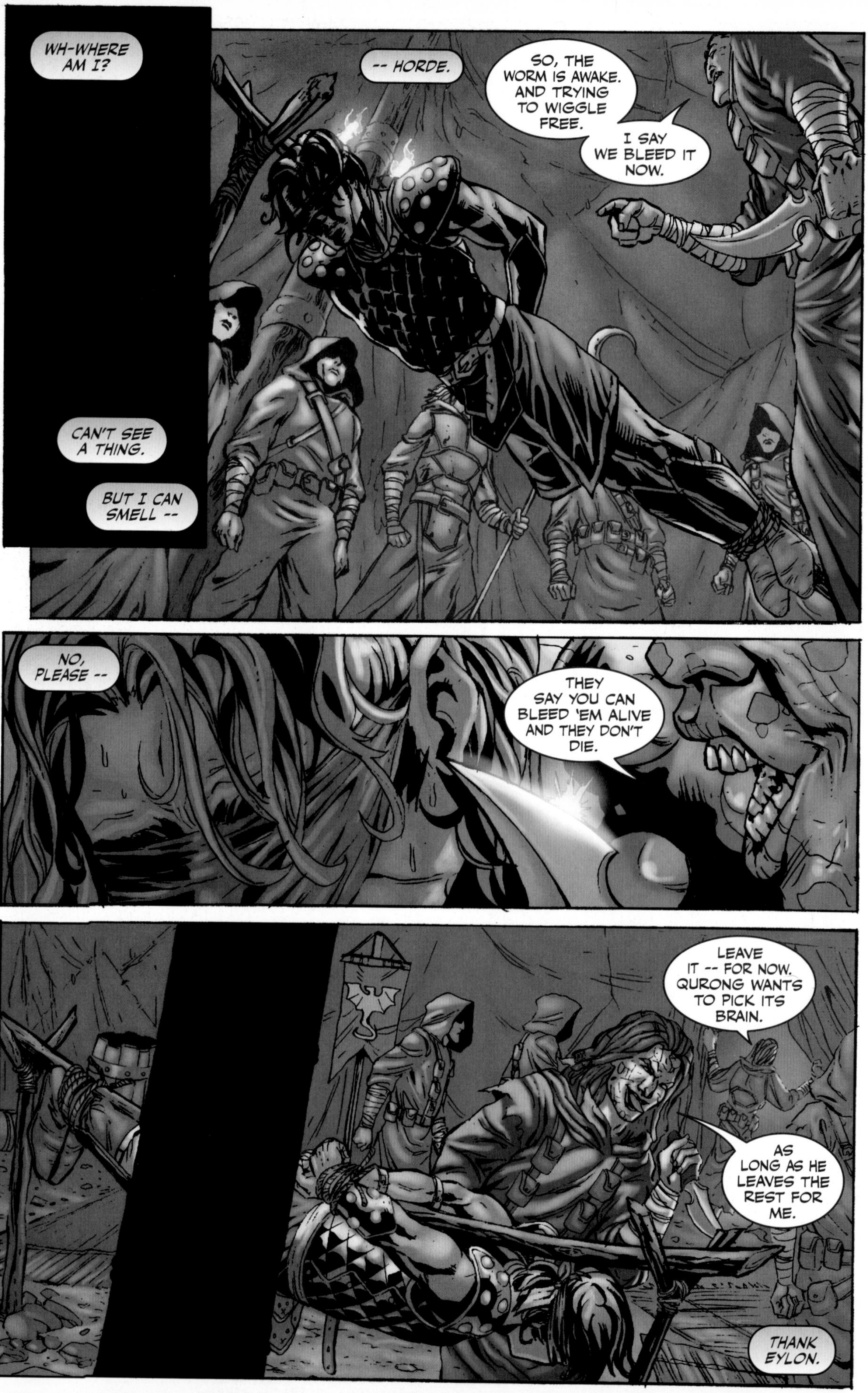
WH-WHERE AM I?
CAN'T SEE A THING.
BUT I CAN SMELL --
-- HORDE.
SO, THE WORM IS AWAKE. AND TRYING TO WIGGLE FREE.
I SAY WE BLEED IT NOW.
NO, PLEASE --
THEY SAY YOU CAN BLEED 'EM ALIVE AND THEY DON'T DIE.
LEAVE IT -- FOR NOW. QURONG WANTS TO PICK ITS BRAIN.
AS LONG AS HE LEAVES THE REST FOR ME.
THANK EYLON.

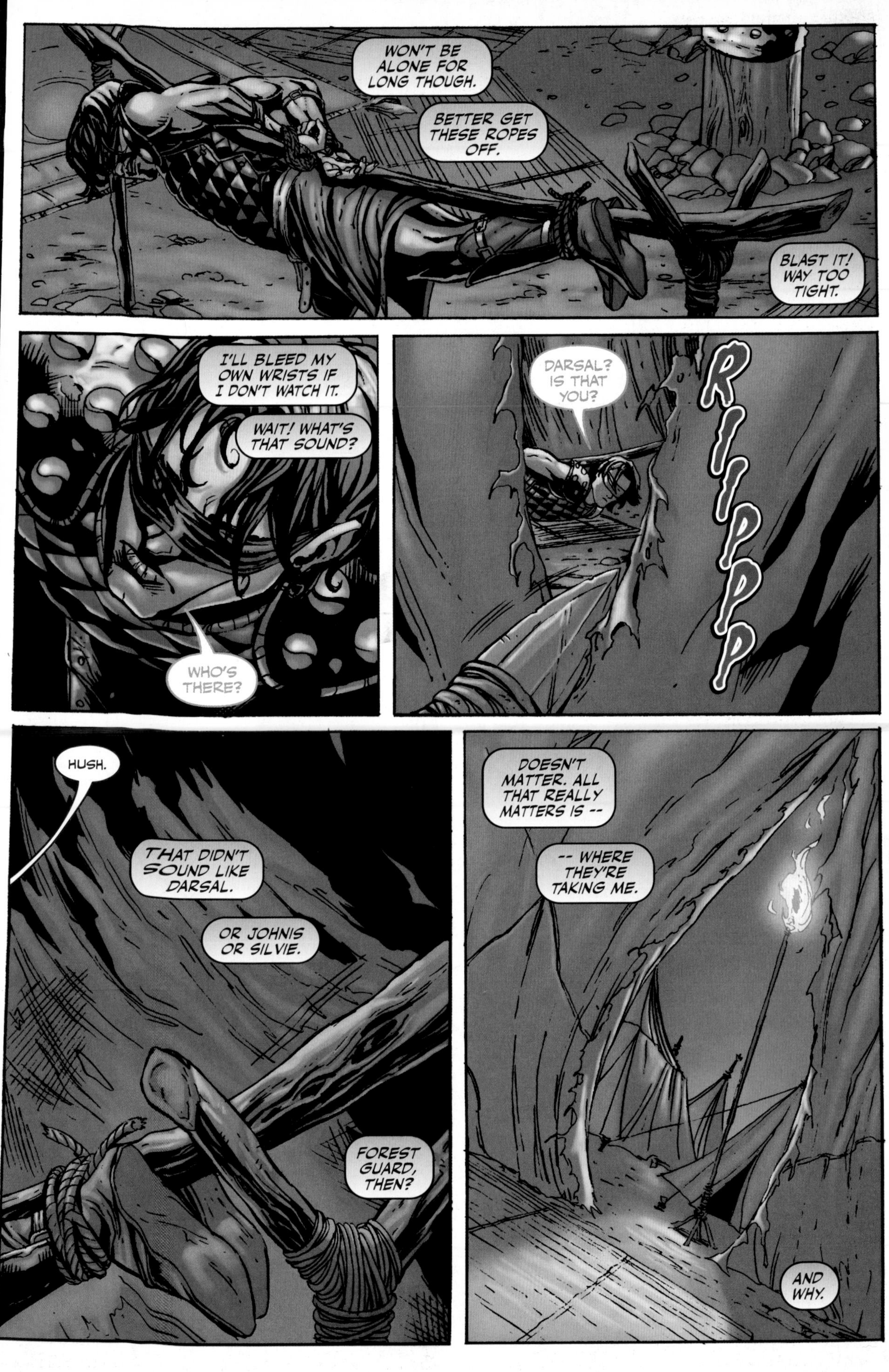
WON'T BE ALONE FOR LONG THOUGH.
BETTER GET THESE ROPES OFF.
BLAST IT! WAY TOO TIGHT.
I'LL BLEED MY OWN WRISTS IF I DON'T WATCH IT.
WAIT! WHAT'S THAT SOUND?
WHO'S THERE?
DARSAL? IS THAT YOU?
RIIPPP
HUSH.
THAT DIDN'T SOUND LIKE DARSAL.
OR JOHNIS OR SILVIE.
FOREST GUARD, THEN?
DOESN'T MATTER. ALL THAT REALLY MATTERS IS --
-- WHERE THEY'RE TAKING ME.
AND WHY.

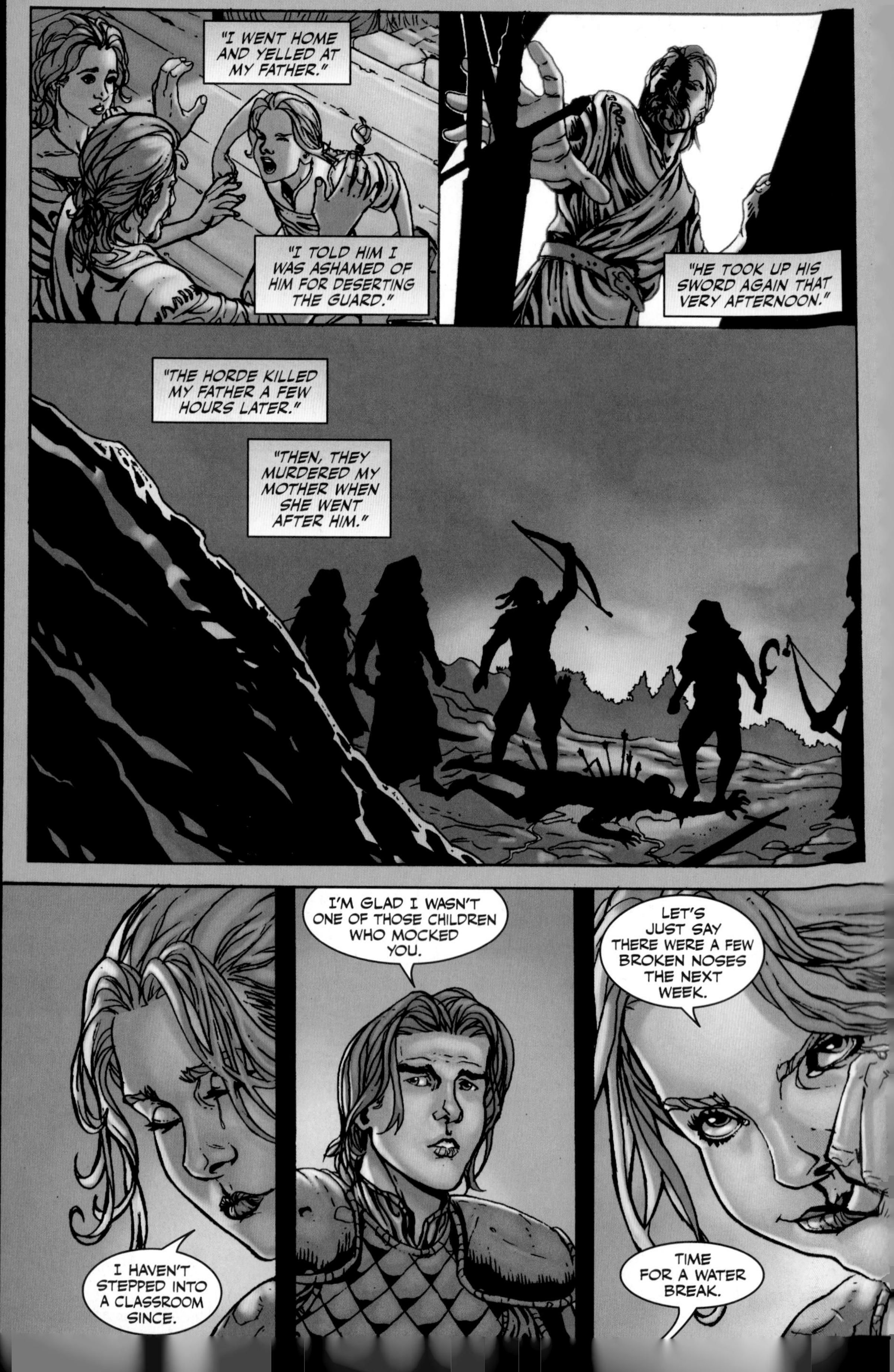
"I WENT HOME AND YELLED AT MY FATHER."
"I TOLD HIM I WAS ASHAMED OF HIM FOR DESERTING THE GUARD."
"HE TOOK UP HIS SWORD AGAIN THAT VERY AFTERNOON."
"THE HORDE KILLED MY FATHER A FEW HOURS LATER."
"THEN, THEY MURDERED MY MOTHER WHEN SHE WENT AFTER HIM."
I HAVEN'T STEPPED INTO A CLASSROOM SINCE.
I'M GLAD I WASN'T ONE OF THOSE CHILDREN WHO MOCKED YOU.
LET'S JUST SAY THERE WERE A FEW BROKEN NOSES THE NEXT WEEK.
TIME FOR A WATER BREAK.

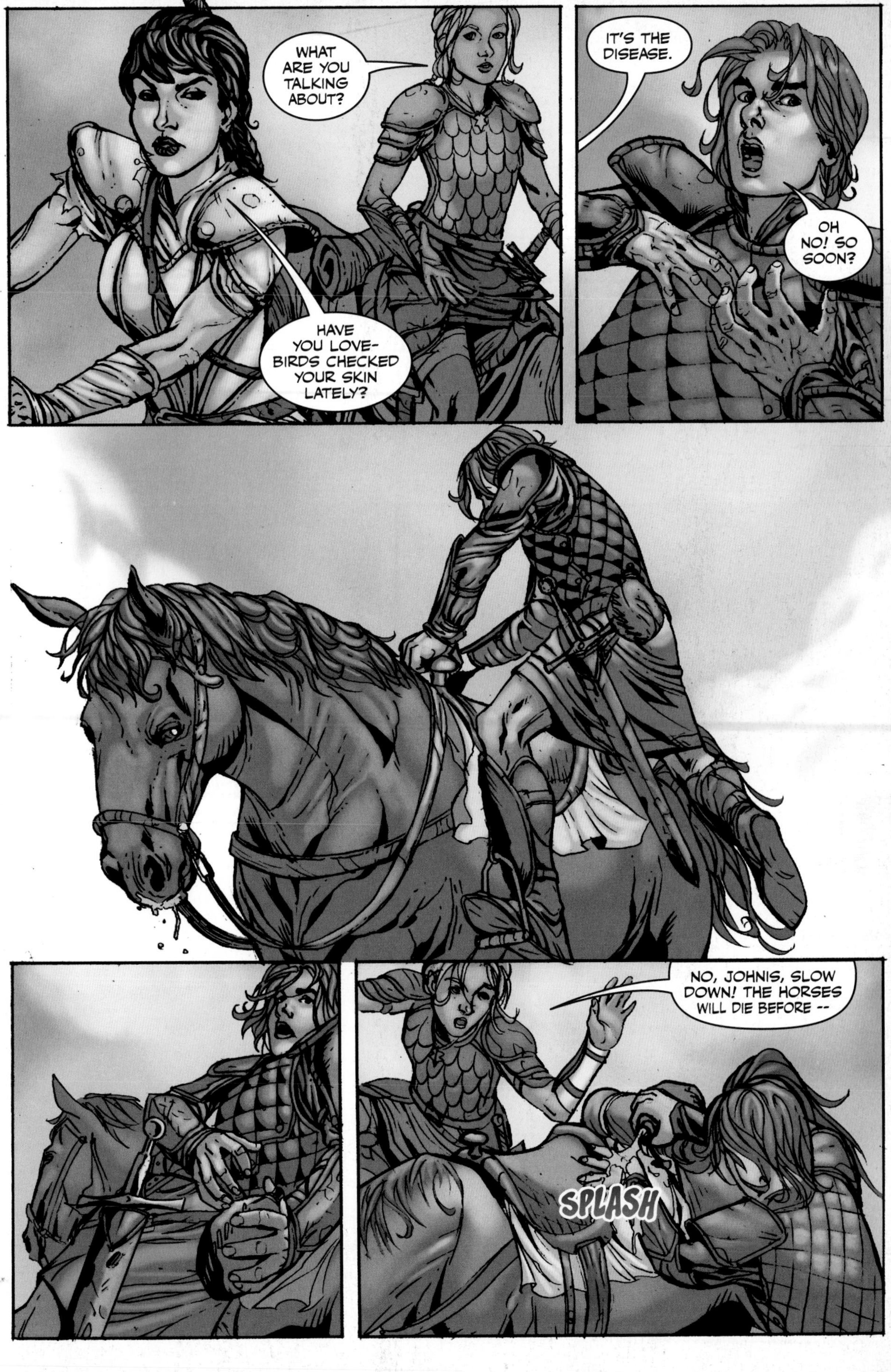
WHAT ARE YOU TALKING ABOUT?
HAVE YOU LOVE-BIRDS CHECKED YOUR SKIN LATELY?
IT'S THE DISEASE.
OH NO! SO SOON?
NO, JOHNIS, SLOW DOWN! THE HORSES WILL DIE BEFORE --
SPLASH

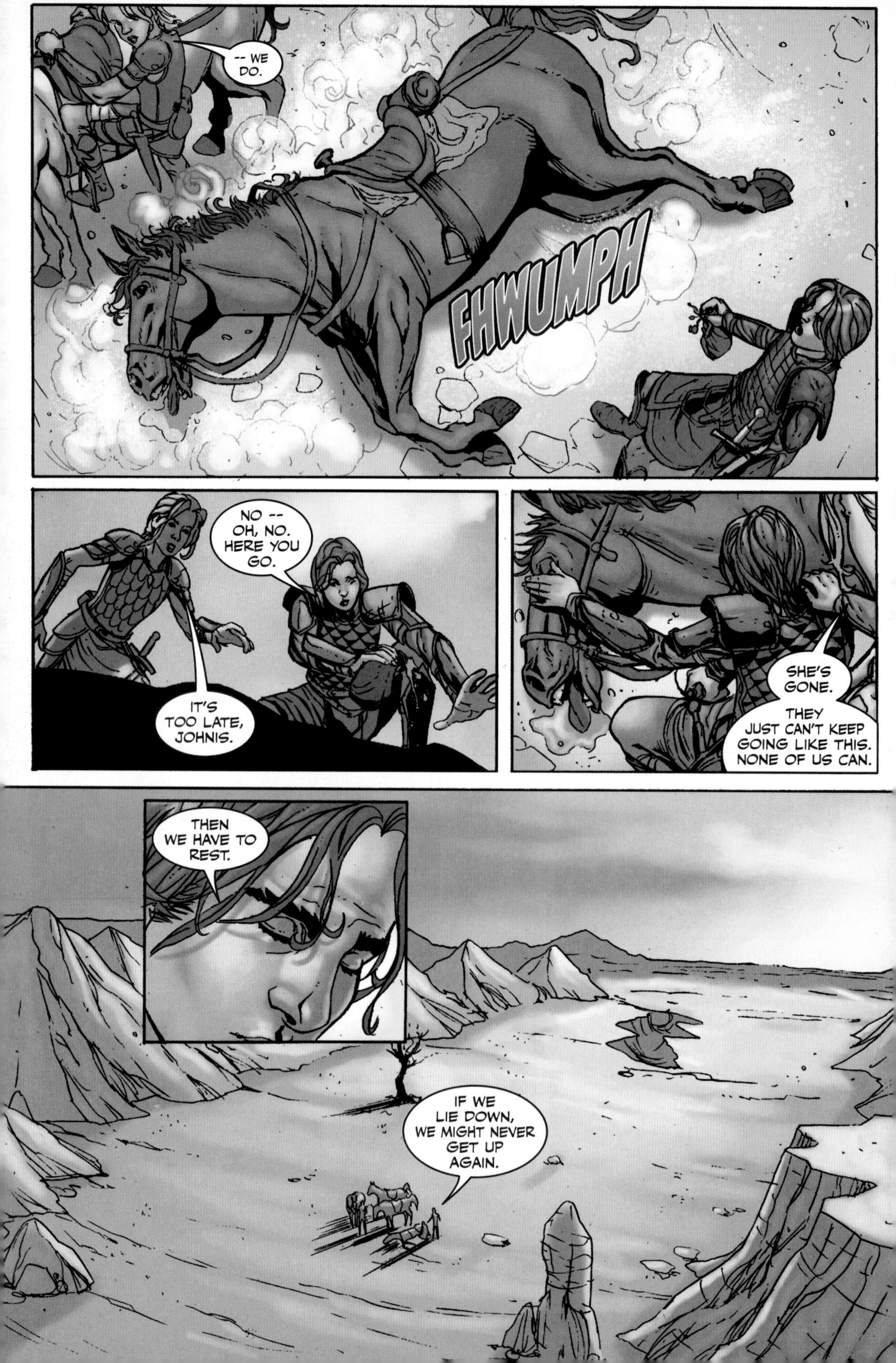
-- WE DO.
FHWUMPH
NO -- OH, NO. HERE YOU GO.
IT'S TOO LATE, JOHNIS.
SHE'S GONE.
THEY JUST CAN'T KEEP GOING LIKE THIS. NONE OF US CAN.
THEN WE HAVE TO REST.
IF WE LIE DOWN, WE MIGHT NEVER GET UP AGAIN.

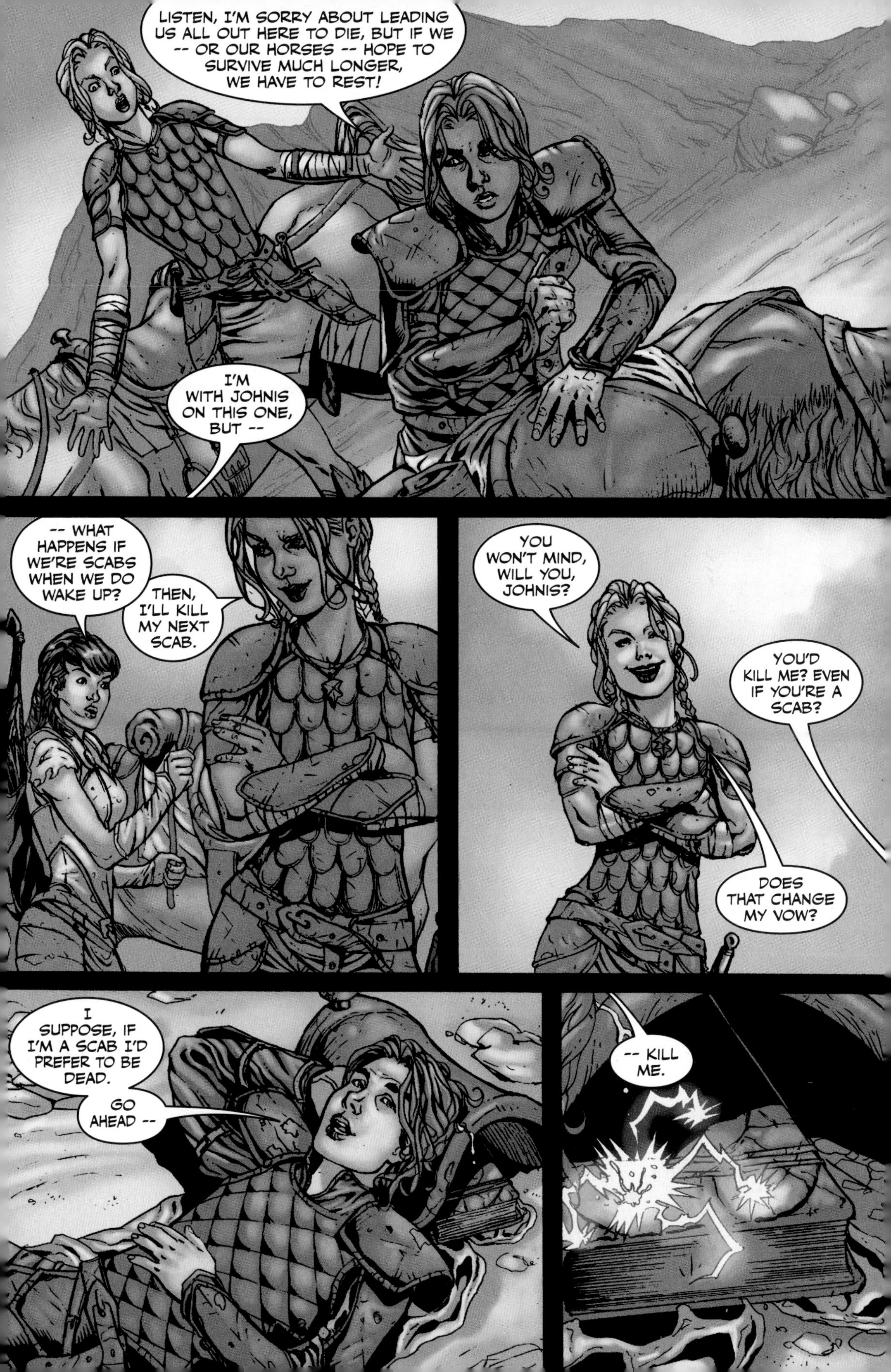
LISTEN, I'M SORRY ABOUT LEADING US ALL OUT HERE TO DIE, BUT IF WE -- OR OUR HORSES -- HOPE TO SURVIVE MUCH LONGER, WE HAVE TO REST!
I'M WITH JOHNIS ON THIS ONE, BUT --
-- WHAT HAPPENS IF WE'RE SCABS WHEN WE DO WAKE UP?
THEN, I'LL KILL MY NEXT SCAB.
YOU WON'T MIND, WILL YOU, JOHNIS?
YOU'D KILL ME? EVEN IF YOU'RE A SCAB?
DOES THAT CHANGE MY VOW?
I SUPPOSE, IF I'M A SCAB I'D PREFER TO BE DEAD.
GO AHEAD --
-- KILL ME.

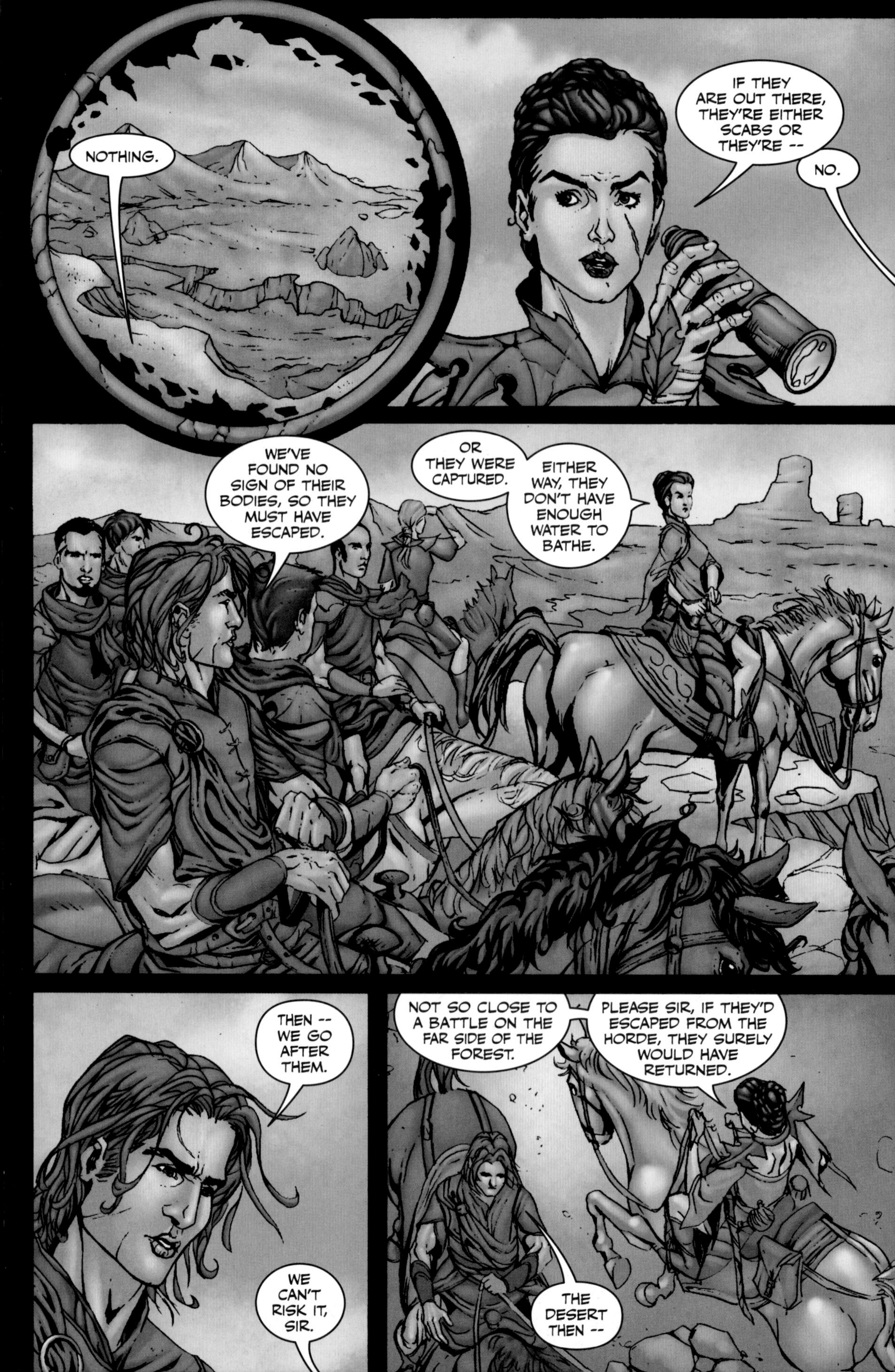
NOTHING.
IF THEY ARE OUT THERE, THEY'RE EITHER SCABS OR THEY'RE --
NO.
WE'VE FOUND NO SIGN OF THEIR BODIES, SO THEY MUST HAVE ESCAPED.
OR THEY WERE CAPTURED.
EITHER WAY, THEY DON'T HAVE ENOUGH WATER TO BATHE.
THEN -- WE GO AFTER THEM.
WE CAN'T RISK IT, SIR.
NOT SO CLOSE TO A BATTLE ON THE FAR SIDE OF THE FOREST.
PLEASE SIR, IF THEY'D ESCAPED FROM THE HORDE, THEY SURELY WOULD HAVE RETURNED.
THE DESERT THEN --

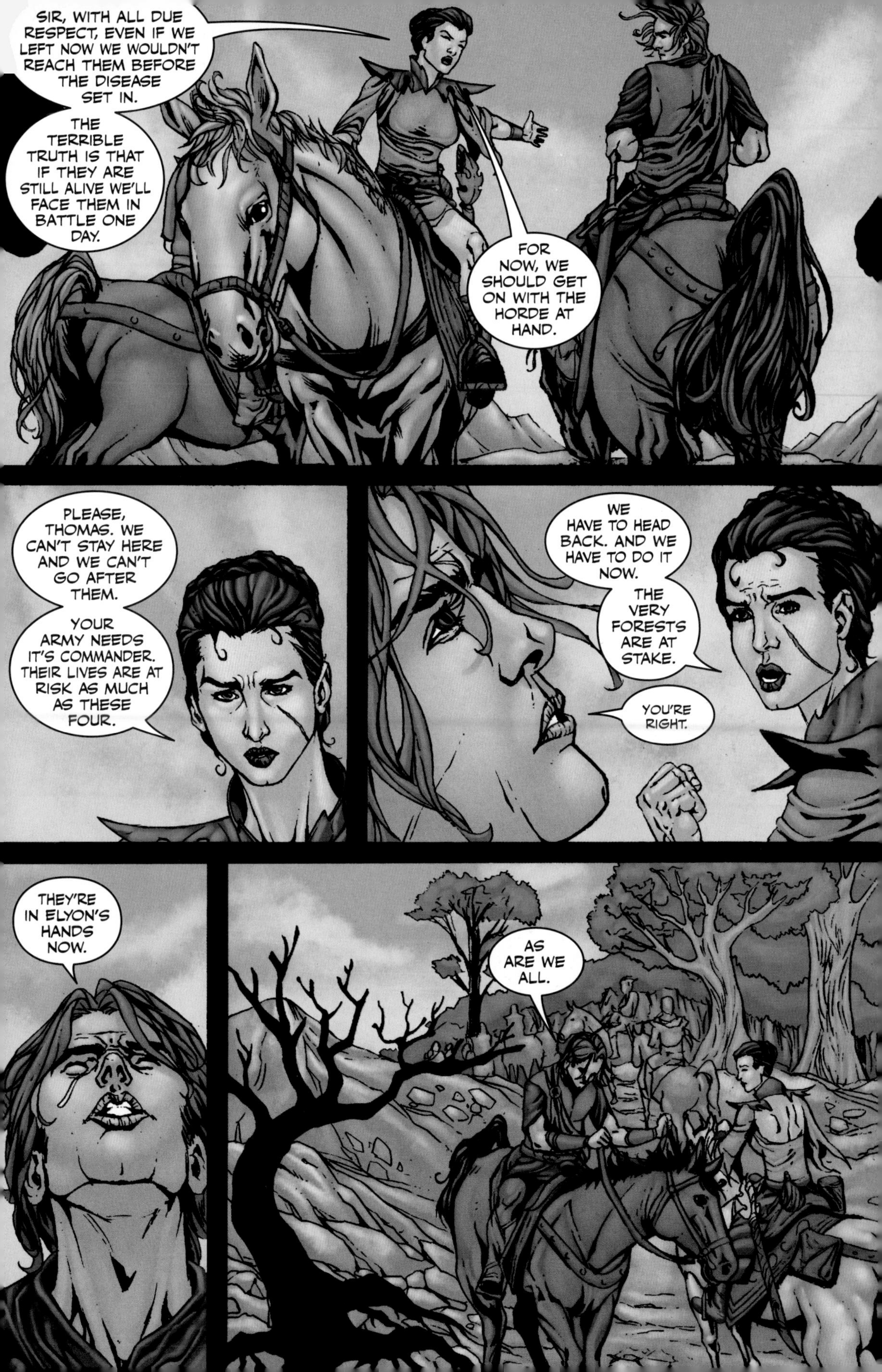
SIR, WITH ALL DUE RESPECT, EVEN IF WE LEFT NOW WE WOULDN'T REACH THEM BEFORE THE DISEASE SET IN.
THE TERRIBLE TRUTH IS THAT IF THEY ARE STILL ALIVE WE'LL FACE THEM IN BATTLE ONE DAY.
FOR NOW, WE SHOULD GET ON WITH THE HORDE AT HAND.
PLEASE, THOMAS. WE CAN'T STAY HERE AND WE CAN'T GO AFTER THEM.
YOUR ARMY NEEDS IT'S COMMANDER. THEIR LIVES ARE AT RISK AS MUCH AS THESE FOUR.
WE HAVE TO HEAD BACK. AND WE HAVE TO DO IT NOW.
THE VERY FORESTS ARE AT STAKE.
YOU'RE RIGHT.
THEY'RE IN ELYON'S HANDS NOW.
AS ARE WE ALL.

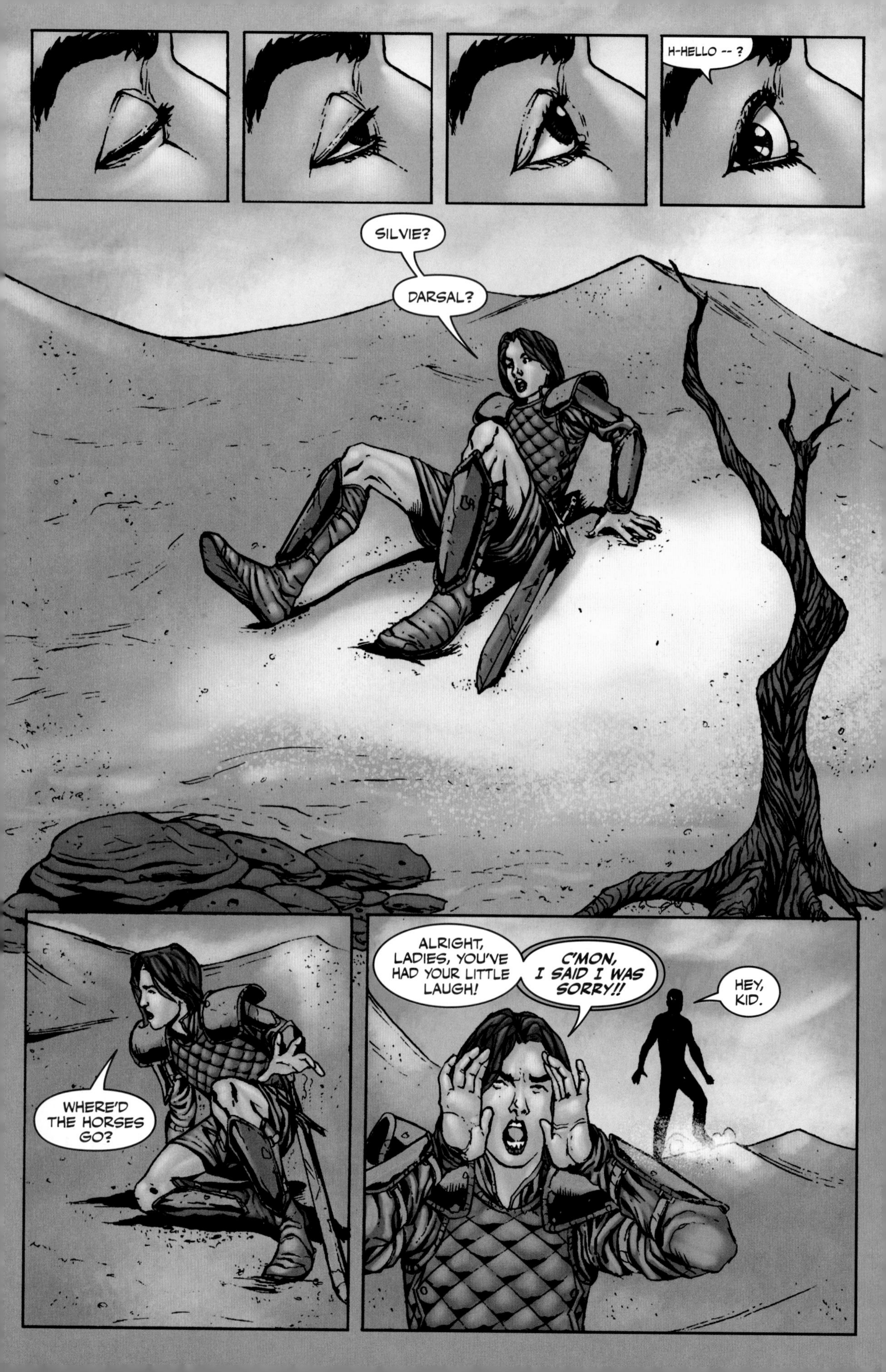
H-HELLO -- ?
SILVIE?
DARSAL?
WHERE'D THE HORSES GO?
ALRIGHT, LADIES, YOU'VE HAD YOUR LITTLE LAUGH!
C'MON, I SAID I WAS SORRY!!
HEY, KID.

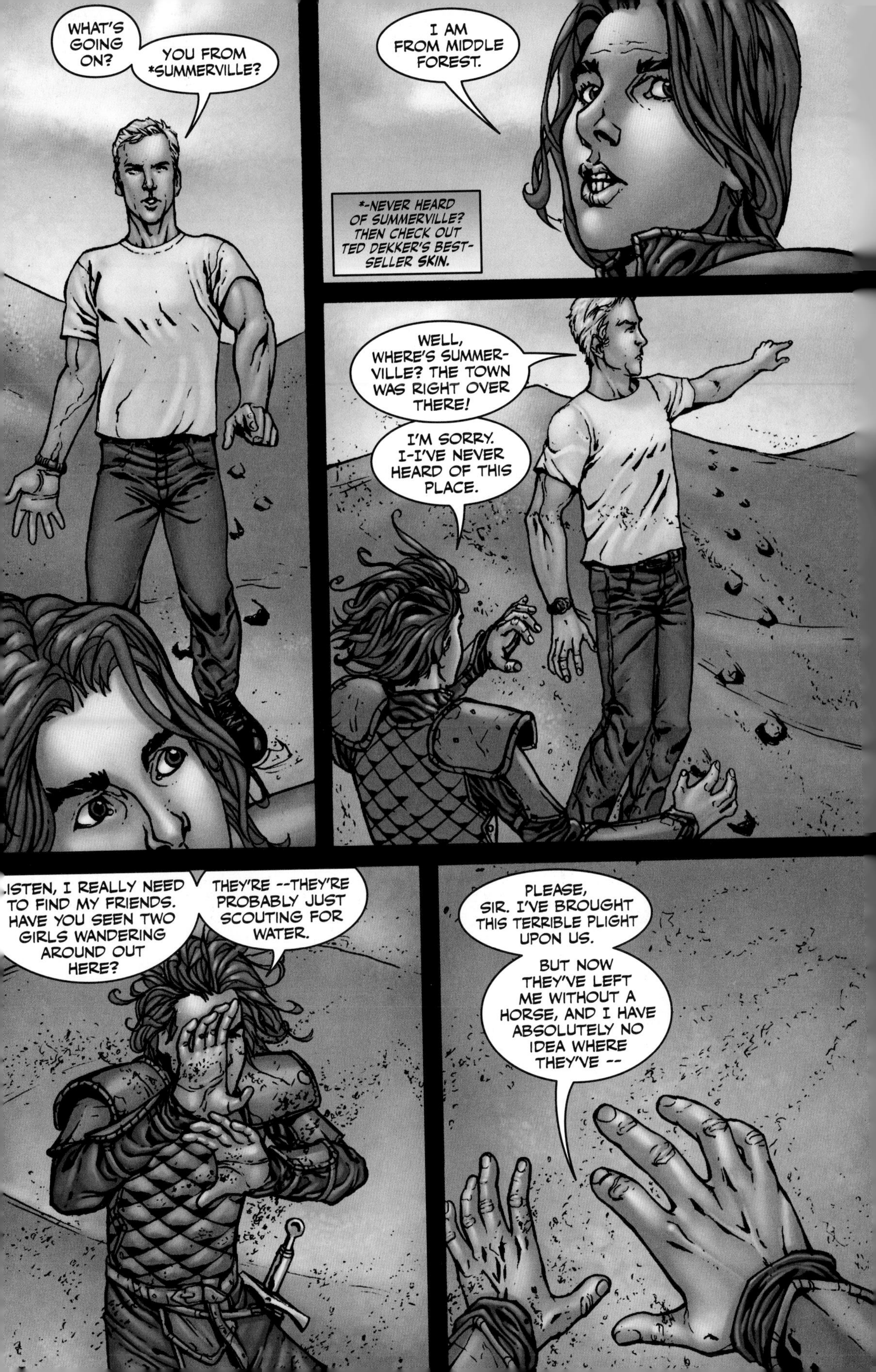
WHAT'S GOING ON?
YOU FROM *SUMMERVILLE?
I AM FROM MIDDLE FOREST.
*-NEVER HEARD OF SUMMERVILLE? THEN CHECK OUT TED DEKKER'S BEST-SELLER SKIN.
WELL, WHERE'S SUMMER-VILLE? THE TOWN WAS RIGHT OVER THERE!
I'M SORRY. I-I'VE NEVER HEARD OF THIS PLACE.
ISTEN, I REALLY NEED TO FIND MY FRIENDS. HAVE YOU SEEN TWO GIRLS WANDERING AROUND OUT HERE?
THEY'RE --THEY'RE PROBABLY JUST SCOUTING FOR WATER.
PLEASE, SIR. I'VE BROUGHT THIS TERRIBLE PLIGHT UPON US.
BUT NOW THEY'VE LEFT ME WITHOUT A HORSE, AND I HAVE ABSOLUTELY NO IDEA WHERE THEY'VE --

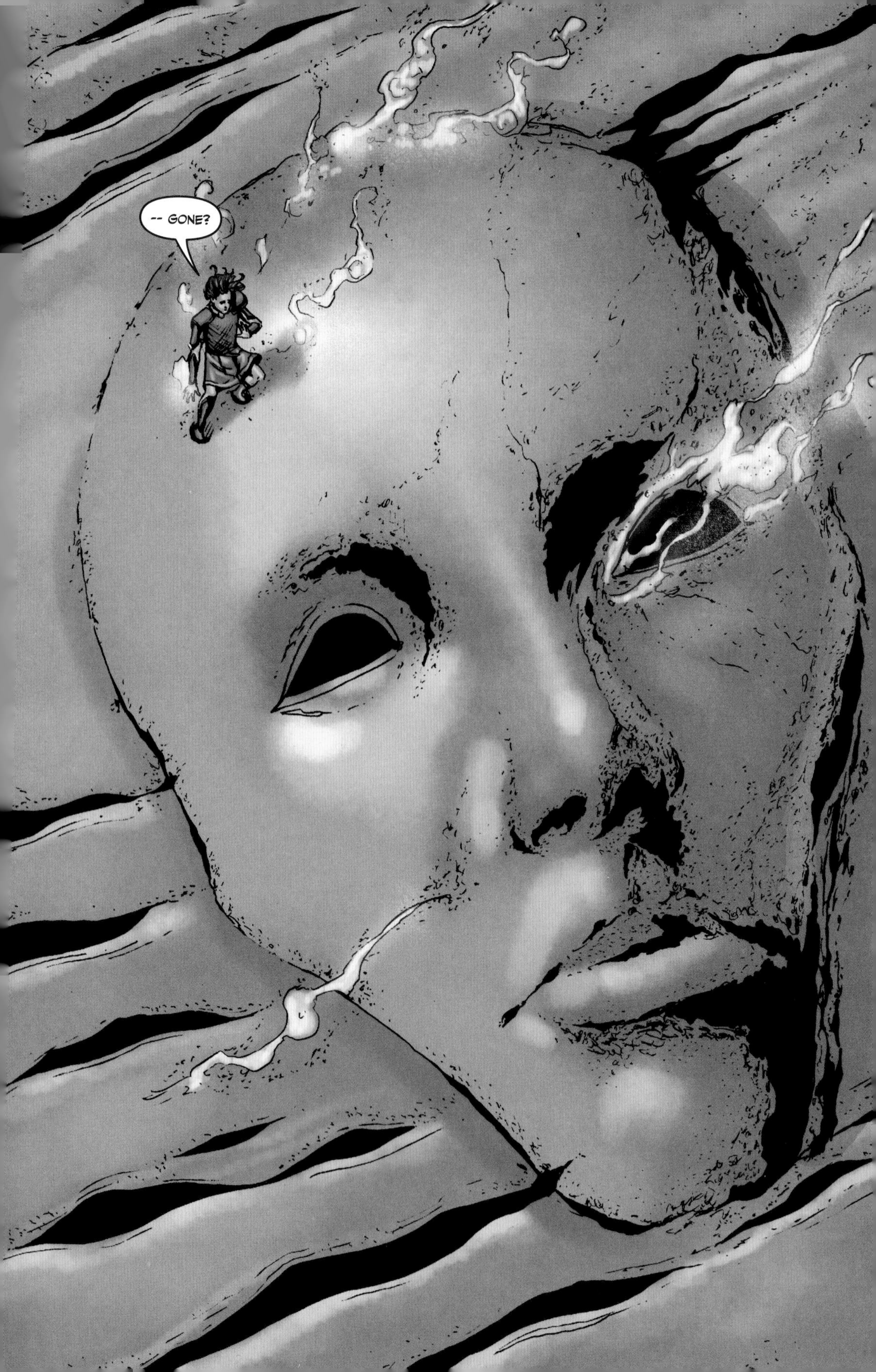
-- GONE?

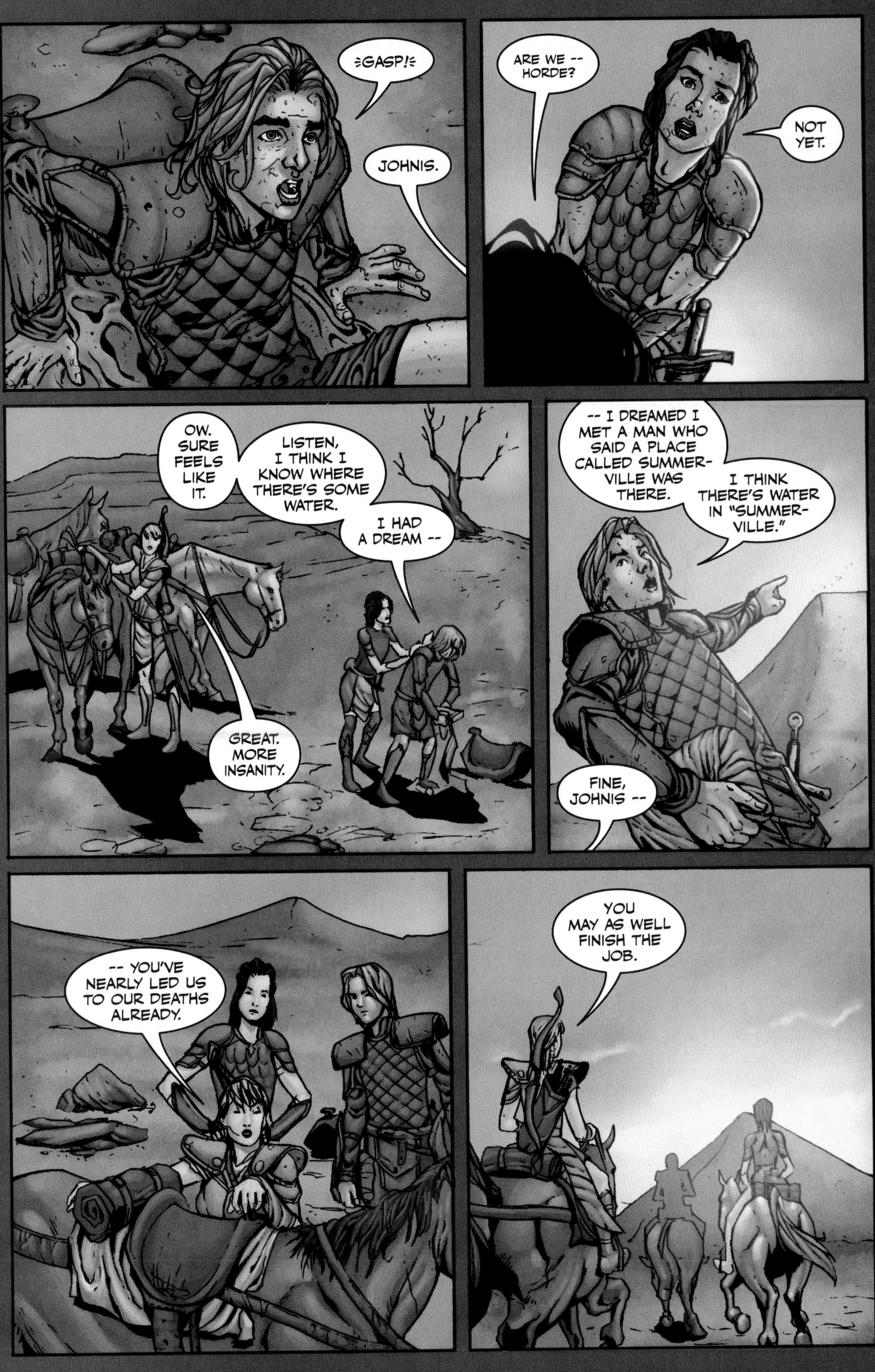

≋GASP!≋
JOHNIS.
ARE WE -- HORDE?
NOT YET.
OW. SURE FEELS LIKE IT.
LISTEN, I THINK I KNOW WHERE THERE'S SOME WATER.
I HAD A DREAM --
GREAT. MORE INSANITY.
-- I DREAMED I MET A MAN WHO SAID A PLACE CALLED SUMMER-VILLE WAS THERE.
I THINK THERE'S WATER IN "SUMMER-VILLE."
FINE, JOHNIS --
-- YOU'VE NEARLY LED US TO OUR DEATHS ALREADY.
YOU MAY AS WELL FINISH THE JOB.

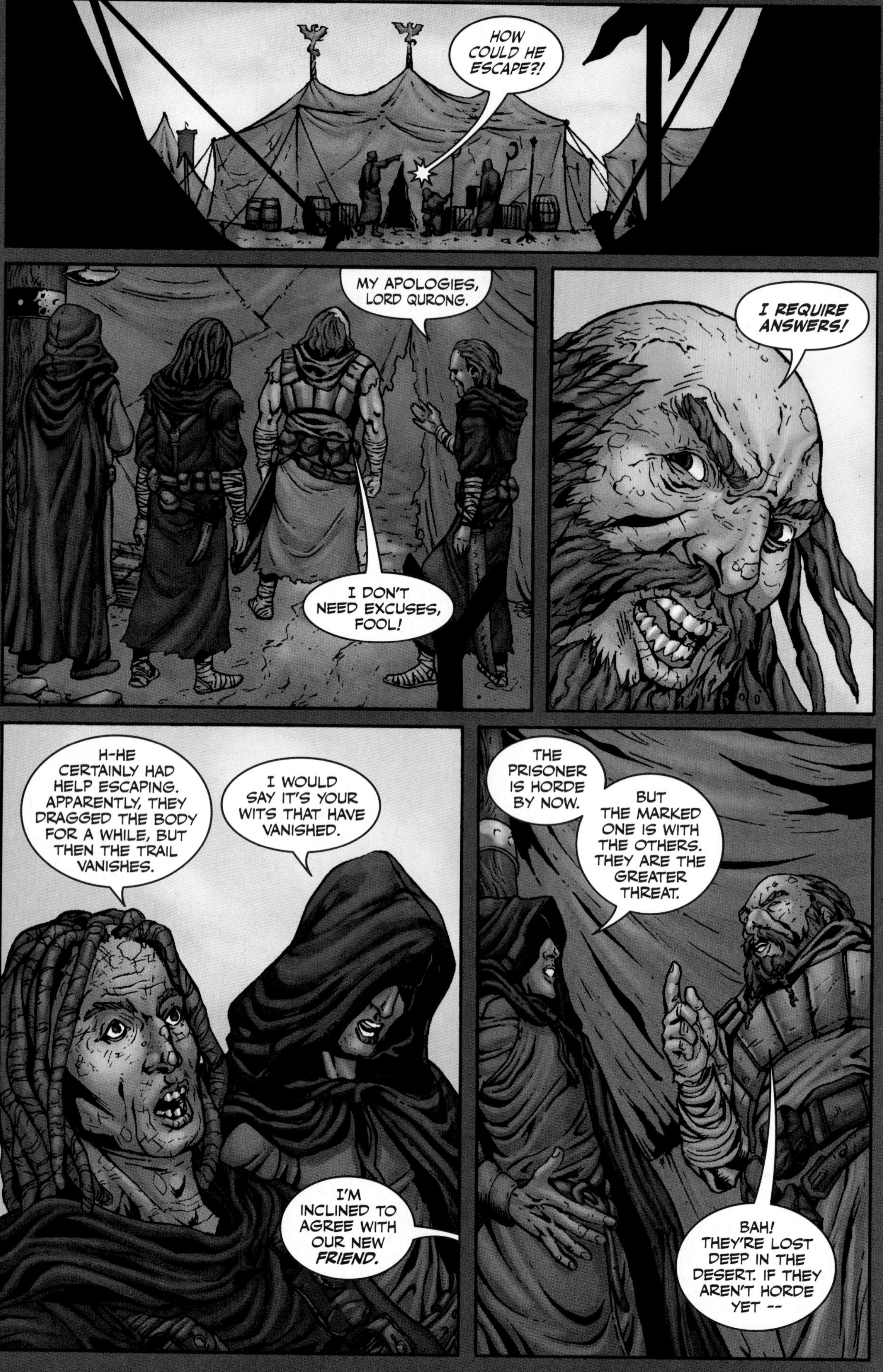
HOW COULD HE ESCAPE?!
MY APOLOGIES, LORD QURONG.
I DON'T NEED EXCUSES, FOOL!
I REQUIRE ANSWERS!
H-HE CERTAINLY HAD HELP ESCAPING. APPARENTLY, THEY DRAGGED THE BODY FOR A WHILE, BUT THEN THE TRAIL VANISHES.
I WOULD SAY IT'S YOUR WITS THAT HAVE VANISHED.
I'M INCLINED TO AGREE WITH OUR NEW *FRIEND*.
THE PRISONER IS HORDE BY NOW.
BUT THE MARKED ONE IS WITH THE OTHERS. THEY ARE THE GREATER THREAT.
BAH! THEY'RE LOST DEEP IN THE DESERT. IF THEY AREN'T HORDE YET --

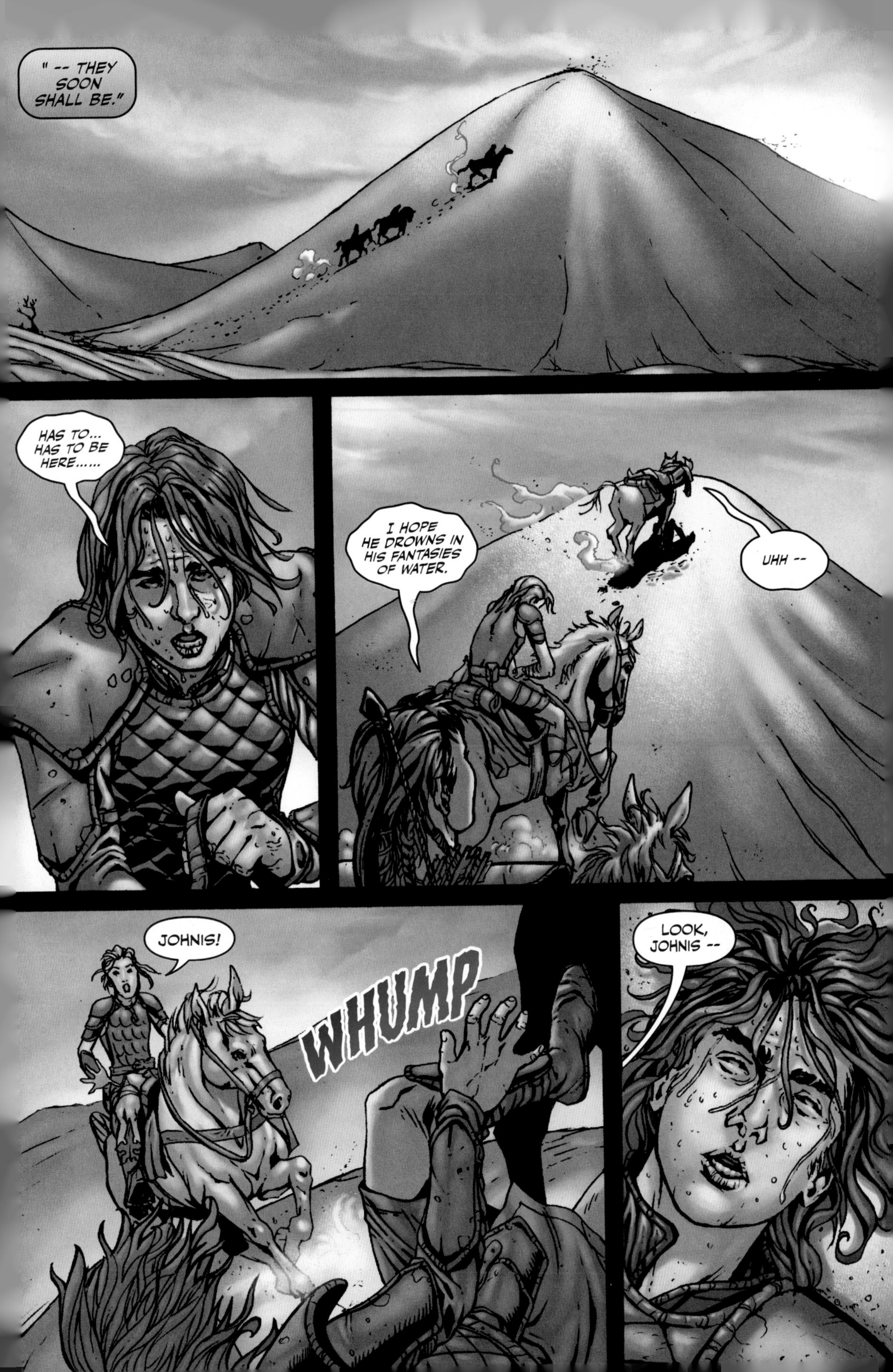
" -- THEY SOON SHALL BE."
HAS TO... HAS TO BE HERE......
I HOPE HE DROWNS IN HIS FANTASIES OF WATER.
UHH --
JOHNIS!
WHUMP
LOOK, JOHNIS --

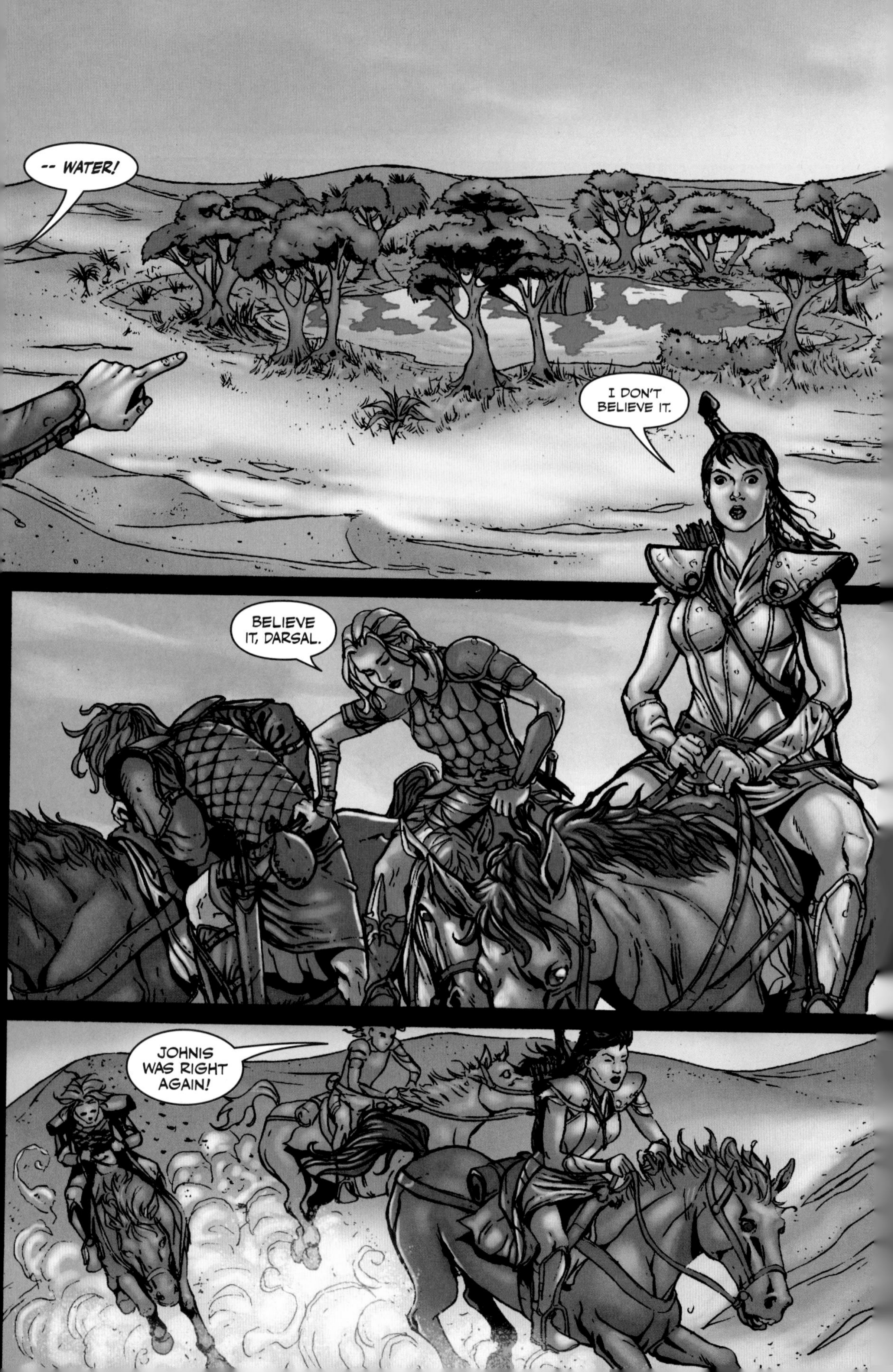
-- WATER!
I DON'T BELIEVE IT.
BELIEVE IT, DARSAL.
JOHNIS WAS RIGHT AGAIN!

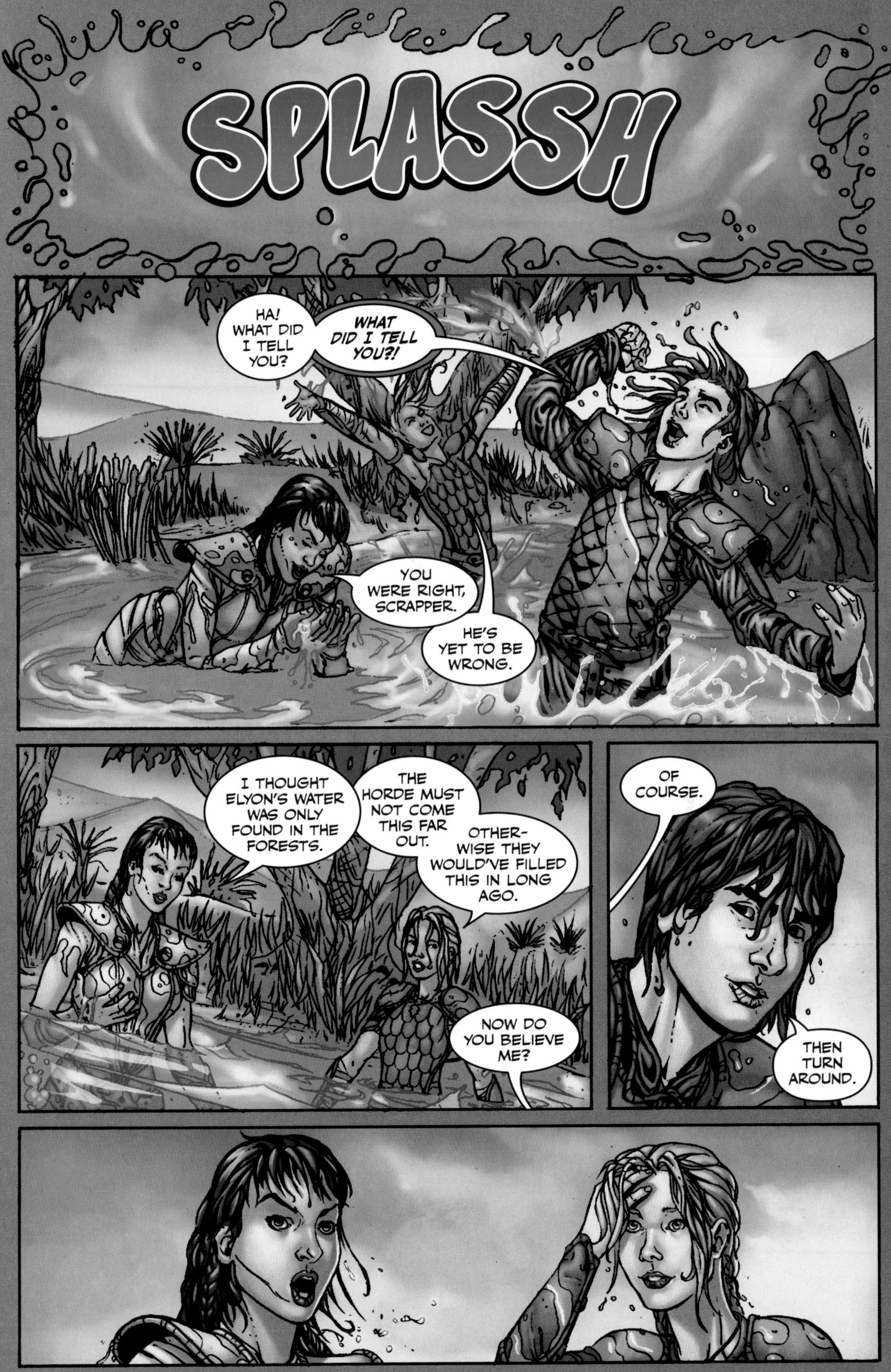
SPLASSH
HA! WHAT DID I TELL YOU?
WHAT DID I TELL YOU?!
YOU WERE RIGHT, SCRAPPER.
HE'S YET TO BE WRONG.
I THOUGHT ELYON'S WATER WAS ONLY FOUND IN THE FORESTS.
THE HORDE MUST NOT COME THIS FAR OUT.
OTHER-WISE THEY WOULD'VE FILLED THIS IN LONG AGO.
NOW DO YOU BELIEVE ME?
OF COURSE.
THEN TURN AROUND.

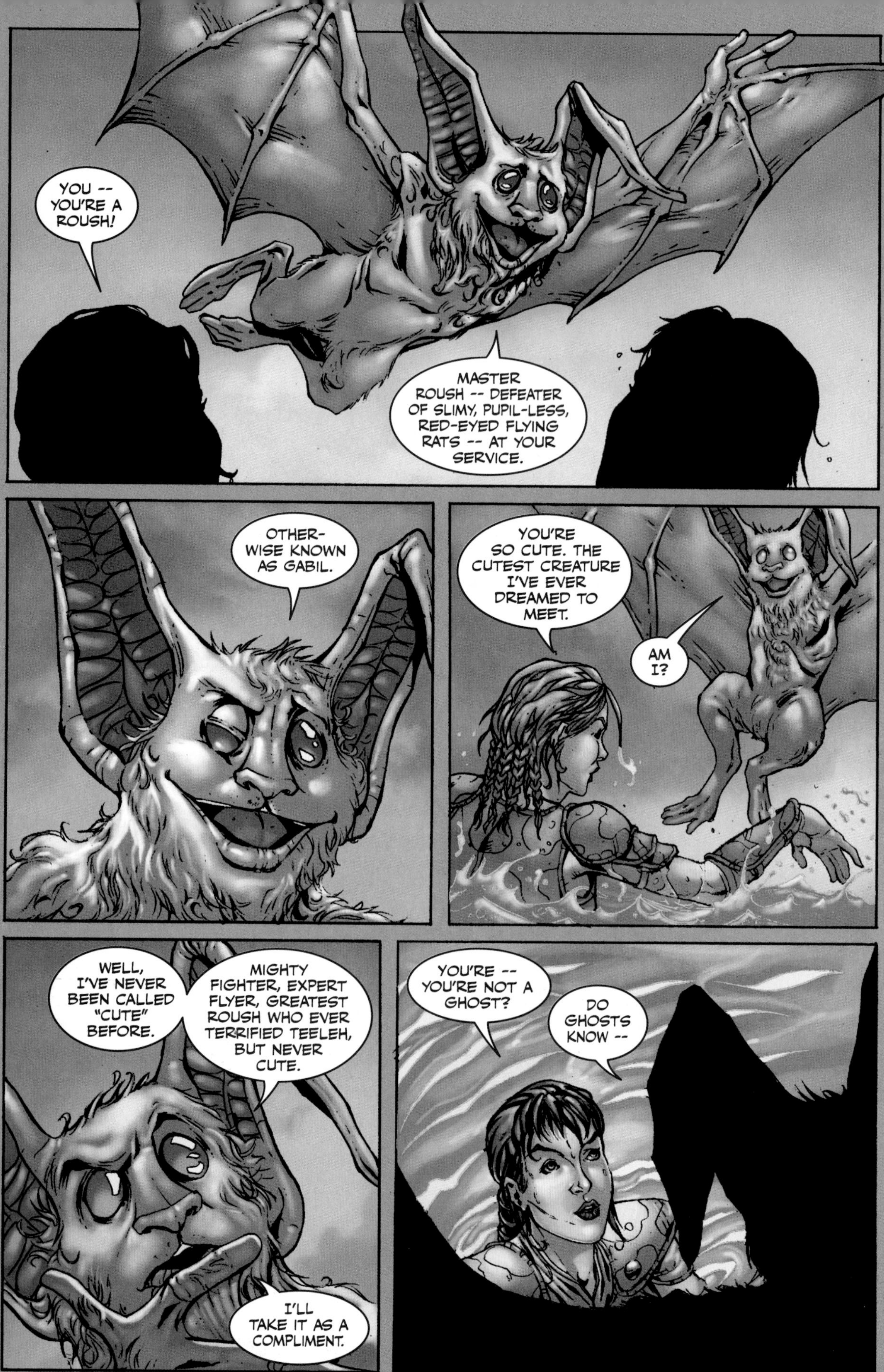
YOU -- YOU'RE A ROUSH!
MASTER ROUSH -- DEFEATER OF SLIMY, PUPIL-LESS, RED-EYED FLYING RATS -- AT YOUR SERVICE.
OTHER-WISE KNOWN AS GABIL.
YOU'RE SO CUTE. THE CUTEST CREATURE I'VE EVER DREAMED TO MEET.
AM I?
WELL, I'VE NEVER BEEN CALLED "CUTE" BEFORE.
MIGHTY FIGHTER, EXPERT FLYER, GREATEST ROUSH WHO EVER TERRIFIED TEELEH, BUT NEVER CUTE.
I'LL TAKE IT AS A COMPLIMENT.
YOU'RE -- YOU'RE NOT A GHOST?
DO GHOSTS KNOW --

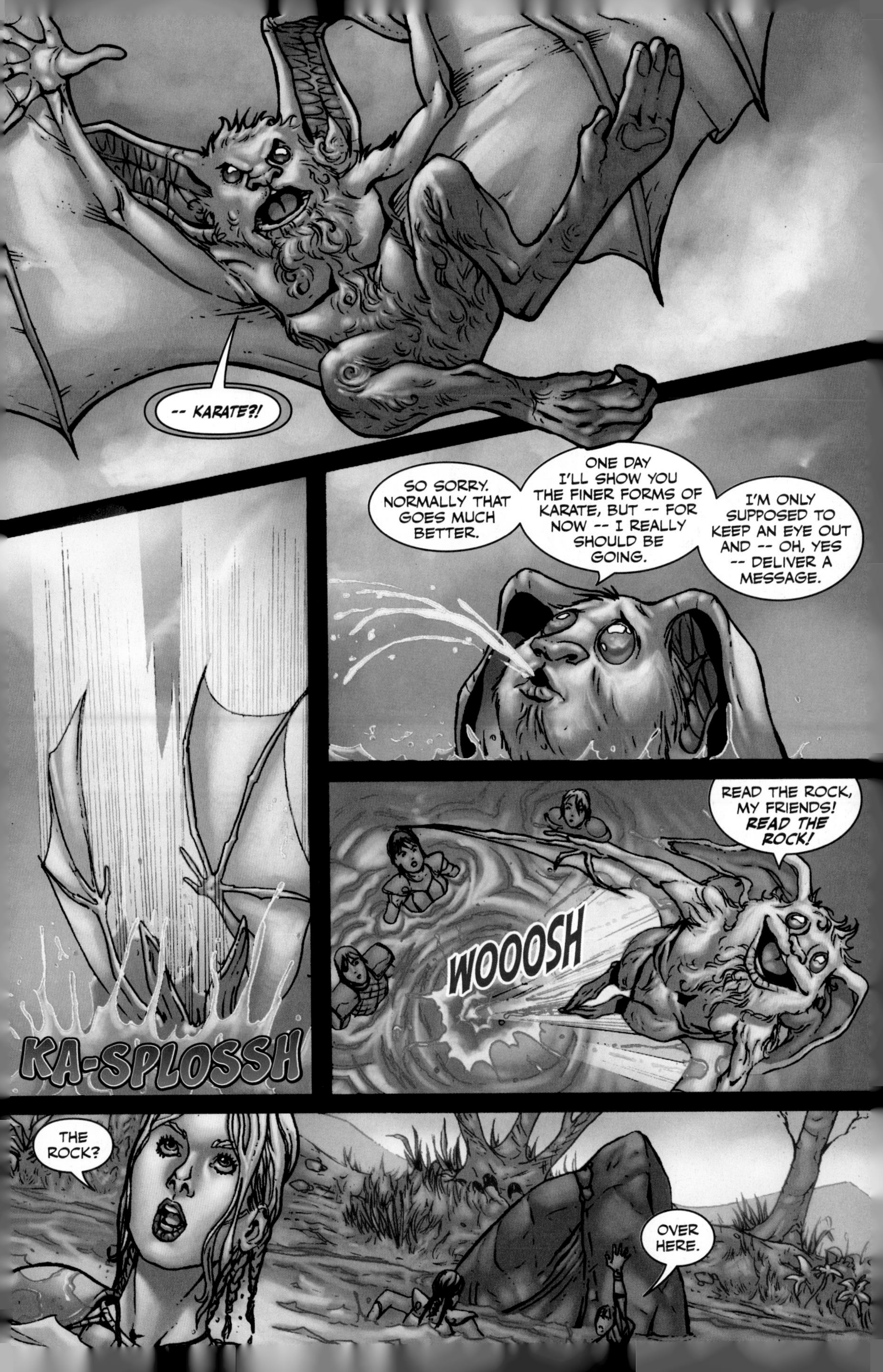

-- KARATE?!
SO SORRY. NORMALLY THAT GOES MUCH BETTER.
ONE DAY I'LL SHOW YOU THE FINER FORMS OF KARATE, BUT -- FOR NOW -- I REALLY SHOULD BE GOING.
I'M ONLY SUPPOSED TO KEEP AN EYE OUT AND -- OH, YES -- DELIVER A MESSAGE.
KA-SPLOSSH
READ THE ROCK, MY FRIENDS! READ THE ROCK!
WOOOSH
THE ROCK?
OVER HERE.

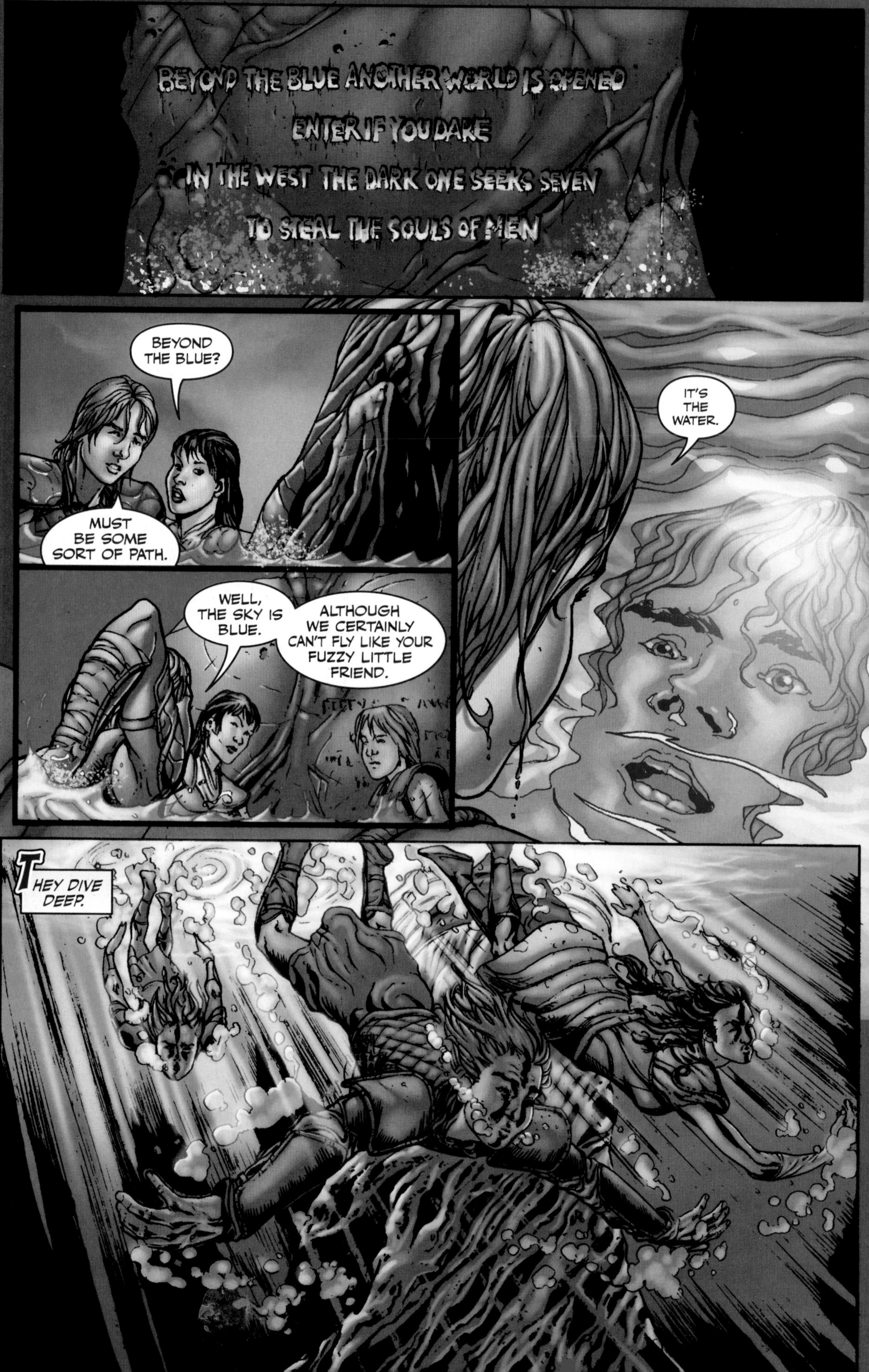
BEYOND THE BLUE ANOTHER WORLD IS OPENED
ENTER IF YOU DARE
IN THE WEST THE DARK ONE SEEKS SEVEN
TO STEAL THE SOULS OF MEN
BEYOND THE BLUE?
MUST BE SOME SORT OF PATH.
IT'S THE WATER.
WELL, THE SKY IS BLUE.
ALTHOUGH WE CERTAINLY CAN'T FLY LIKE YOUR FUZZY LITTLE FRIEND.
THEY DIVE DEEP.

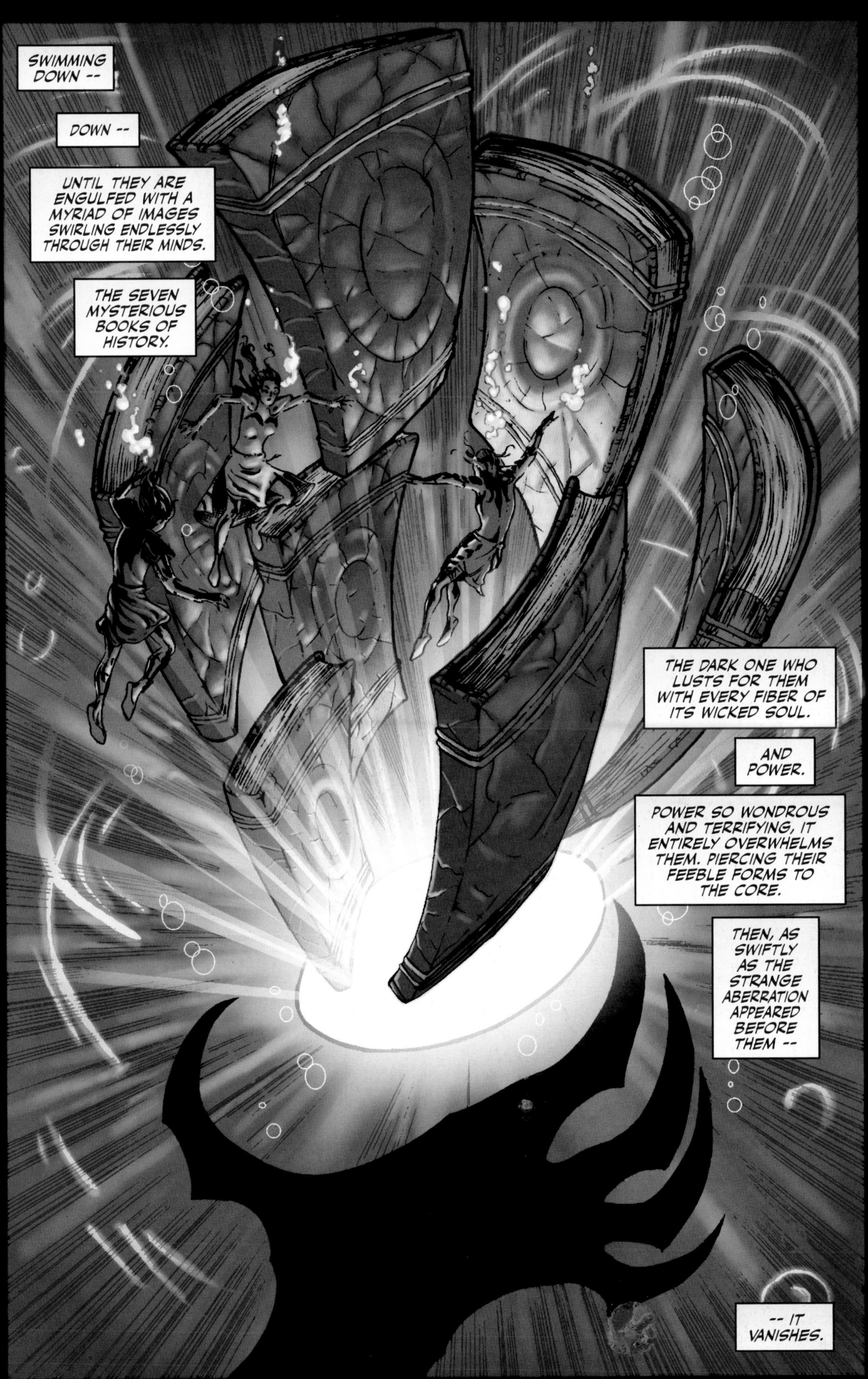
SWIMMING DOWN --
DOWN --
UNTIL THEY ARE ENGULFED WITH A MYRIAD OF IMAGES SWIRLING ENDLESSLY THROUGH THEIR MINDS.
THE SEVEN MYSTERIOUS BOOKS OF HISTORY.
THE DARK ONE WHO LUSTS FOR THEM WITH EVERY FIBER OF ITS WICKED SOUL.
AND POWER.
POWER SO WONDROUS AND TERRIFYING, IT ENTIRELY OVERWHELMS THEM. PIERCING THEIR FEEBLE FORMS TO THE CORE.
THEN, AS SWIFTLY AS THE STRANGE ABERRATION APPEARED BEFORE THEM --
-- IT VANISHES.

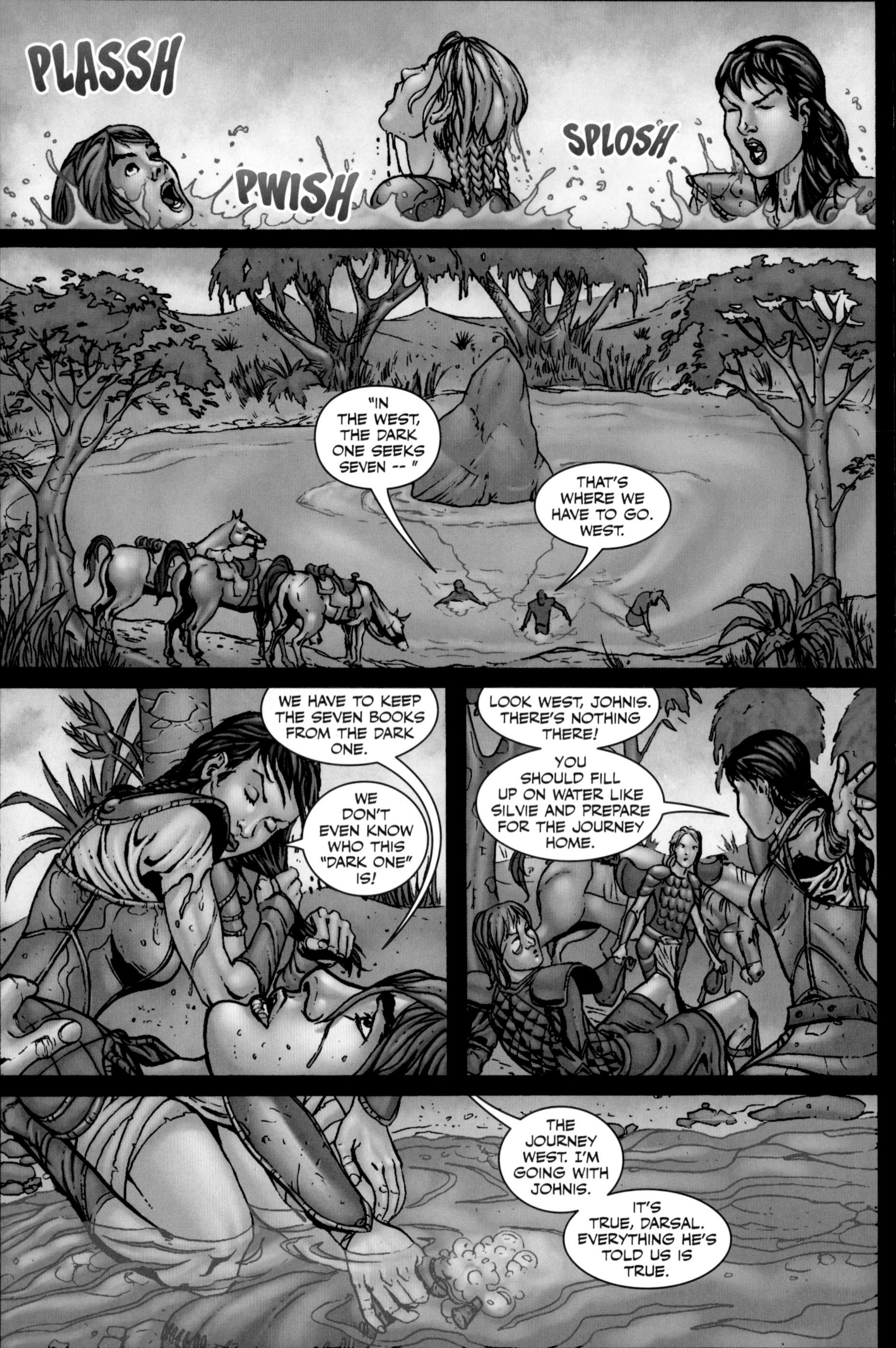
PLASSH
PWISH
SPLOSH
"IN THE WEST, THE DARK ONE SEEKS SEVEN -- "
THAT'S WHERE WE HAVE TO GO. WEST.
WE HAVE TO KEEP THE SEVEN BOOKS FROM THE DARK ONE.
WE DON'T EVEN KNOW WHO THIS "DARK ONE" IS!
LOOK WEST, JOHNIS. THERE'S NOTHING THERE!
YOU SHOULD FILL UP ON WATER LIKE SILVIE AND PREPARE FOR THE JOURNEY HOME.
THE JOURNEY WEST. I'M GOING WITH JOHNIS.
IT'S TRUE, DARSAL. EVERYTHING HE'S TOLD US IS TRUE.

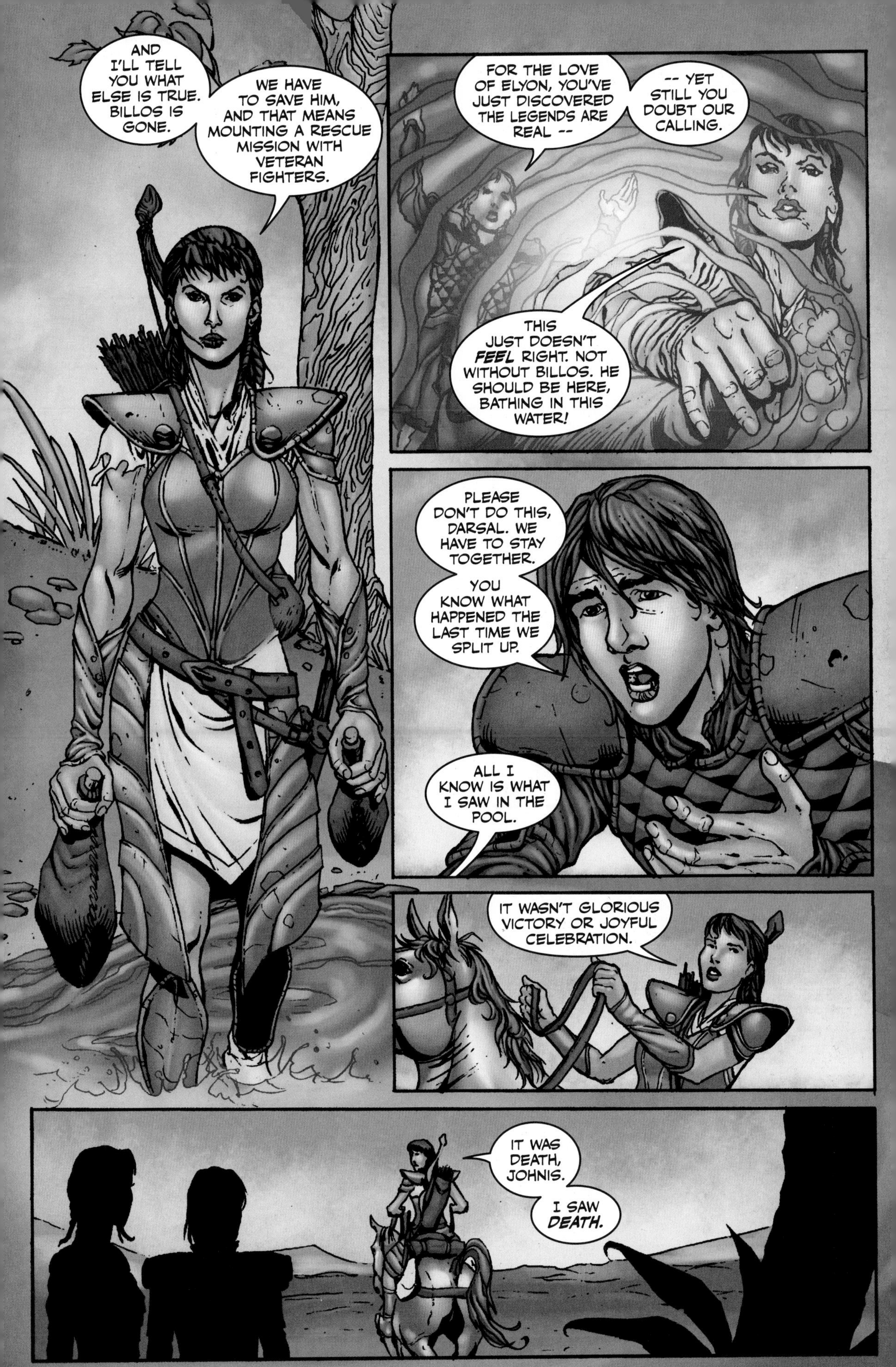
AND I'LL TELL YOU WHAT ELSE IS TRUE. BILLOS IS GONE.
WE HAVE TO SAVE HIM, AND THAT MEANS MOUNTING A RESCUE MISSION WITH VETERAN FIGHTERS.
FOR THE LOVE OF ELYON, YOU'VE JUST DISCOVERED THE LEGENDS ARE REAL --
-- YET STILL YOU DOUBT OUR CALLING.
THIS JUST DOESN'T FEEL RIGHT. NOT WITHOUT BILLOS. HE SHOULD BE HERE, BATHING IN THIS WATER!
PLEASE DON'T DO THIS, DARSAL. WE HAVE TO STAY TOGETHER.
YOU KNOW WHAT HAPPENED THE LAST TIME WE SPLIT UP.
ALL I KNOW IS WHAT I SAW IN THE POOL.
IT WASN'T GLORIOUS VICTORY OR JOYFUL CELEBRATION.
IT WAS DEATH, JOHNIS.
I SAW DEATH.

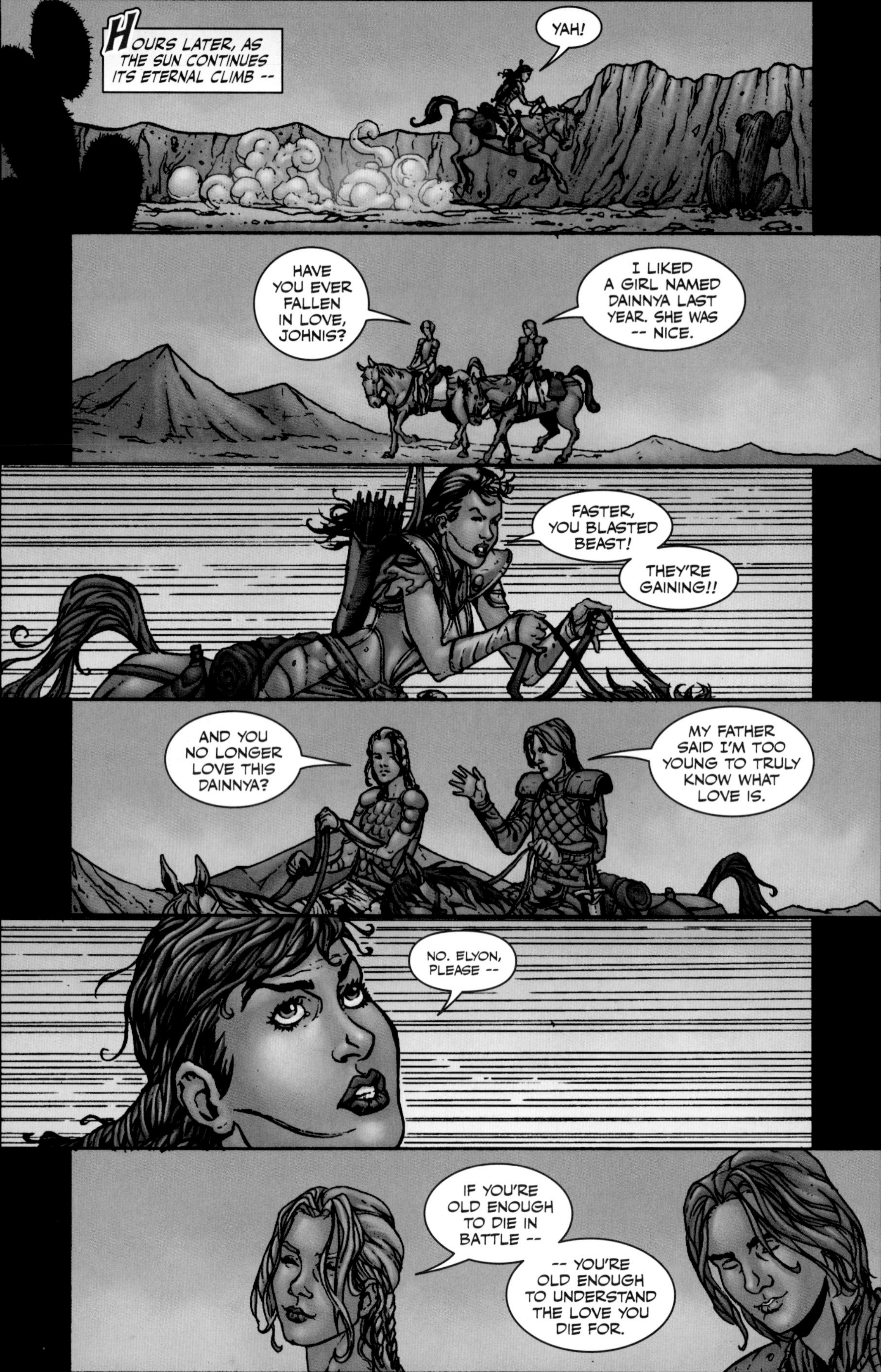
HOURS LATER, AS THE SUN CONTINUES ITS ETERNAL CLIMB --
YAH!
HAVE YOU EVER FALLEN IN LOVE, JOHNIS?
I LIKED A GIRL NAMED DAINNYA LAST YEAR. SHE WAS -- NICE.
FASTER, YOU BLASTED BEAST!
THEY'RE GAINING!!
AND YOU NO LONGER LOVE THIS DAINNYA?
MY FATHER SAID I'M TOO YOUNG TO TRULY KNOW WHAT LOVE IS.
NO. ELYON, PLEASE --
IF YOU'RE OLD ENOUGH TO DIE IN BATTLE --
-- YOU'RE OLD ENOUGH TO UNDERSTAND THE LOVE YOU DIE FOR.

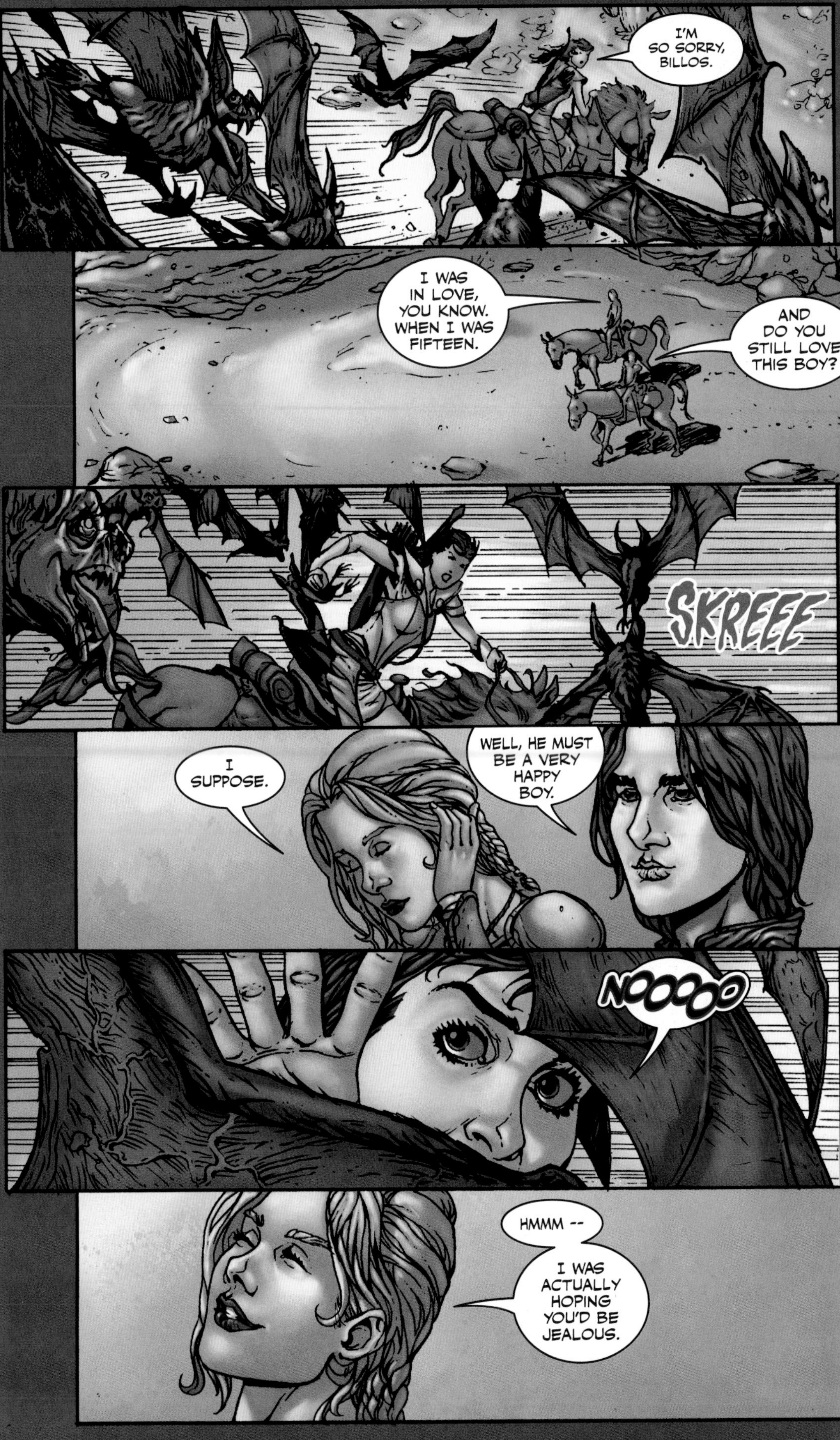
I'M SO SORRY, BILLOS.
I WAS IN LOVE, YOU KNOW. WHEN I WAS FIFTEEN.
AND DO YOU STILL LOVE THIS BOY?
SKREEE
I SUPPOSE.
WELL, HE MUST BE A VERY HAPPY BOY.
NOOOOO
HMMM --
I WAS ACTUALLY HOPING YOU'D BE JEALOUS.

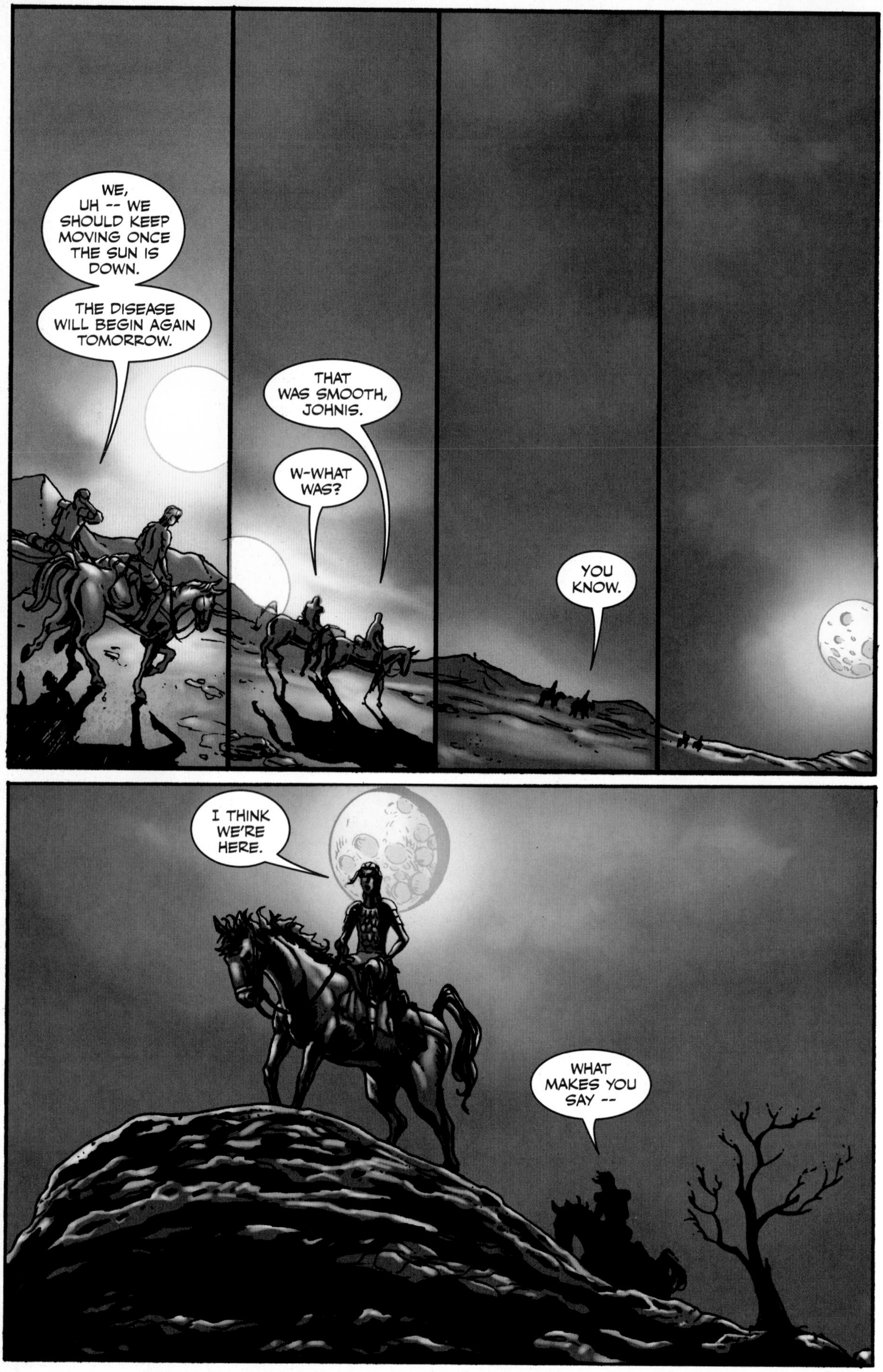
WE, UH -- WE SHOULD KEEP MOVING ONCE THE SUN IS DOWN.
THE DISEASE WILL BEGIN AGAIN TOMORROW.
THAT WAS SMOOTH, JOHNIS.
W-WHAT WAS?
YOU KNOW.
I THINK WE'RE HERE.
WHAT MAKES YOU SAY --

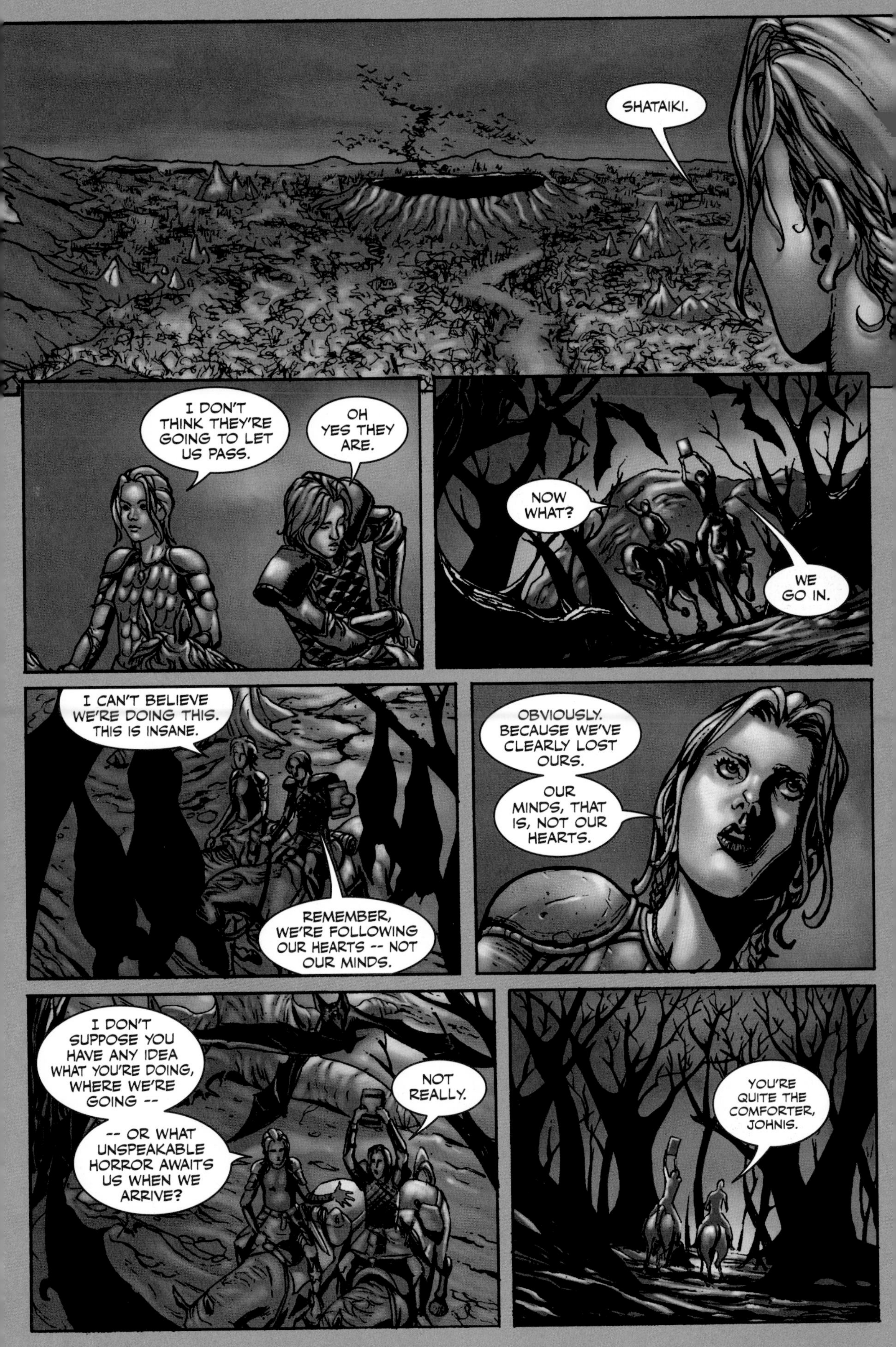
SHATAIKI.
I DON'T THINK THEY'RE GOING TO LET US PASS.
OH YES THEY ARE.
NOW WHAT?
WE GO IN.
I CAN'T BELIEVE WE'RE DOING THIS. THIS IS INSANE.
REMEMBER, WE'RE FOLLOWING OUR HEARTS -- NOT OUR MINDS.
OBVIOUSLY. BECAUSE WE'VE CLEARLY LOST OURS.
OUR MINDS, THAT IS, NOT OUR HEARTS.
I DON'T SUPPOSE YOU HAVE ANY IDEA WHAT YOU'RE DOING, WHERE WE'RE GOING --
-- OR WHAT UNSPEAKABLE HORROR AWAITS US WHEN WE ARRIVE?
NOT REALLY.
YOU'RE QUITE THE COMFORTER, JOHNIS.

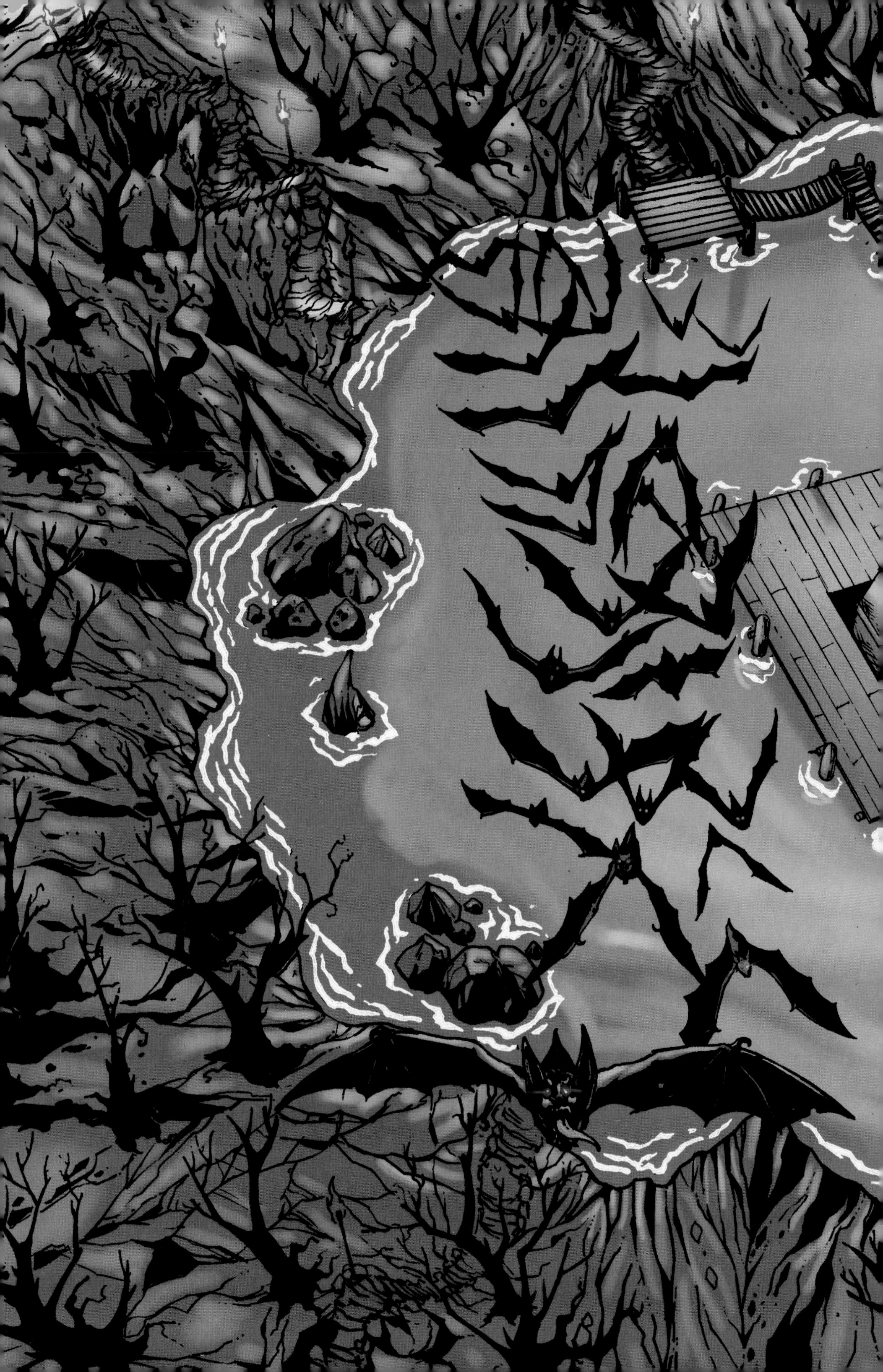

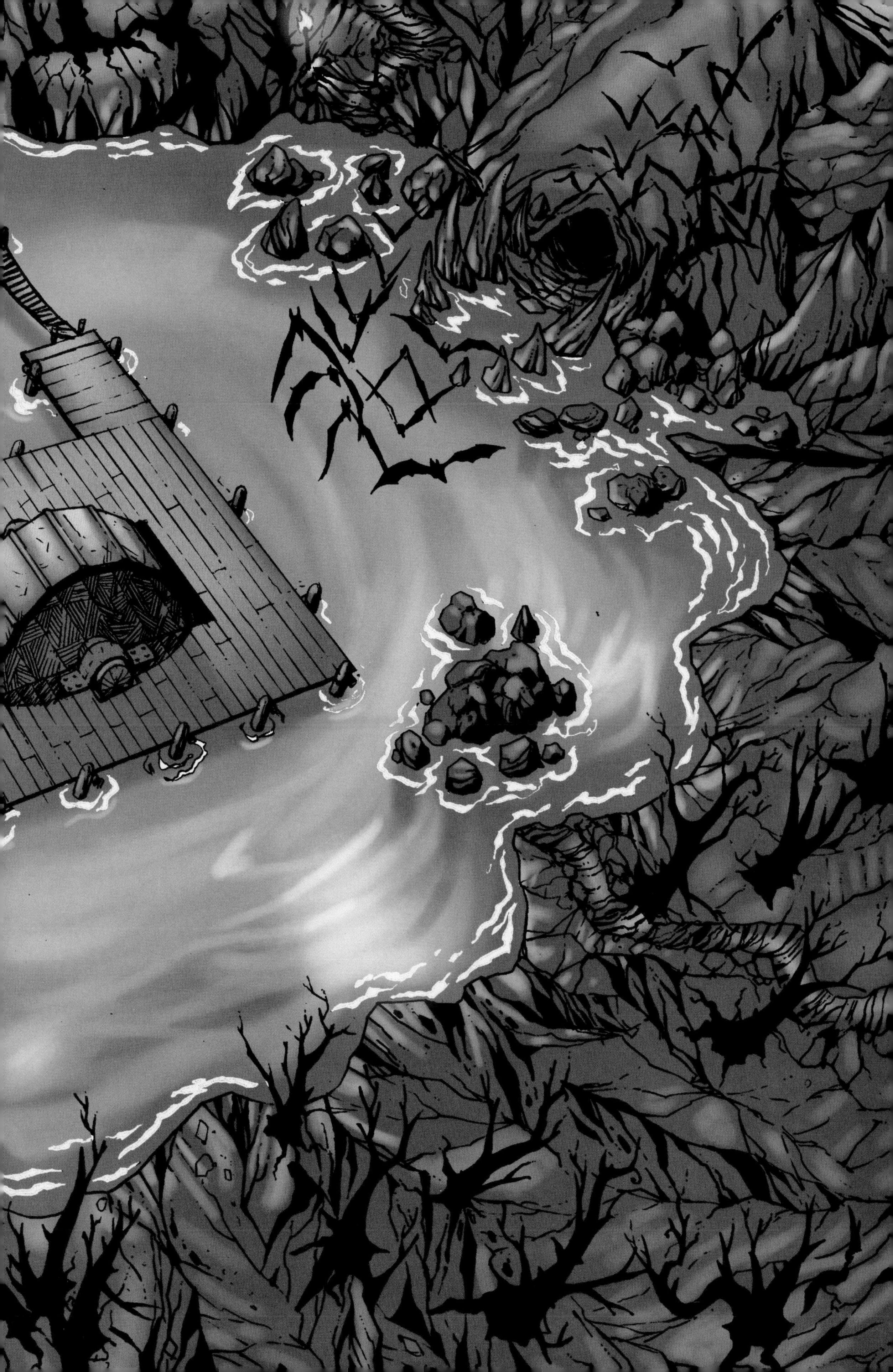

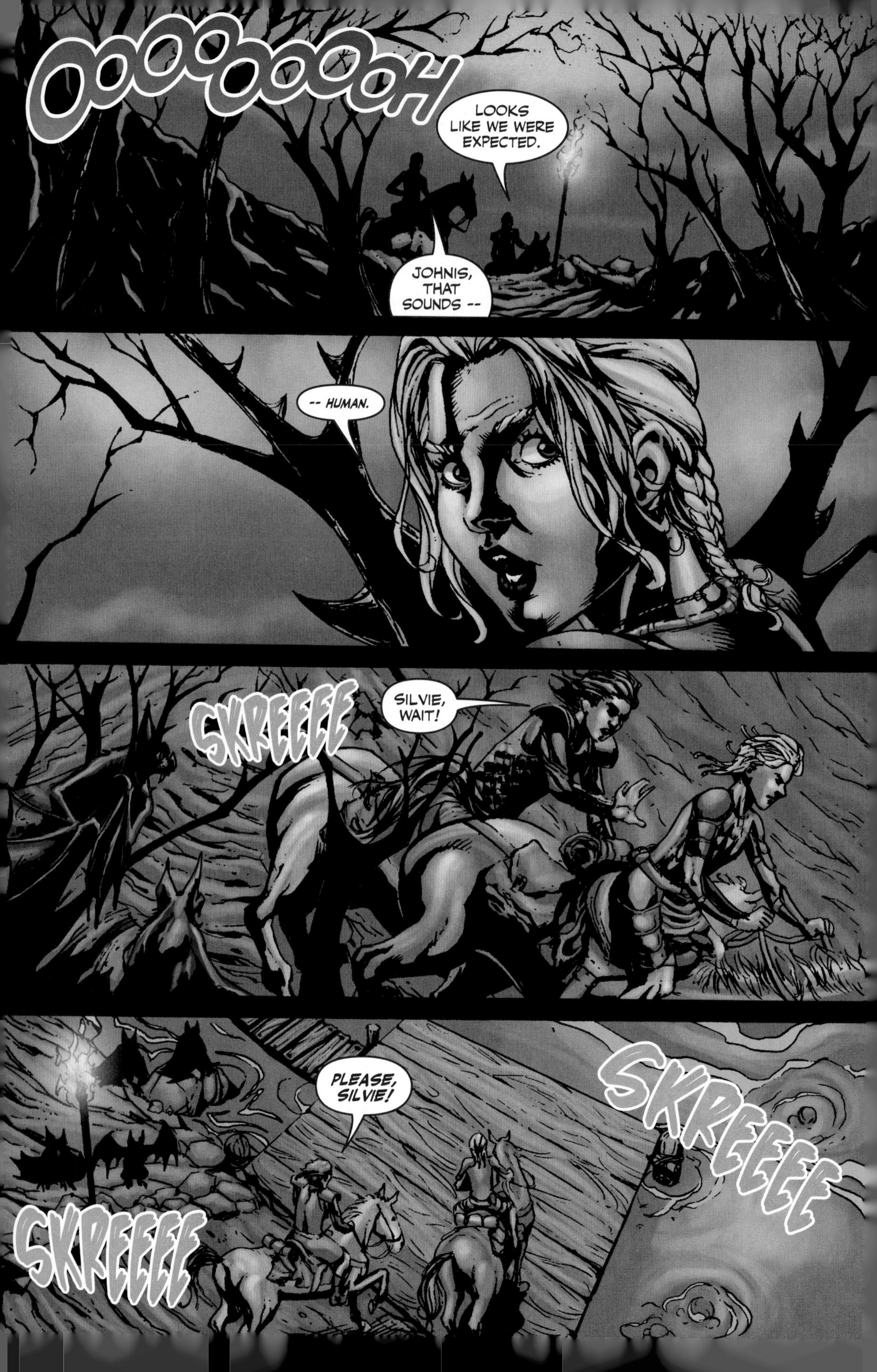
OOOOOOOOOH
LOOKS LIKE WE WERE EXPECTED.
JOHNIS, THAT SOUNDS --
-- HUMAN.
SKREEEE
SILVIE, WAIT!
PLEASE, SILVIE!
SKREEEE
SKREEEEE

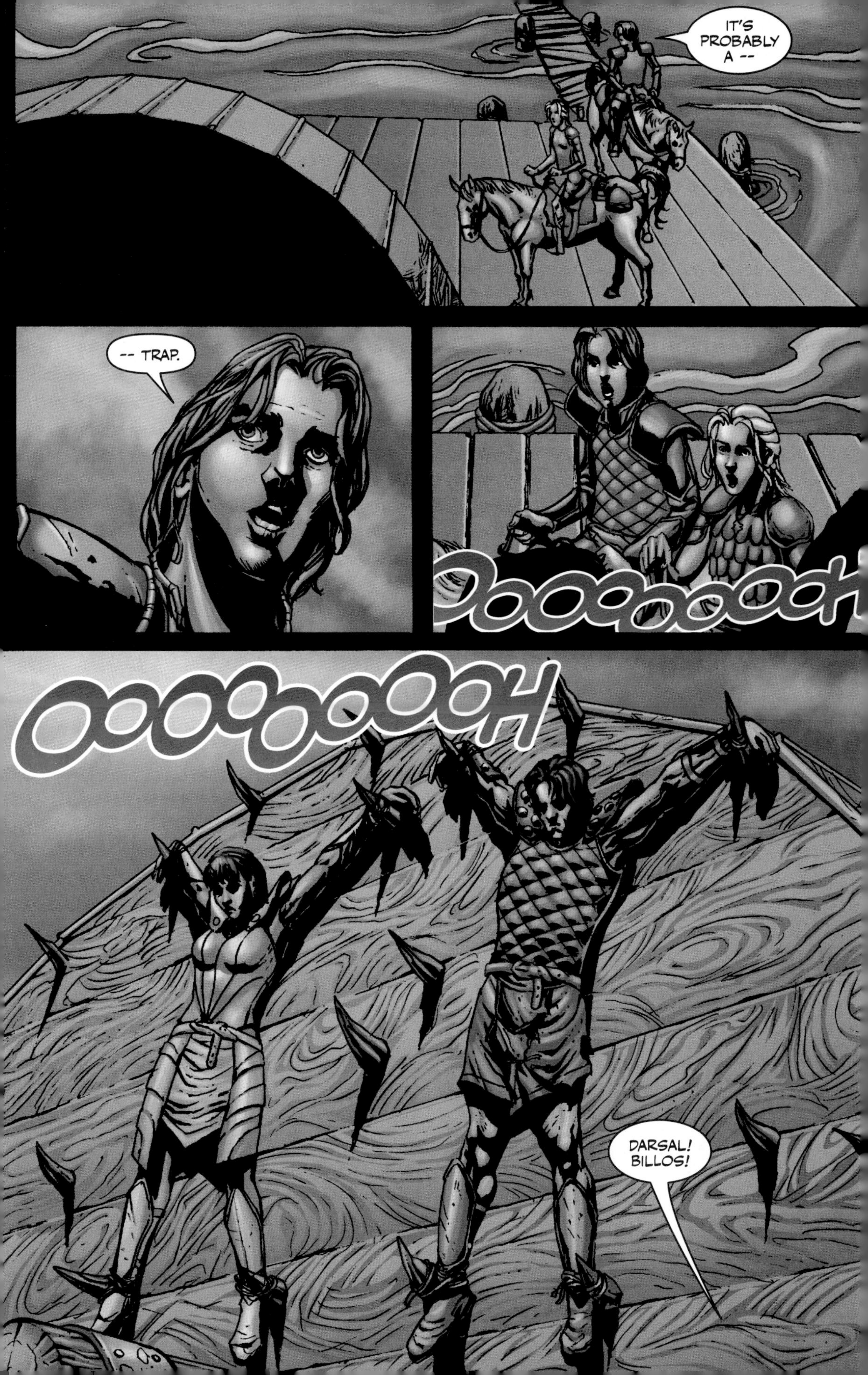
IT'S PROBABLY A --
-- TRAP.
OOOOOOOOOH
OOOOOOOOOH
DARSAL! BILLOS!

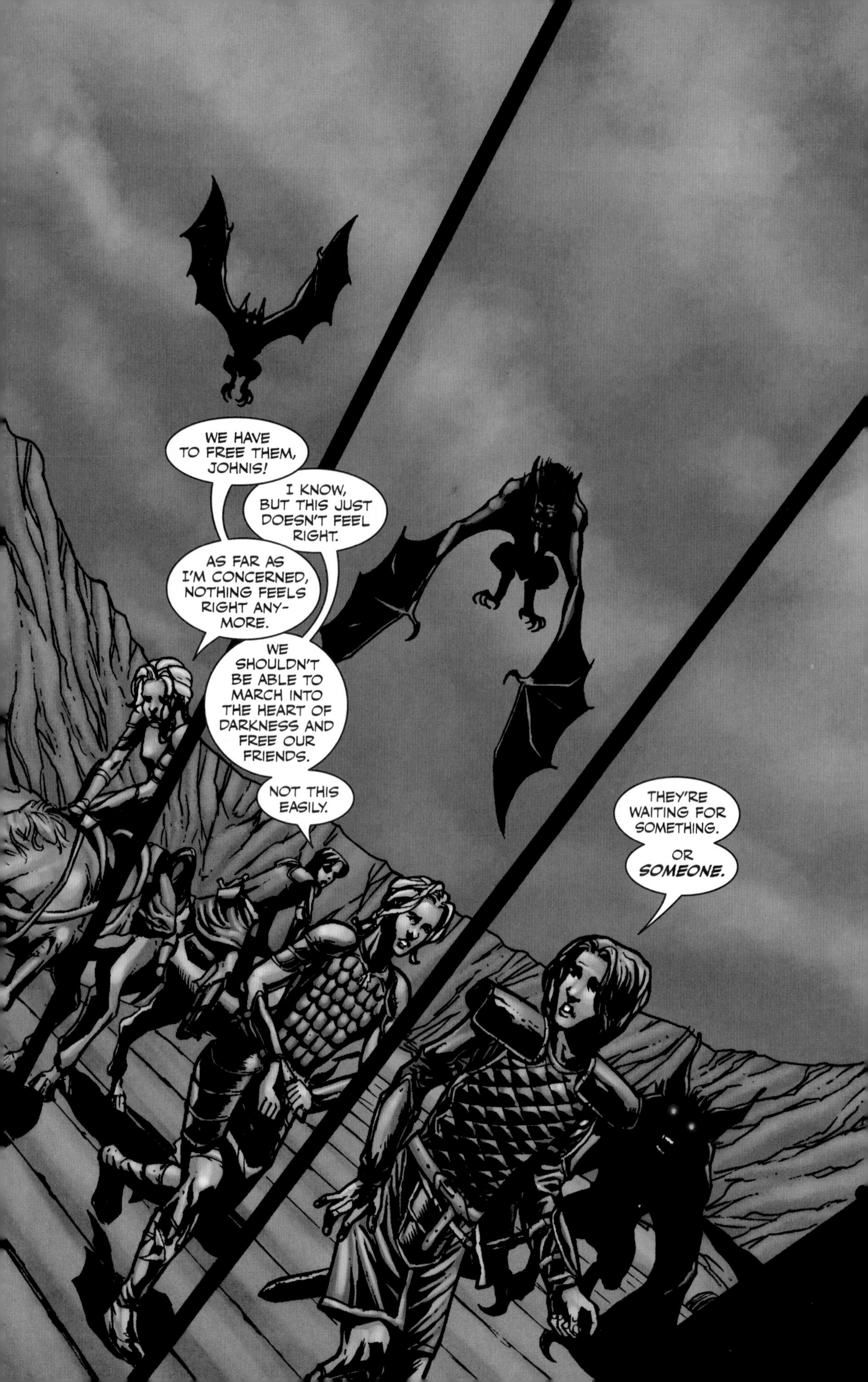
WE HAVE TO FREE THEM, JOHNIS!
I KNOW, BUT THIS JUST DOESN'T FEEL RIGHT.
AS FAR AS I'M CONCERNED, NOTHING FEELS RIGHT ANY-MORE.
WE SHOULDN'T BE ABLE TO MARCH INTO THE HEART OF DARKNESS AND FREE OUR FRIENDS.
NOT THIS EASILY.
THEY'RE WAITING FOR SOMETHING.
OR *SOMEONE.*

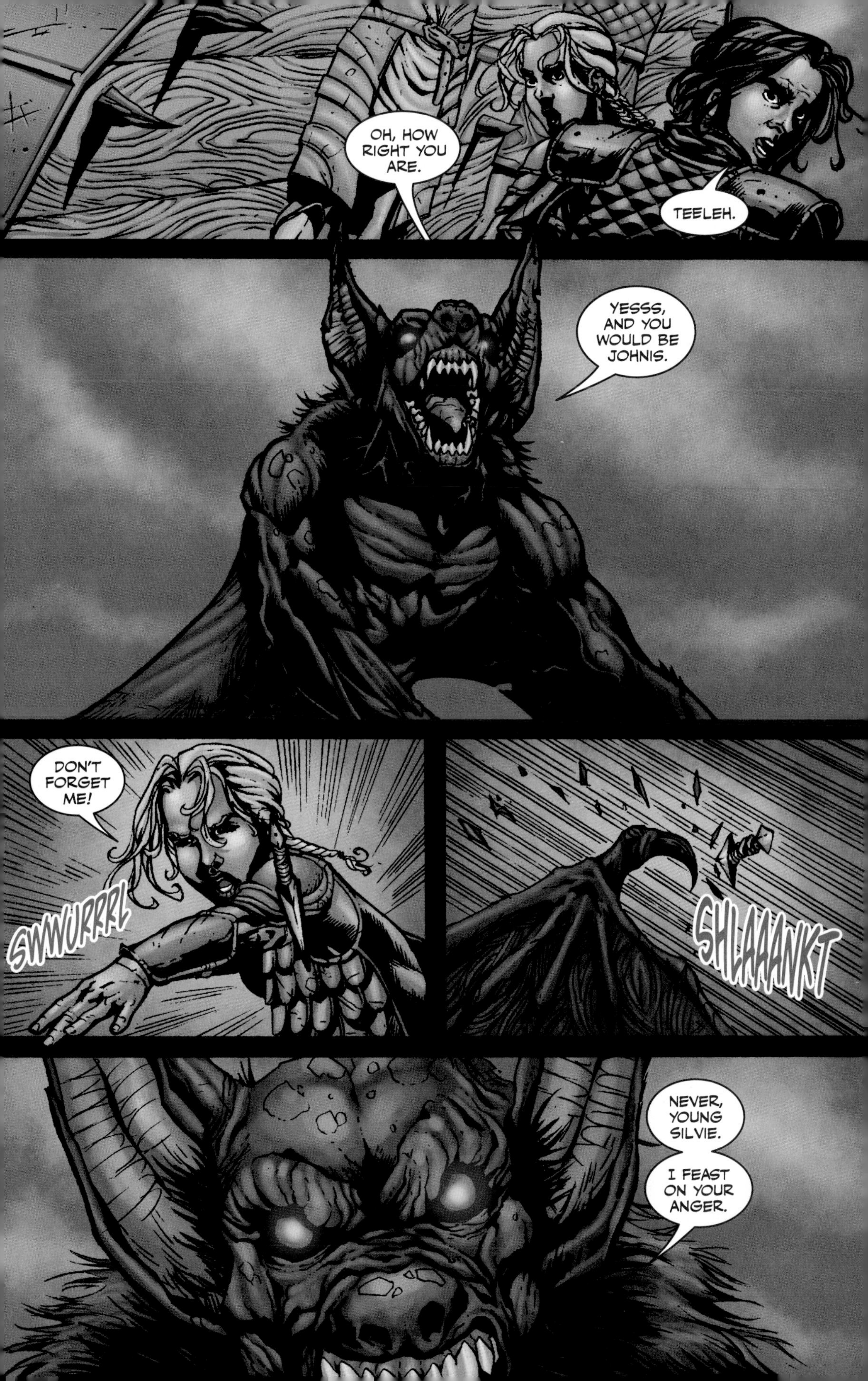
OH, HOW RIGHT YOU ARE.
TEELEH.
YESSS, AND YOU WOULD BE JOHNIS.
DON'T FORGET ME!
SWWURRRL
SHLAAANKT
NEVER, YOUNG SILVIE.
I FEAST ON YOUR ANGER.

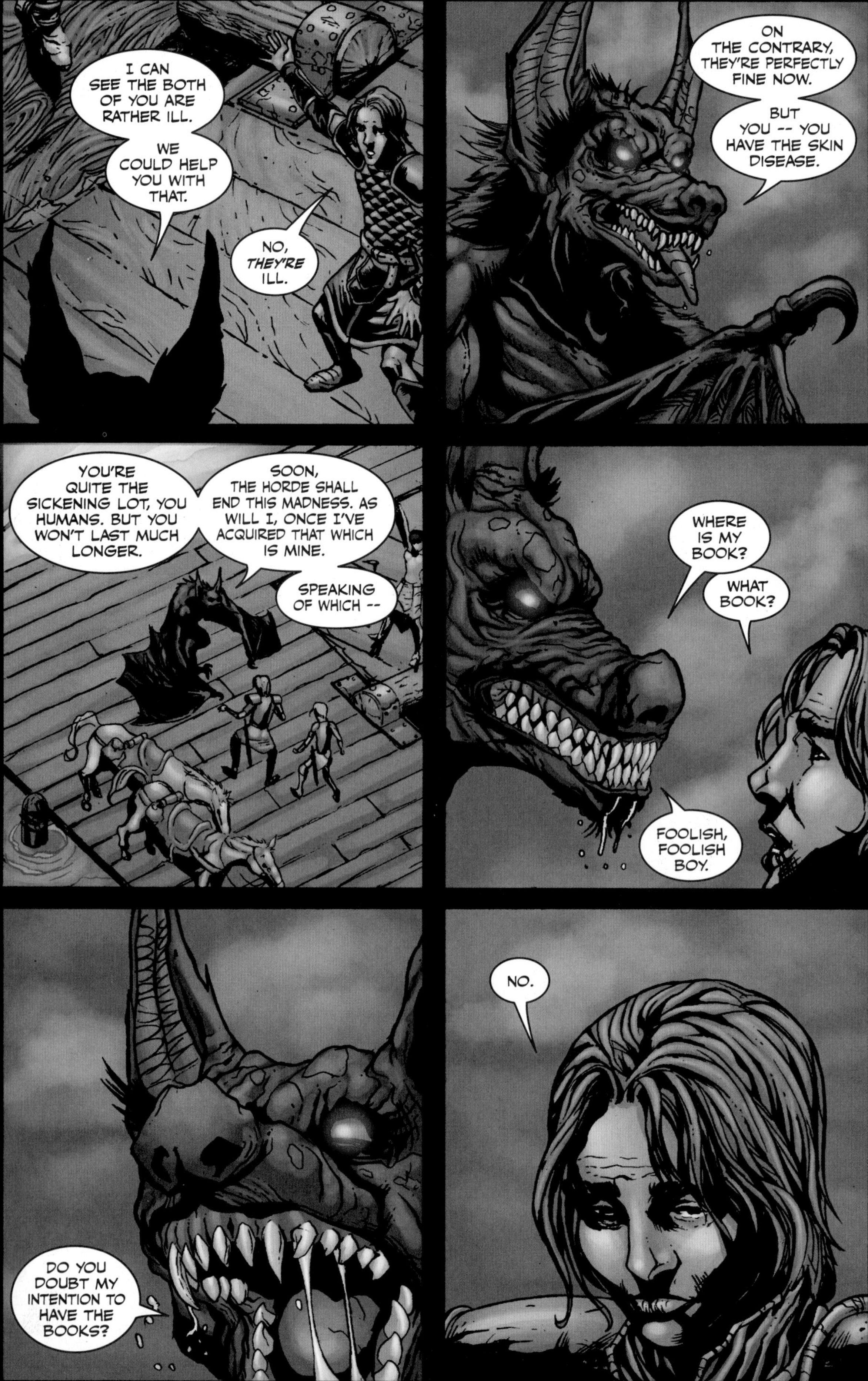
I CAN SEE THE BOTH OF YOU ARE RATHER ILL.
WE COULD HELP YOU WITH THAT.
NO, *THEY'RE* ILL.
ON THE CONTRARY, THEY'RE PERFECTLY FINE NOW.
BUT YOU -- YOU HAVE THE SKIN DISEASE.
YOU'RE QUITE THE SICKENING LOT, YOU HUMANS. BUT YOU WON'T LAST MUCH LONGER.
SOON, THE HORDE SHALL END THIS MADNESS. AS WILL I, ONCE I'VE ACQUIRED THAT WHICH IS MINE.
SPEAKING OF WHICH --
WHERE IS MY BOOK?
WHAT BOOK?
FOOLISH, FOOLISH BOY.
DO YOU DOUBT MY INTENTION TO HAVE THE BOOKS?
NO.

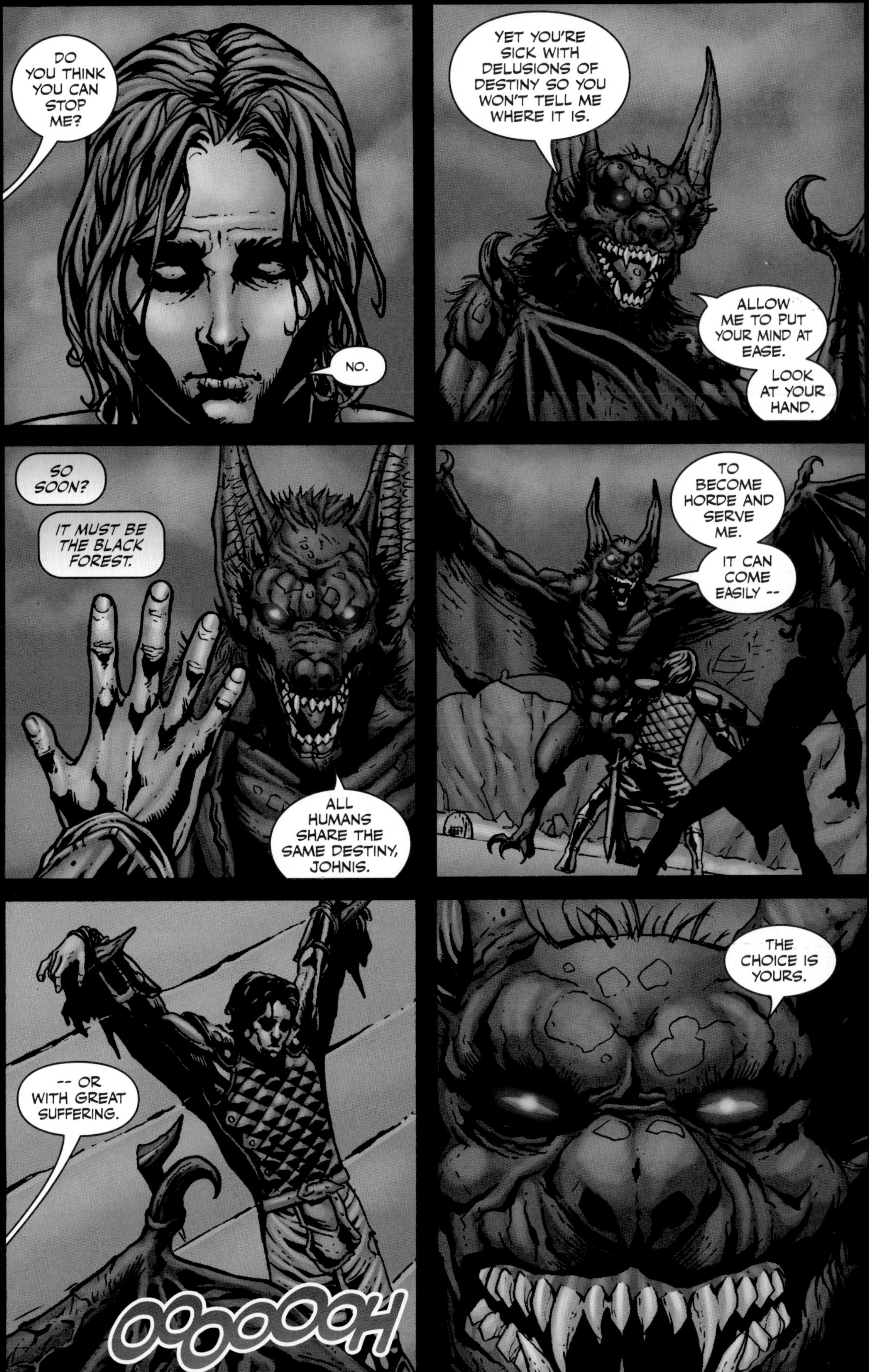
DO YOU THINK YOU CAN STOP ME?
NO.
YET YOU'RE SICK WITH DELUSIONS OF DESTINY SO YOU WON'T TELL ME WHERE IT IS.
ALLOW ME TO PUT YOUR MIND AT EASE.
LOOK AT YOUR HAND.
SO SOON?
IT MUST BE THE BLACK FOREST.
ALL HUMANS SHARE THE SAME DESTINY, JOHNIS.
TO BECOME HORDE AND SERVE ME.
IT CAN COME EASILY --
-- OR WITH GREAT SUFFERING.
OOOOOOH
THE CHOICE IS YOURS.

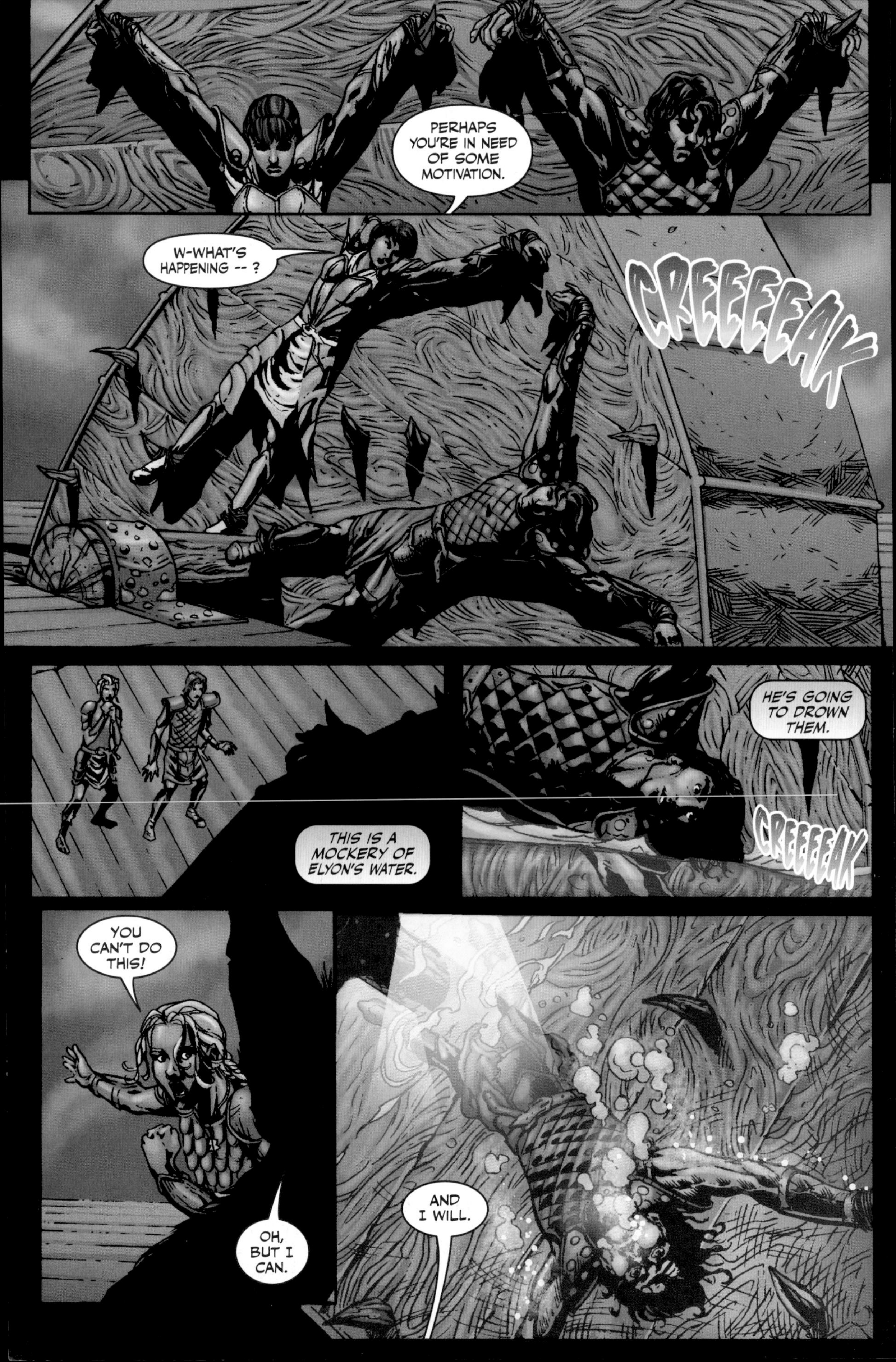
PERHAPS YOU'RE IN NEED OF SOME MOTIVATION.
W-WHAT'S HAPPENING -- ?
CREEEEAK
HE'S GOING TO DROWN THEM.
THIS IS A MOCKERY OF ELYON'S WATER.
CREEEEAK
YOU CAN'T DO THIS!
OH, BUT I CAN.
AND I WILL.

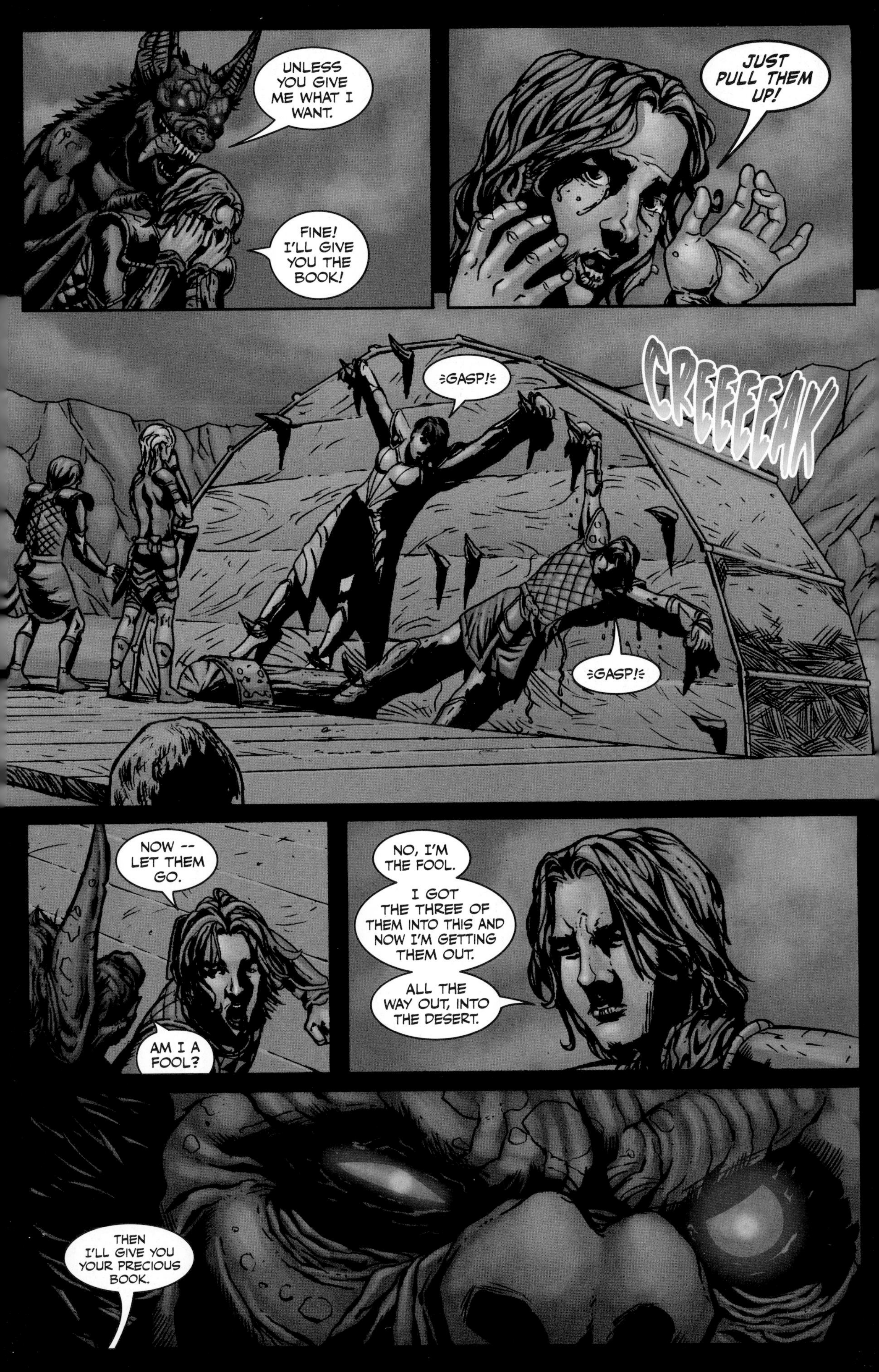
UNLESS YOU GIVE ME WHAT I WANT.
FINE! I'LL GIVE YOU THE BOOK!
JUST PULL THEM UP!
CREEEEAK
≈GASP!≈
≈GASP!≈
NOW -- LET THEM GO.
AM I A FOOL?
NO, I'M THE FOOL.
I GOT THE THREE OF THEM INTO THIS AND NOW I'M GETTING THEM OUT.
ALL THE WAY OUT, INTO THE DESERT.
THEN I'LL GIVE YOU YOUR PRECIOUS BOOK.

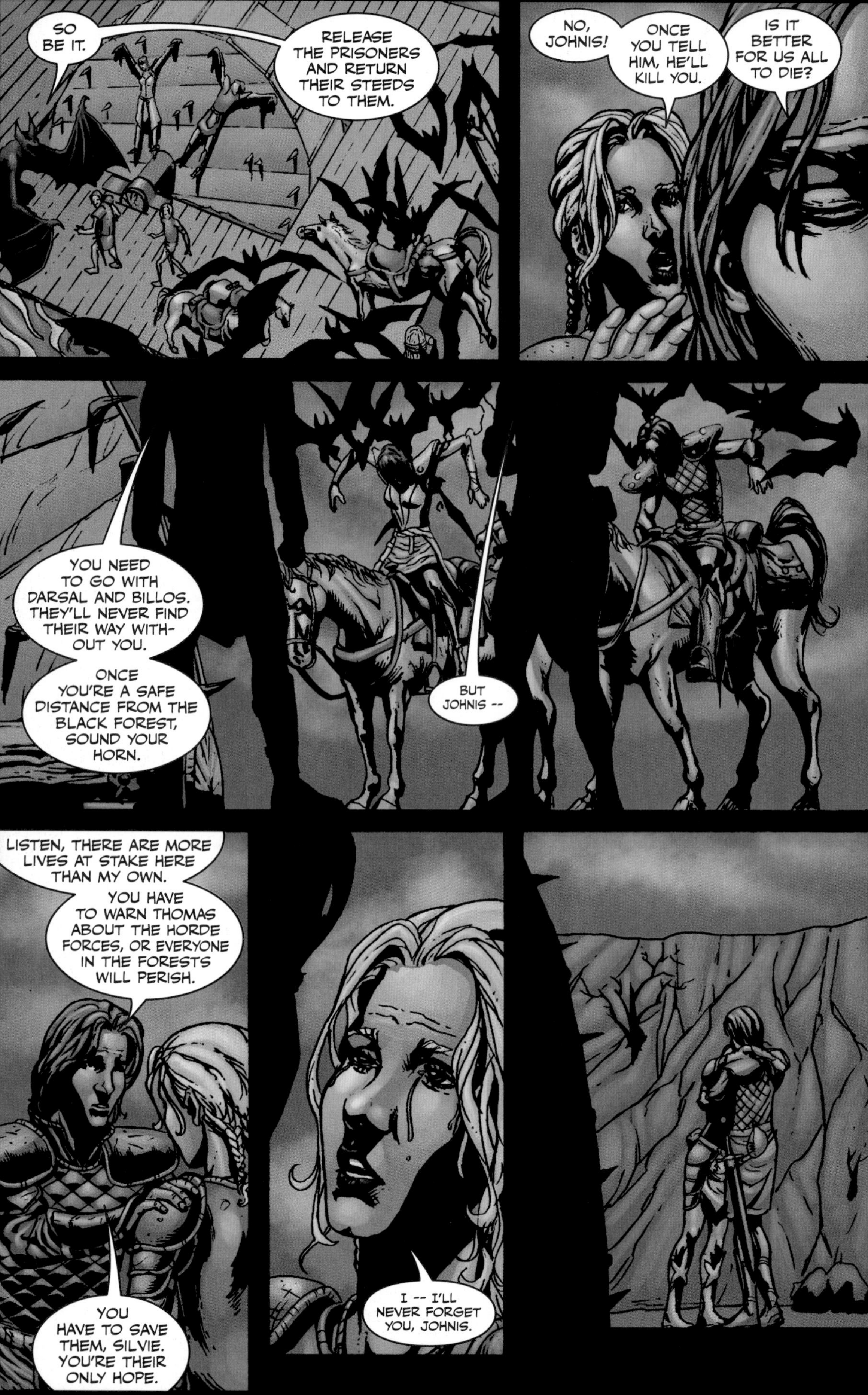

SO BE IT.
RELEASE THE PRISONERS AND RETURN THEIR STEEDS TO THEM.
NO, JOHNIS!
ONCE YOU TELL HIM, HE'LL KILL YOU.
IS IT BETTER FOR US ALL TO DIE?
YOU NEED TO GO WITH DARSAL AND BILLOS. THEY'LL NEVER FIND THEIR WAY WITH-OUT YOU.
ONCE YOU'RE A SAFE DISTANCE FROM THE BLACK FOREST, SOUND YOUR HORN.
BUT JOHNIS --
LISTEN, THERE ARE MORE LIVES AT STAKE HERE THAN MY OWN.
YOU HAVE TO WARN THOMAS ABOUT THE HORDE FORCES, OR EVERYONE IN THE FORESTS WILL PERISH.
YOU HAVE TO SAVE THEM, SILVIE. YOU'RE THEIR ONLY HOPE.
I -- I'LL NEVER FORGET YOU, JOHNIS.

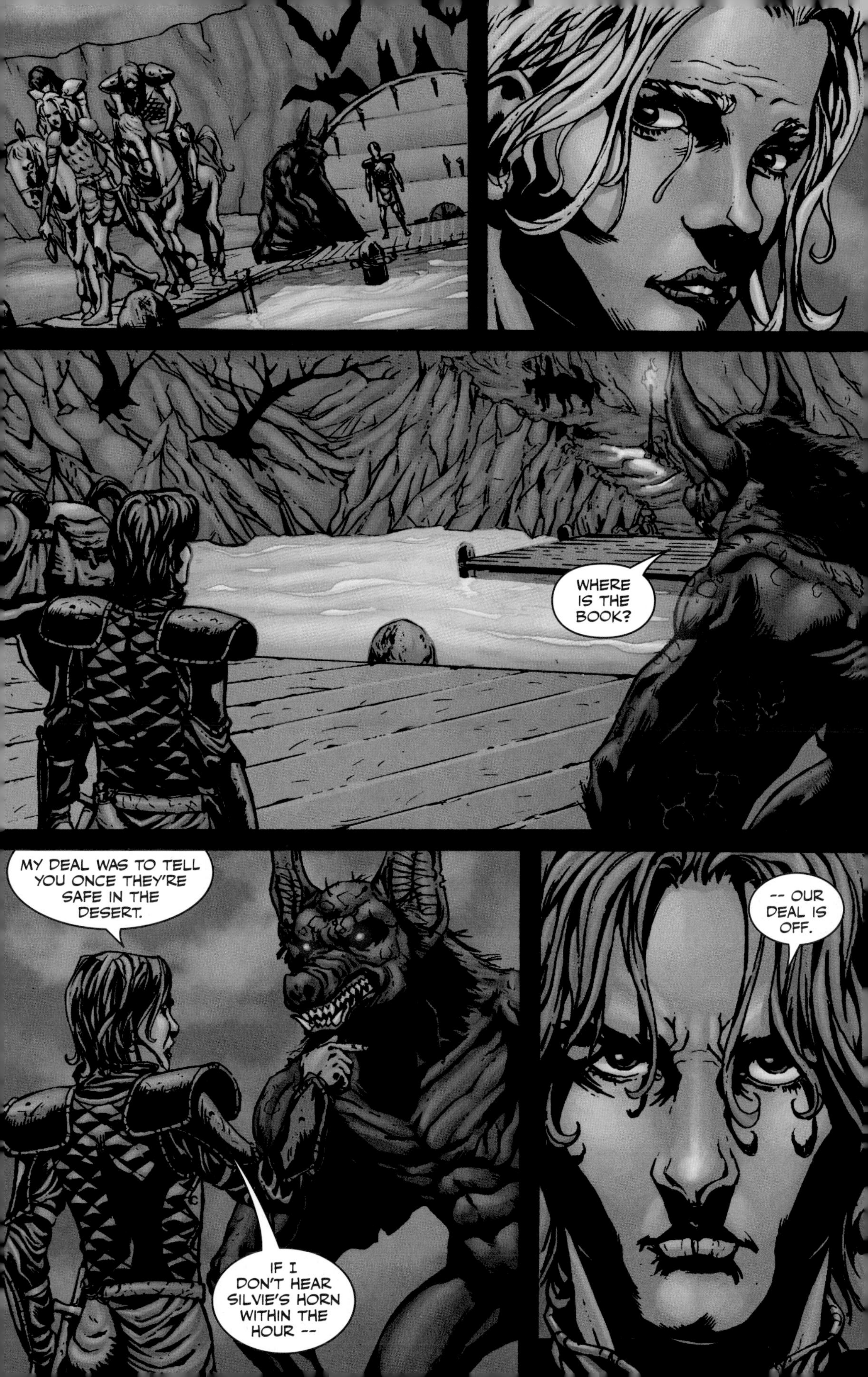
WHERE IS THE BOOK?
MY DEAL WAS TO TELL YOU ONCE THEY'RE SAFE IN THE DESERT.
IF I DON'T HEAR SILVIE'S HORN WITHIN THE HOUR --
-- OUR DEAL IS OFF.

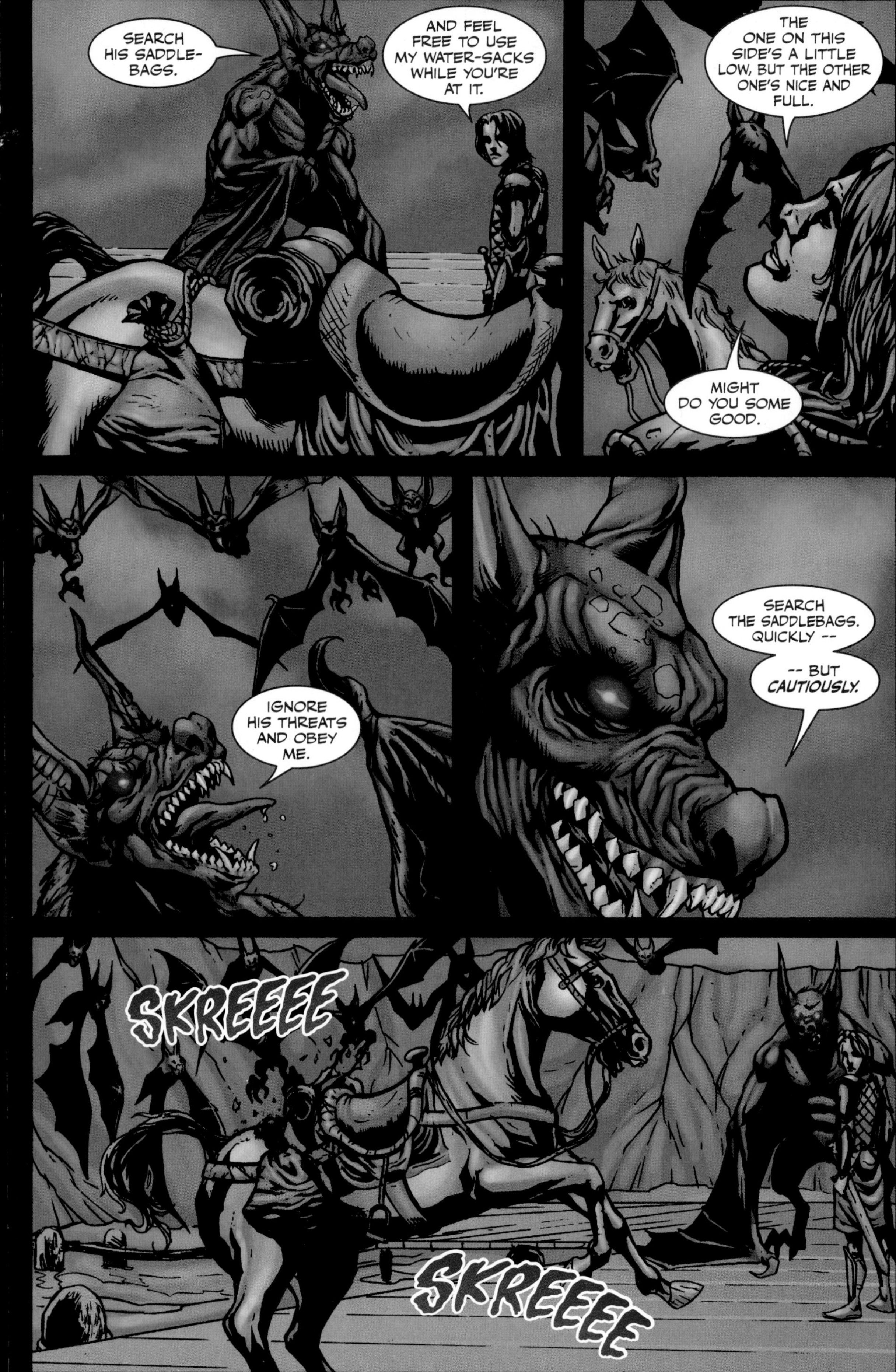
SEARCH HIS SADDLE-BAGS.
AND FEEL FREE TO USE MY WATER-SACKS WHILE YOU'RE AT IT.
THE ONE ON THIS SIDE'S A LITTLE LOW, BUT THE OTHER ONE'S NICE AND FULL.
MIGHT DO YOU SOME GOOD.
IGNORE HIS THREATS AND OBEY ME.
SEARCH THE SADDLEBAGS. QUICKLY --
-- BUT *CAUTIOUSLY.*
SKREEEEE
SKREEEEE

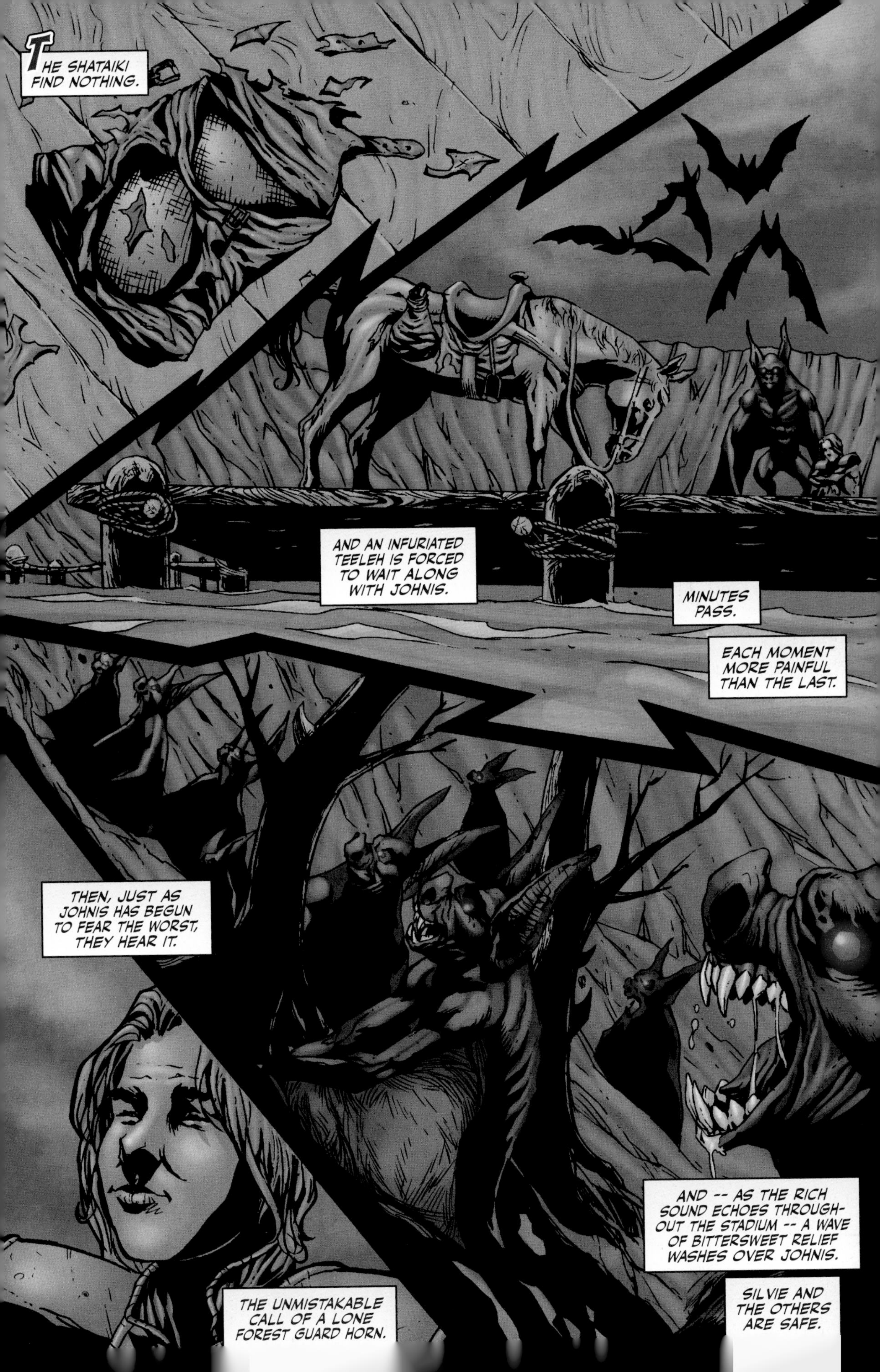
THE SHATAIKI FIND NOTHING.
AND AN INFURIATED TEELEH IS FORCED TO WAIT ALONG WITH JOHNIS.
MINUTES PASS.
EACH MOMENT MORE PAINFUL THAN THE LAST.
THEN, JUST AS JOHNIS HAS BEGUN TO FEAR THE WORST, THEY HEAR IT.
THE UNMISTAKABLE CALL OF A LONE FOREST GUARD HORN.
AND -- AS THE RICH SOUND ECHOES THROUGH-OUT THE STADIUM -- A WAVE OF BITTERSWEET RELIEF WASHES OVER JOHNIS.
SILVIE AND THE OTHERS ARE SAFE.

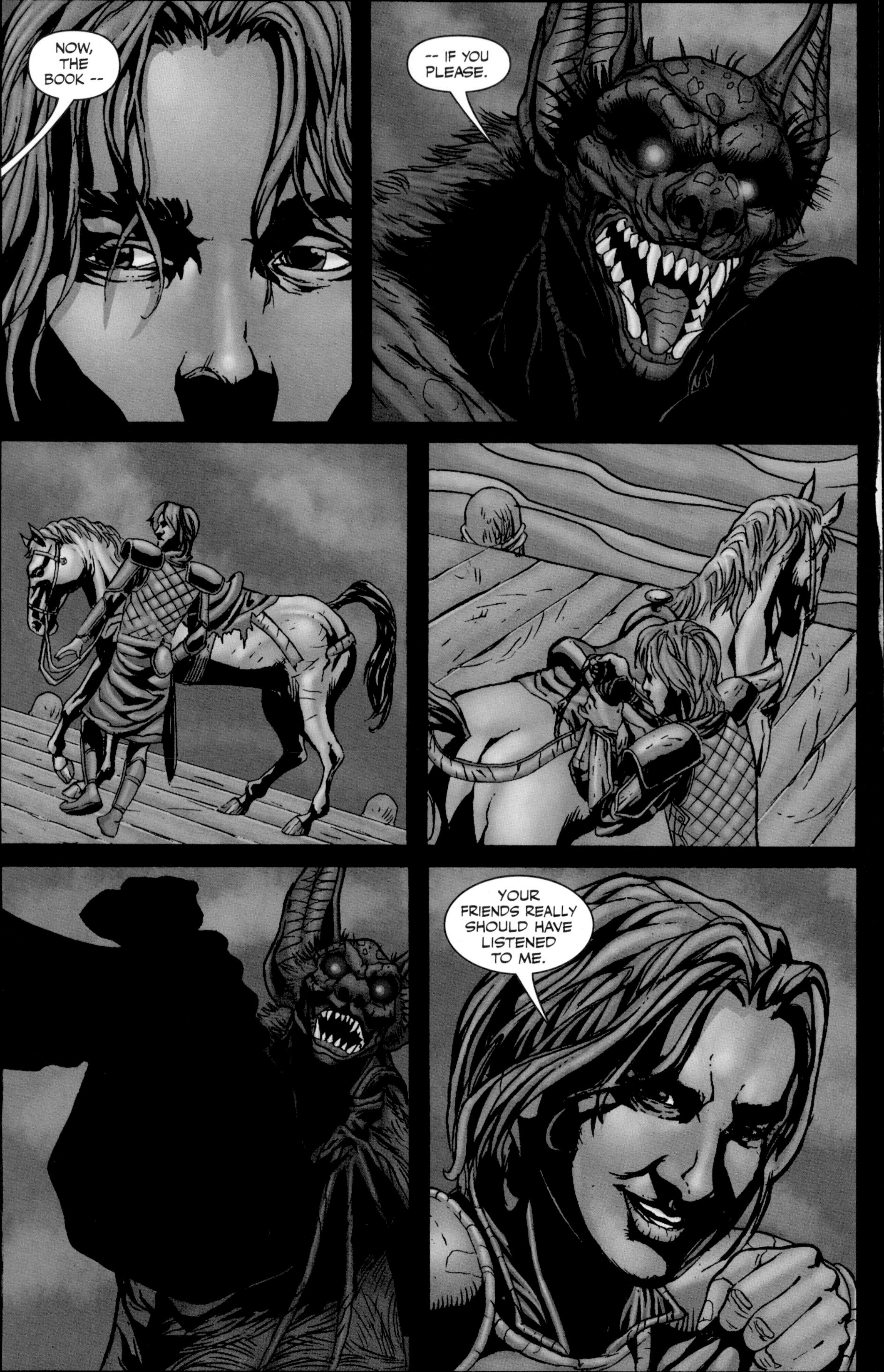
NOW, THE BOOK --
-- IF YOU PLEASE.
YOUR FRIENDS REALLY SHOULD HAVE LISTENED TO ME.

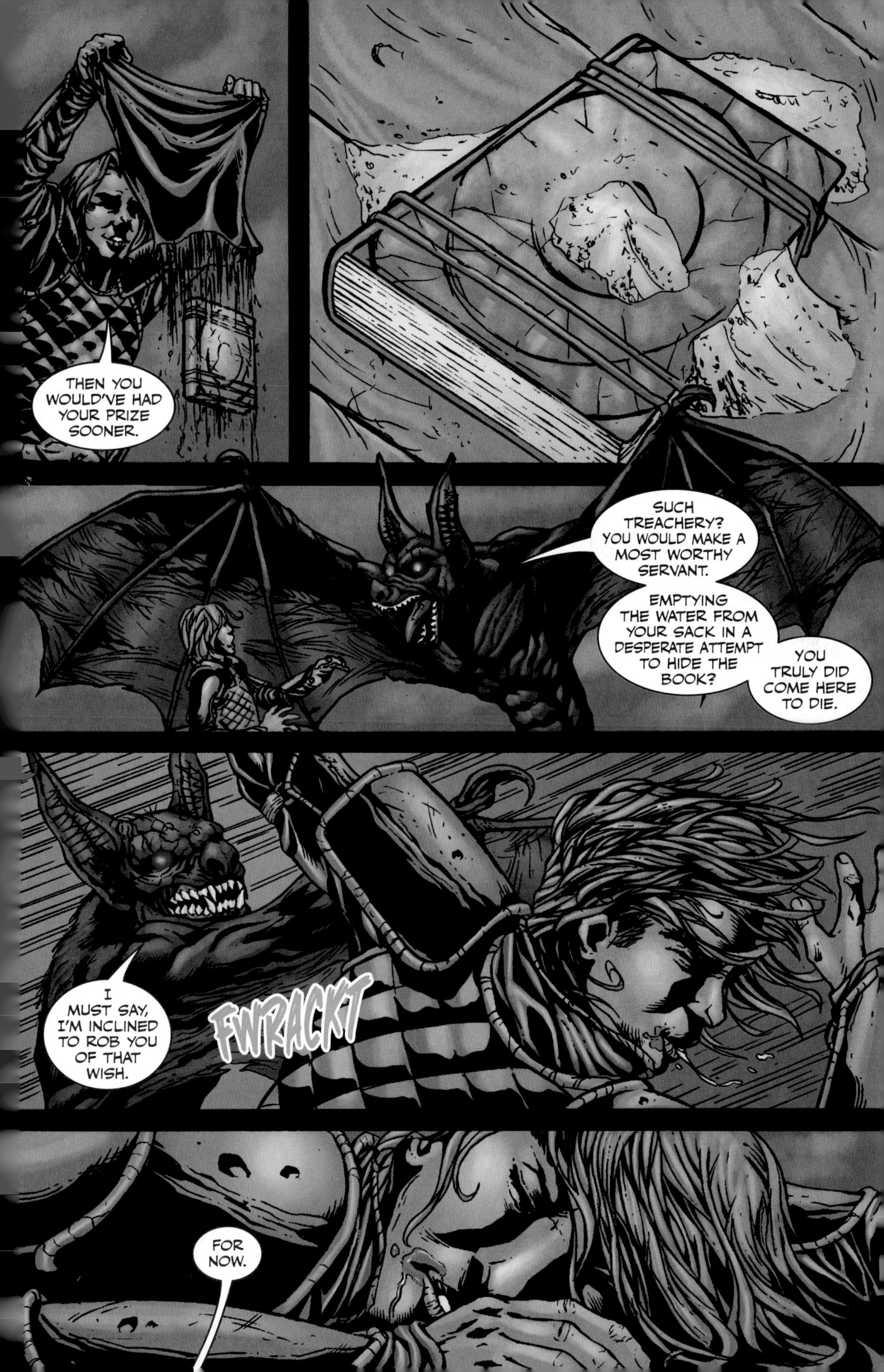
THEN YOU WOULD'VE HAD YOUR PRIZE SOONER.
SUCH TREACHERY? YOU WOULD MAKE A MOST WORTHY SERVANT.
EMPTYING THE WATER FROM YOUR SACK IN A DESPERATE ATTEMPT TO HIDE THE BOOK?
YOU TRULY DID COME HERE TO DIE.
I MUST SAY, I'M INCLINED TO ROB YOU OF THAT WISH.
FWRACKT
FOR NOW.

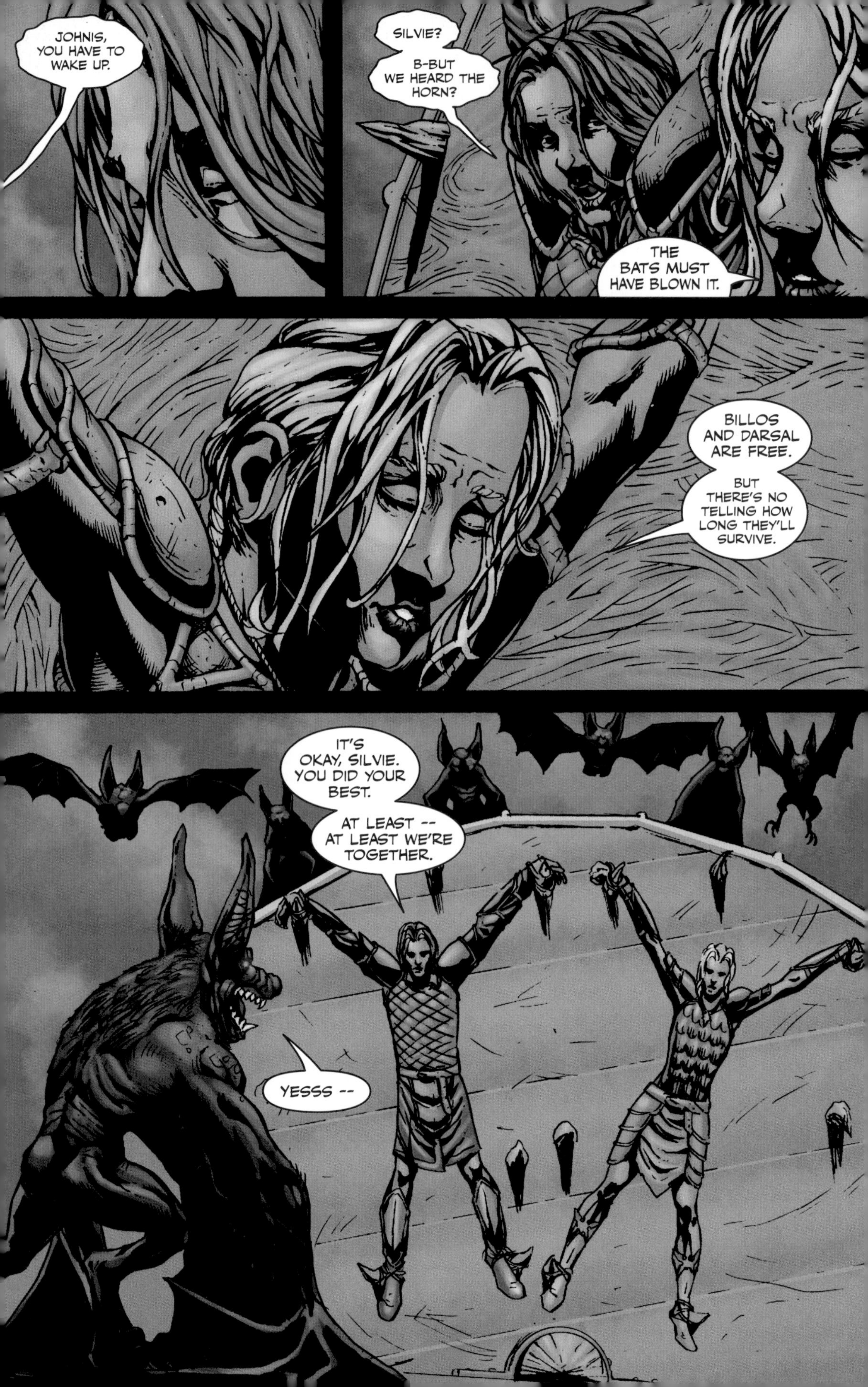
JOHNIS, YOU HAVE TO WAKE UP.
SILVIE?
B-BUT WE HEARD THE HORN?
THE BATS MUST HAVE BLOWN IT.
BILLOS AND DARSAL ARE FREE.
BUT THERE'S NO TELLING HOW LONG THEY'LL SURVIVE.
IT'S OKAY, SILVIE. YOU DID YOUR BEST.
AT LEAST -- AT LEAST WE'RE TOGETHER.
YESSS --

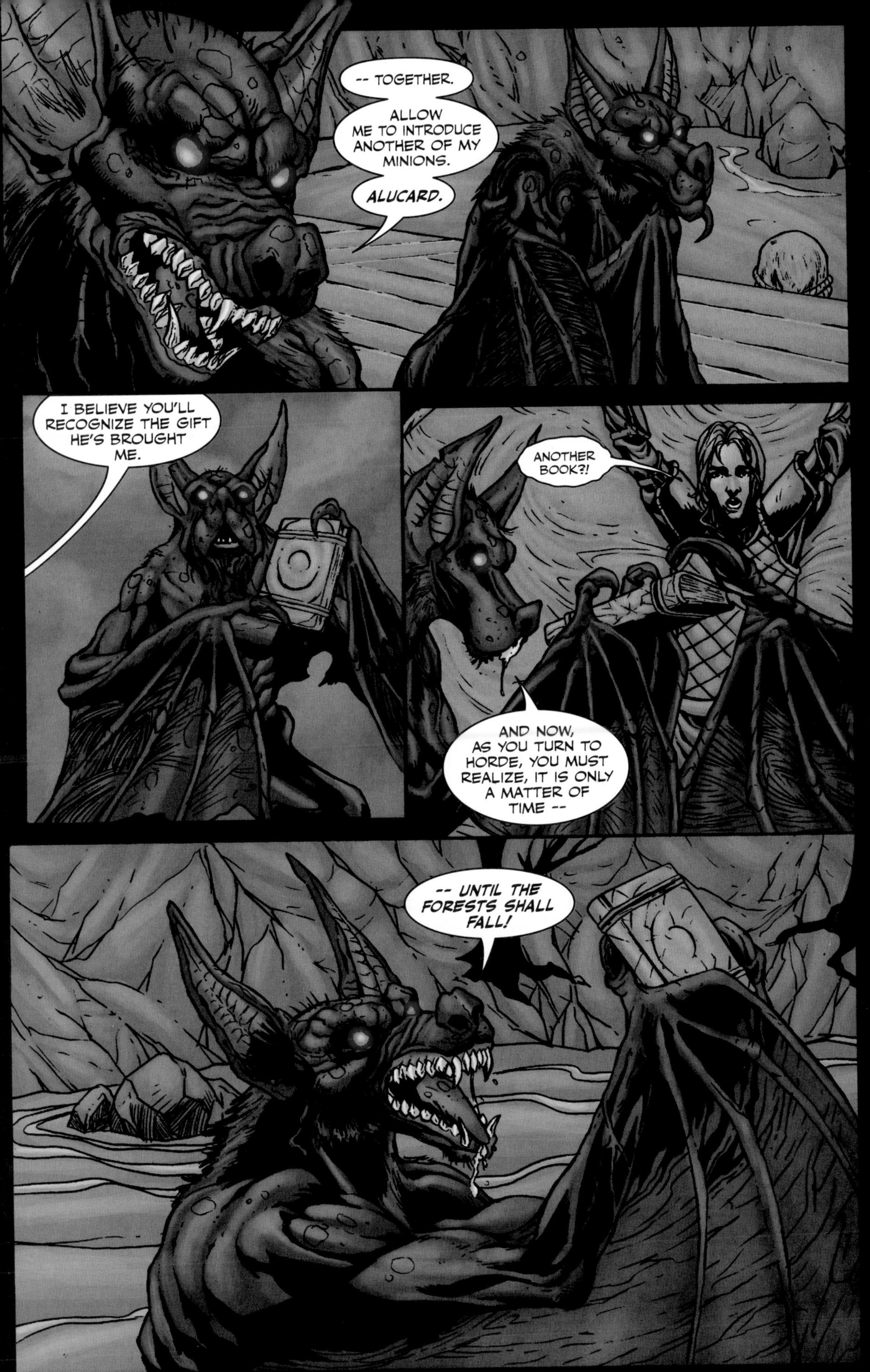
-- TOGETHER.
ALLOW ME TO INTRODUCE ANOTHER OF MY MINIONS.
ALUCARD.
I BELIEVE YOU'LL RECOGNIZE THE GIFT HE'S BROUGHT ME.
ANOTHER BOOK?!
AND NOW, AS YOU TURN TO HORDE, YOU MUST REALIZE, IT IS ONLY A MATTER OF TIME --
-- UNTIL THE FORESTS SHALL FALL!

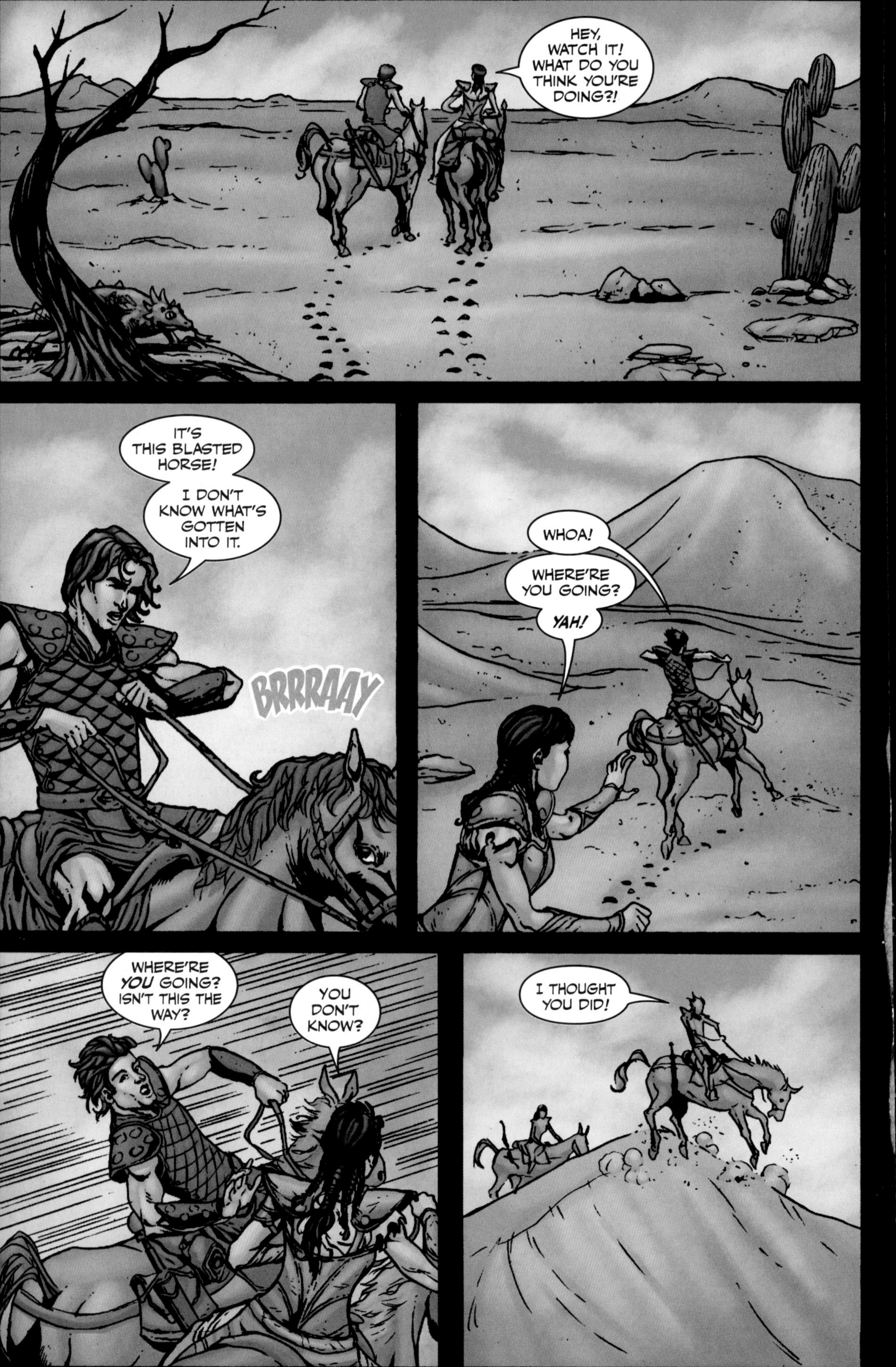
HEY, WATCH IT! WHAT DO YOU THINK YOU'RE DOING?!
IT'S THIS BLASTED HORSE!
I DON'T KNOW WHAT'S GOTTEN INTO IT.
BRRRAAY
WHOA!
WHERE'RE YOU GOING?
YAH!
WHERE'RE *YOU* GOING? ISN'T THIS THE WAY?
YOU DON'T KNOW?
I THOUGHT YOU DID!

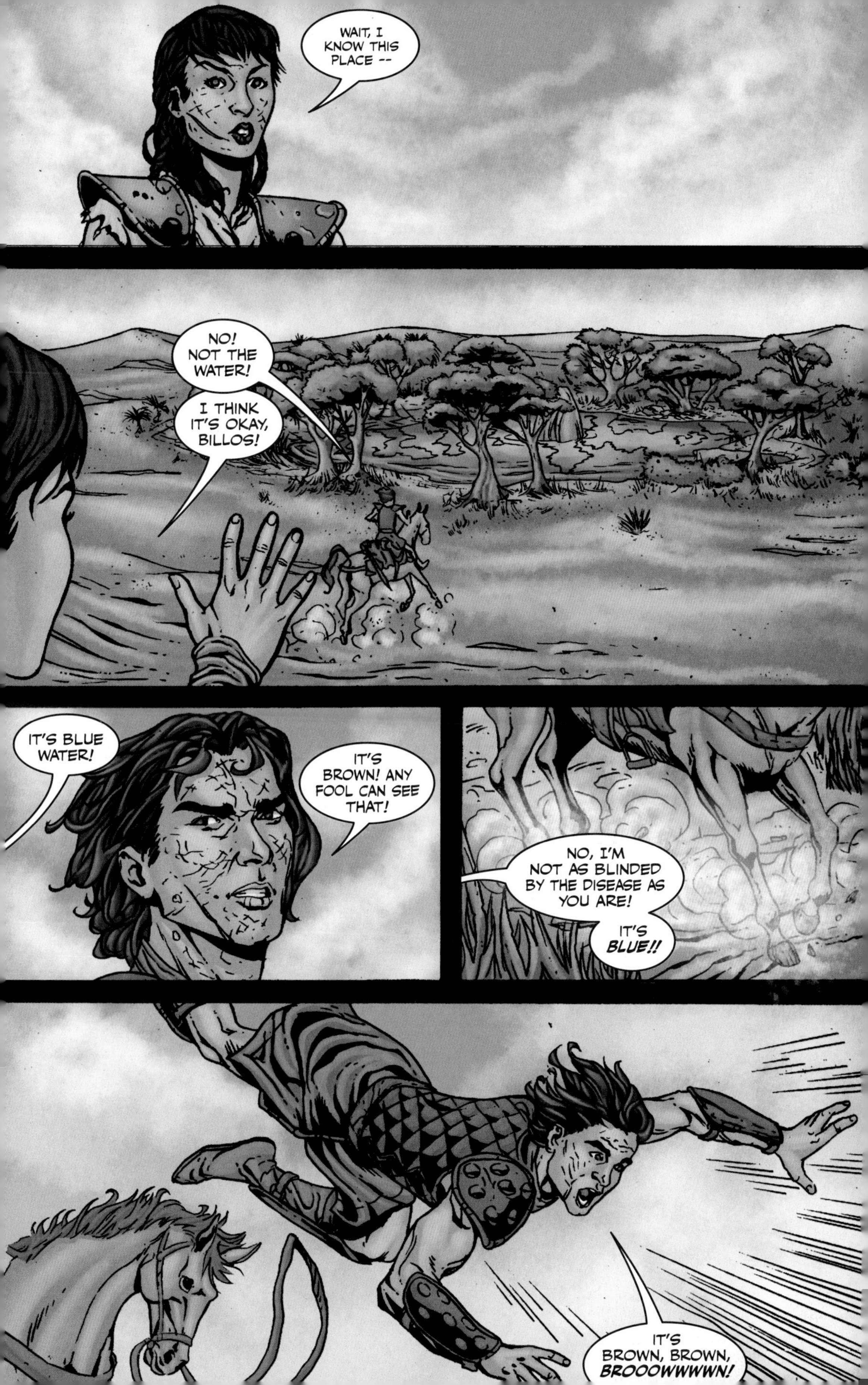
WAIT, I KNOW THIS PLACE --
NO! NOT THE WATER!
I THINK IT'S OKAY, BILLOS!
IT'S BLUE WATER!
IT'S BROWN! ANY FOOL CAN SEE THAT!
NO, I'M NOT AS BLINDED BY THE DISEASE AS YOU ARE!
IT'S *BLUE!!*
IT'S BROWN, BROWN, ***BROOOWWWWN!***

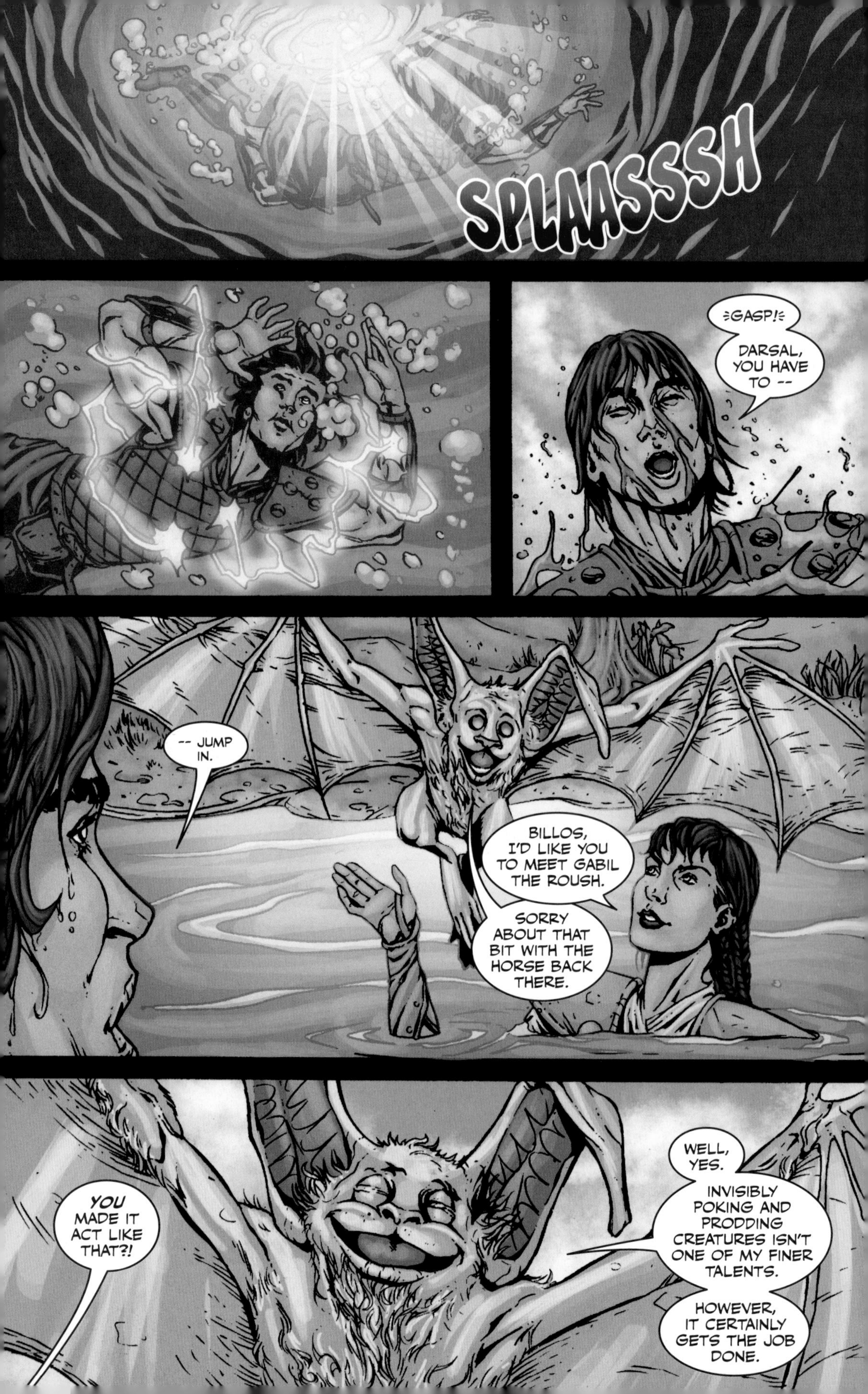
SPLAASSSH
GASP!
DARSAL, YOU HAVE TO --
-- JUMP IN.
BILLOS, I'D LIKE YOU TO MEET GABIL THE ROUSH.
SORRY ABOUT THAT BIT WITH THE HORSE BACK THERE.
YOU MADE IT ACT LIKE THAT?!
WELL, YES.
INVISIBLY POKING AND PRODDING CREATURES ISN'T ONE OF MY FINER TALENTS.
HOWEVER, IT CERTAINLY GETS THE JOB DONE.

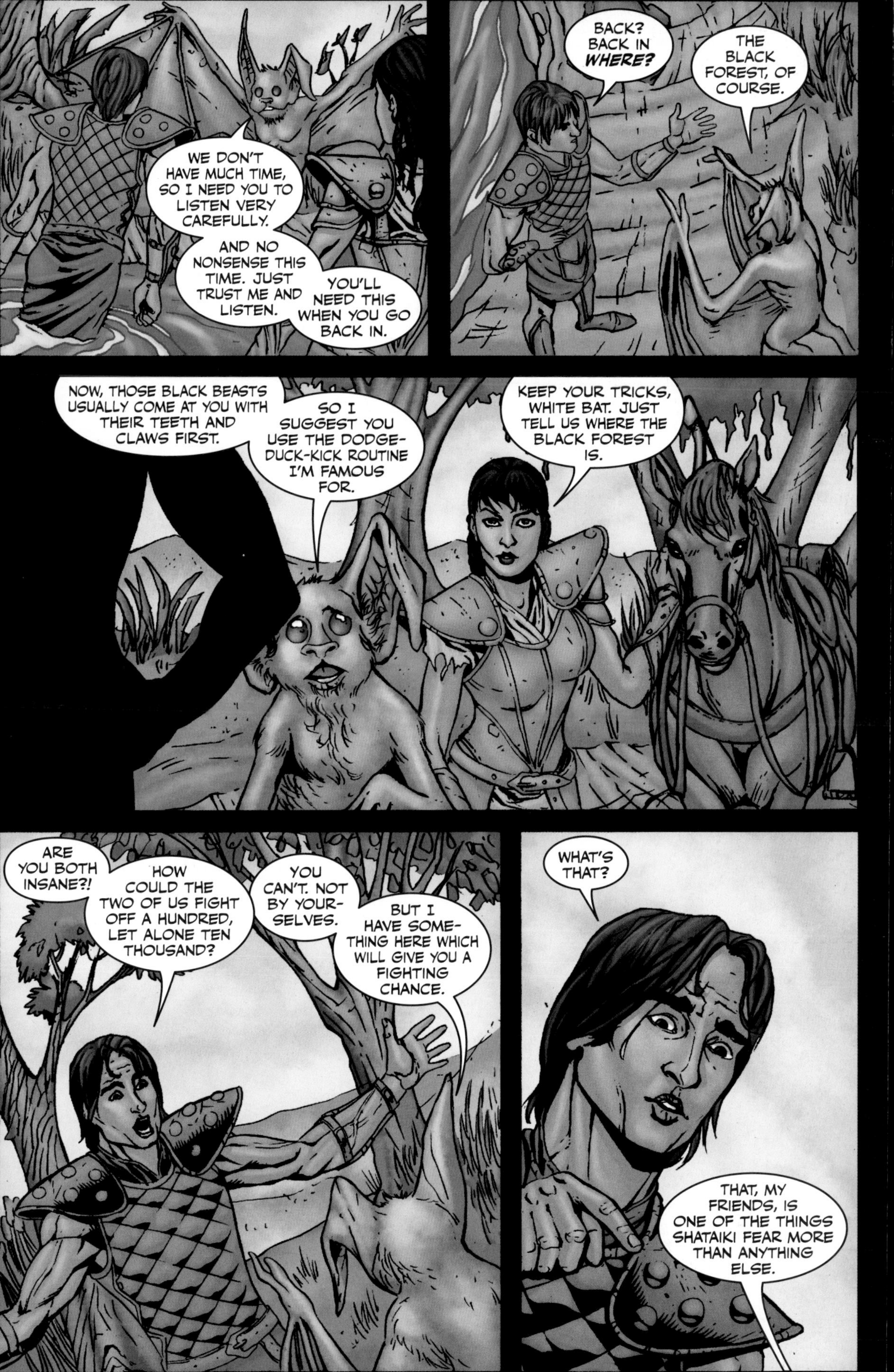
WE DON'T HAVE MUCH TIME, SO I NEED YOU TO LISTEN VERY CAREFULLY.
AND NO NONSENSE THIS TIME. JUST TRUST ME AND LISTEN.
YOU'LL NEED THIS WHEN YOU GO BACK IN.
BACK? BACK IN WHERE?
THE BLACK FOREST, OF COURSE.
NOW, THOSE BLACK BEASTS USUALLY COME AT YOU WITH THEIR TEETH AND CLAWS FIRST.
SO I SUGGEST YOU USE THE DODGE-DUCK-KICK ROUTINE I'M FAMOUS FOR.
KEEP YOUR TRICKS, WHITE BAT. JUST TELL US WHERE THE BLACK FOREST IS.
ARE YOU BOTH INSANE?!
HOW COULD THE TWO OF US FIGHT OFF A HUNDRED, LET ALONE TEN THOUSAND?
YOU CAN'T. NOT BY YOURSELVES.
BUT I HAVE SOMETHING HERE WHICH WILL GIVE YOU A FIGHTING CHANCE.
WHAT'S THAT?
THAT, MY FRIENDS, IS ONE OF THE THINGS SHATAIKI FEAR MORE THAN ANYTHING ELSE.

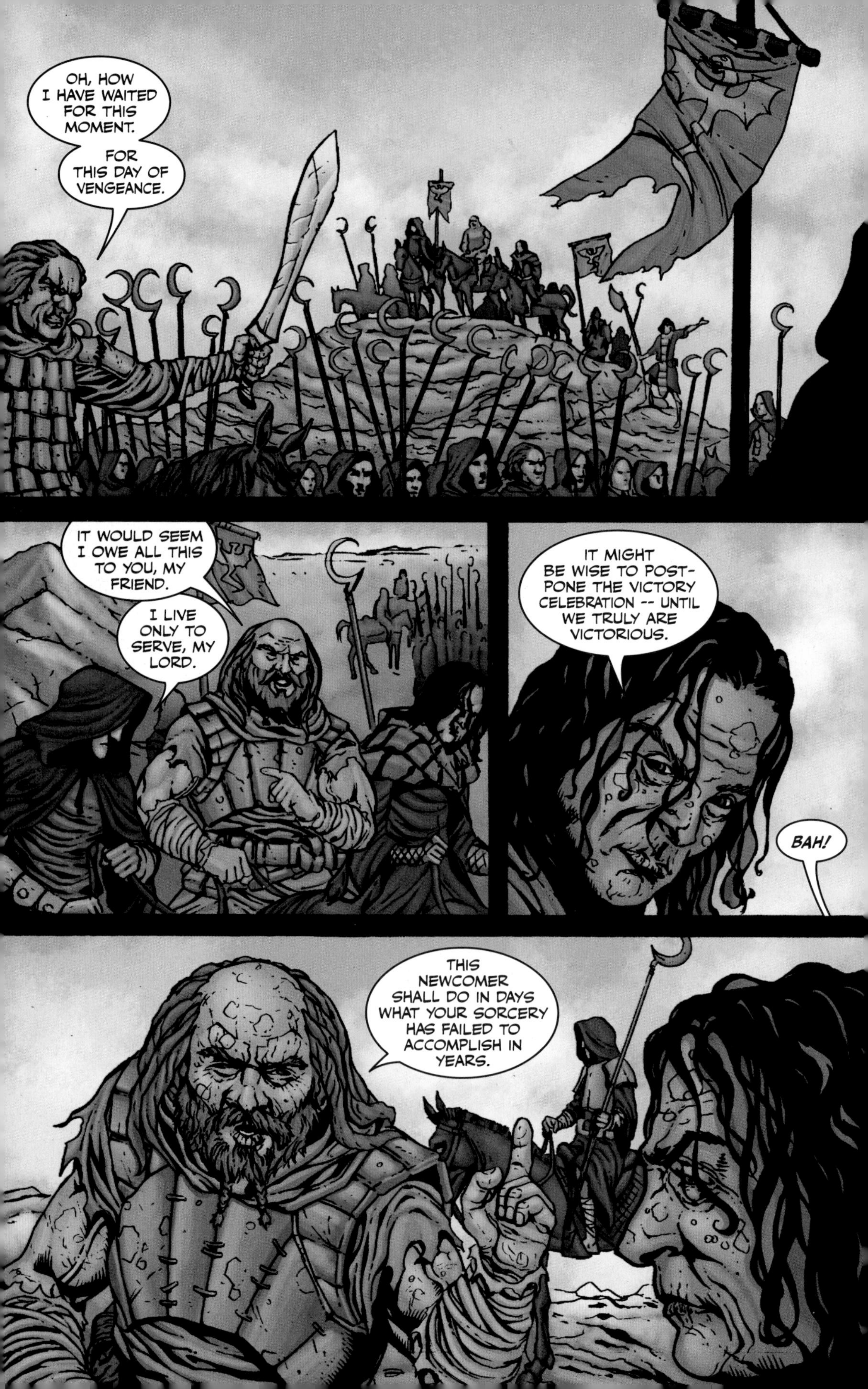
OH, HOW I HAVE WAITED FOR THIS MOMENT.
FOR THIS DAY OF VENGEANCE.
IT WOULD SEEM I OWE ALL THIS TO YOU, MY FRIEND.
I LIVE ONLY TO SERVE, MY LORD.
IT MIGHT BE WISE TO POST-PONE THE VICTORY CELEBRATION -- UNTIL WE TRULY ARE VICTORIOUS.
BAH!
THIS NEWCOMER SHALL DO IN DAYS WHAT YOUR SORCERY HAS FAILED TO ACCOMPLISH IN YEARS.

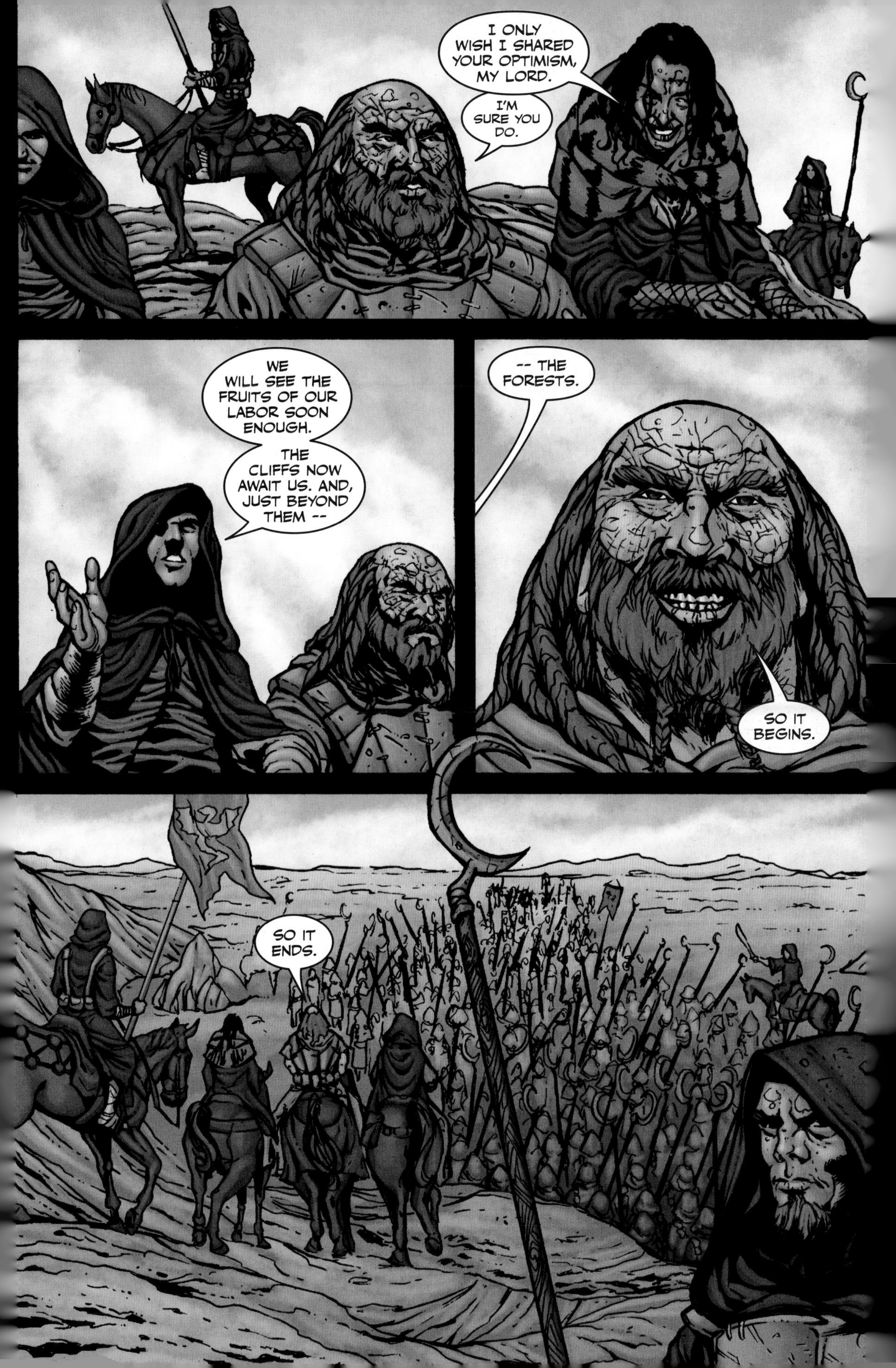
I ONLY WISH I SHARED YOUR OPTIMISM, MY LORD.
I'M SURE YOU DO.
WE WILL SEE THE FRUITS OF OUR LABOR SOON ENOUGH.
THE CLIFFS NOW AWAIT US. AND, JUST BEYOND THEM --
-- THE FORESTS.
SO IT BEGINS.
SO IT ENDS.

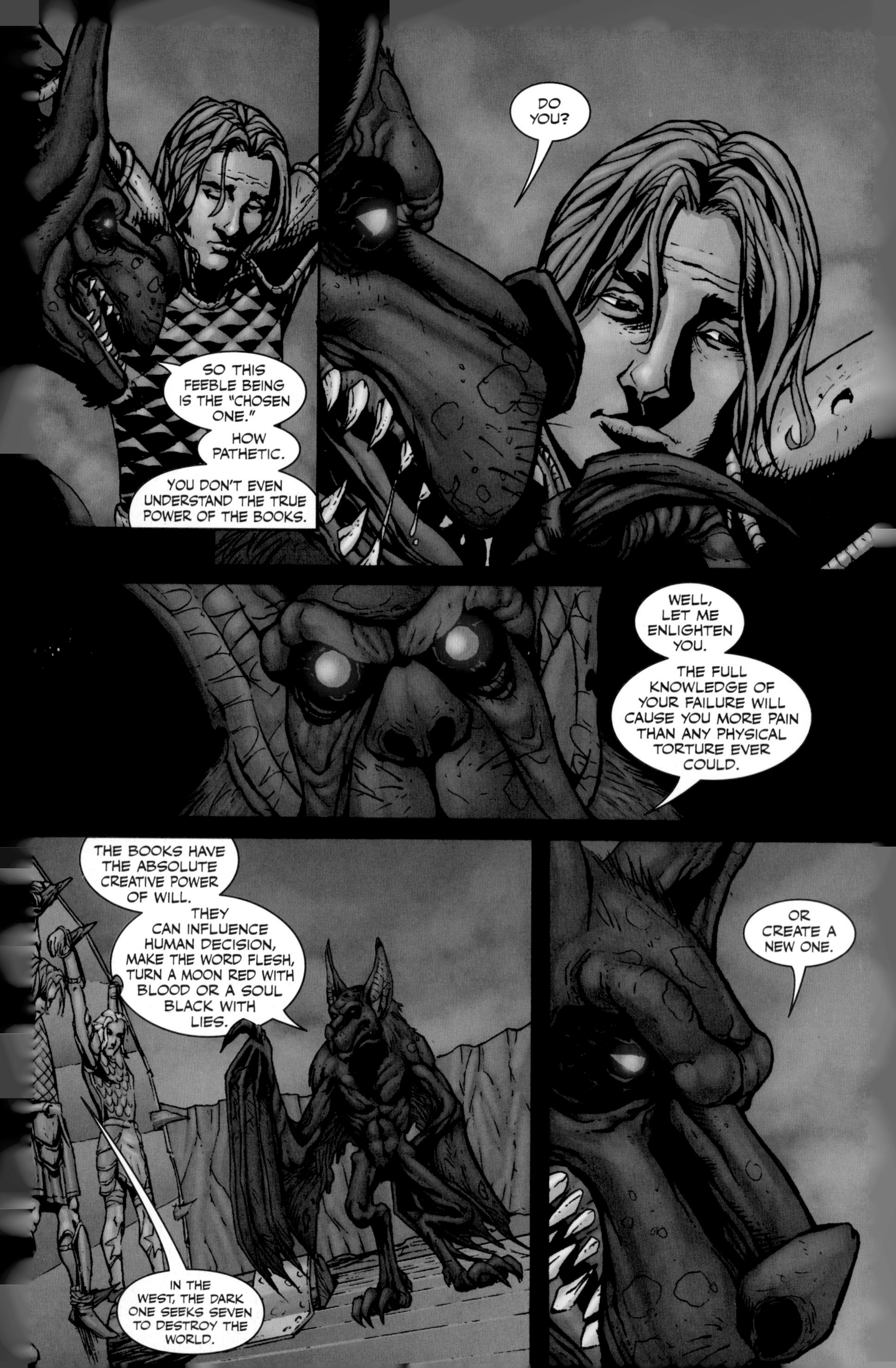
SO THIS FEEBLE BEING IS THE "CHOSEN ONE."
HOW PATHETIC.
YOU DON'T EVEN UNDERSTAND THE TRUE POWER OF THE BOOKS.
DO YOU?
WELL, LET ME ENLIGHTEN YOU.
THE FULL KNOWLEDGE OF YOUR FAILURE WILL CAUSE YOU MORE PAIN THAN ANY PHYSICAL TORTURE EVER COULD.
THE BOOKS HAVE THE ABSOLUTE CREATIVE POWER OF WILL.
THEY CAN INFLUENCE HUMAN DECISION, MAKE THE WORD FLESH, TURN A MOON RED WITH BLOOD OR A SOUL BLACK WITH LIES.
IN THE WEST, THE DARK ONE SEEKS SEVEN TO DESTROY THE WORLD.
OR CREATE A NEW ONE.

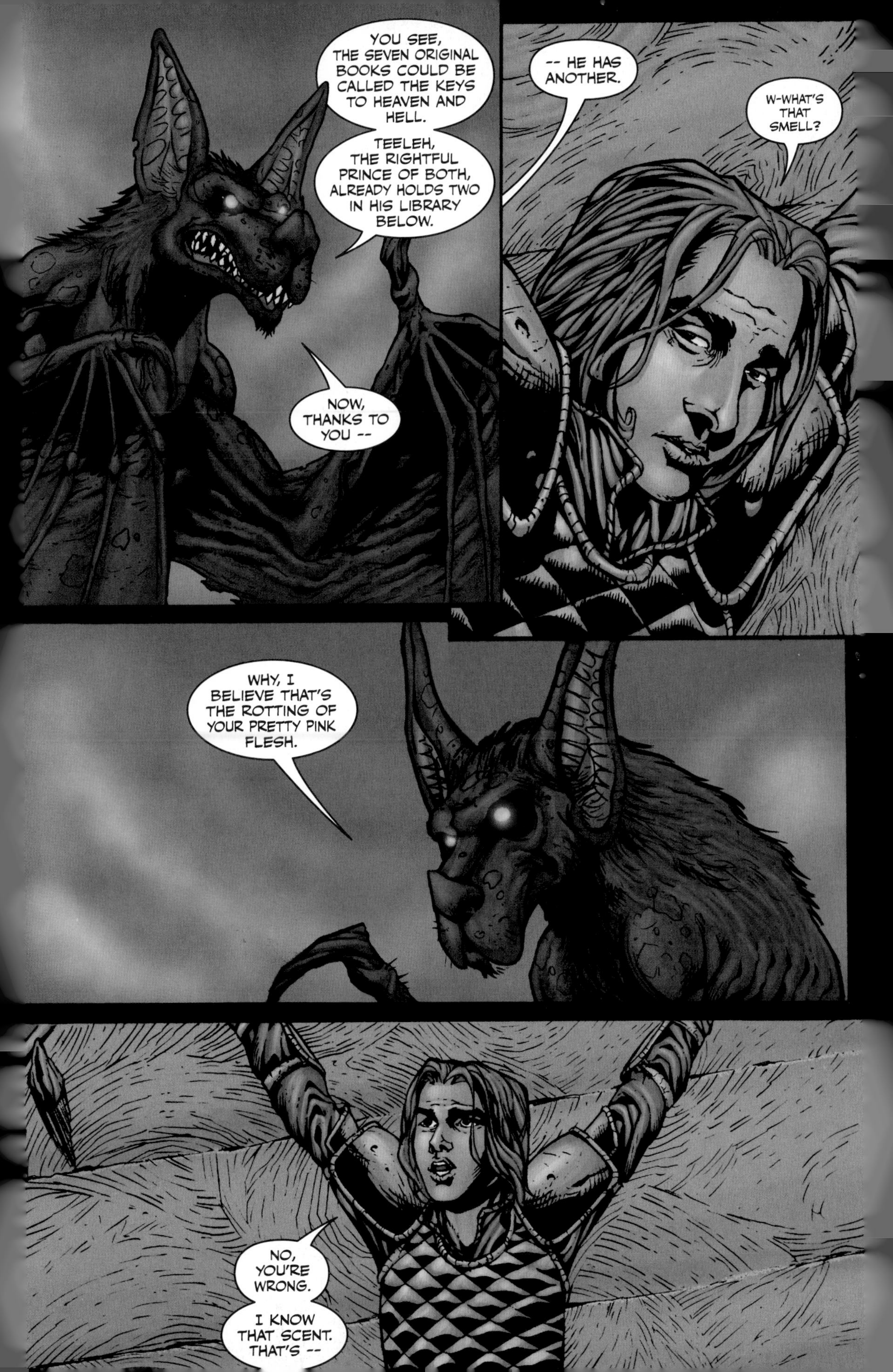
YOU SEE, THE SEVEN ORIGINAL BOOKS COULD BE CALLED THE KEYS TO HEAVEN AND HELL.
TEELEH, THE RIGHTFUL PRINCE OF BOTH, ALREADY HOLDS TWO IN HIS LIBRARY BELOW.
NOW, THANKS TO YOU --
-- HE HAS ANOTHER.
W-WHAT'S THAT SMELL?
WHY, I BELIEVE THAT'S THE ROTTING OF YOUR PRETTY PINK FLESH.
NO, YOU'RE WRONG.
I KNOW THAT SCENT. THAT'S --

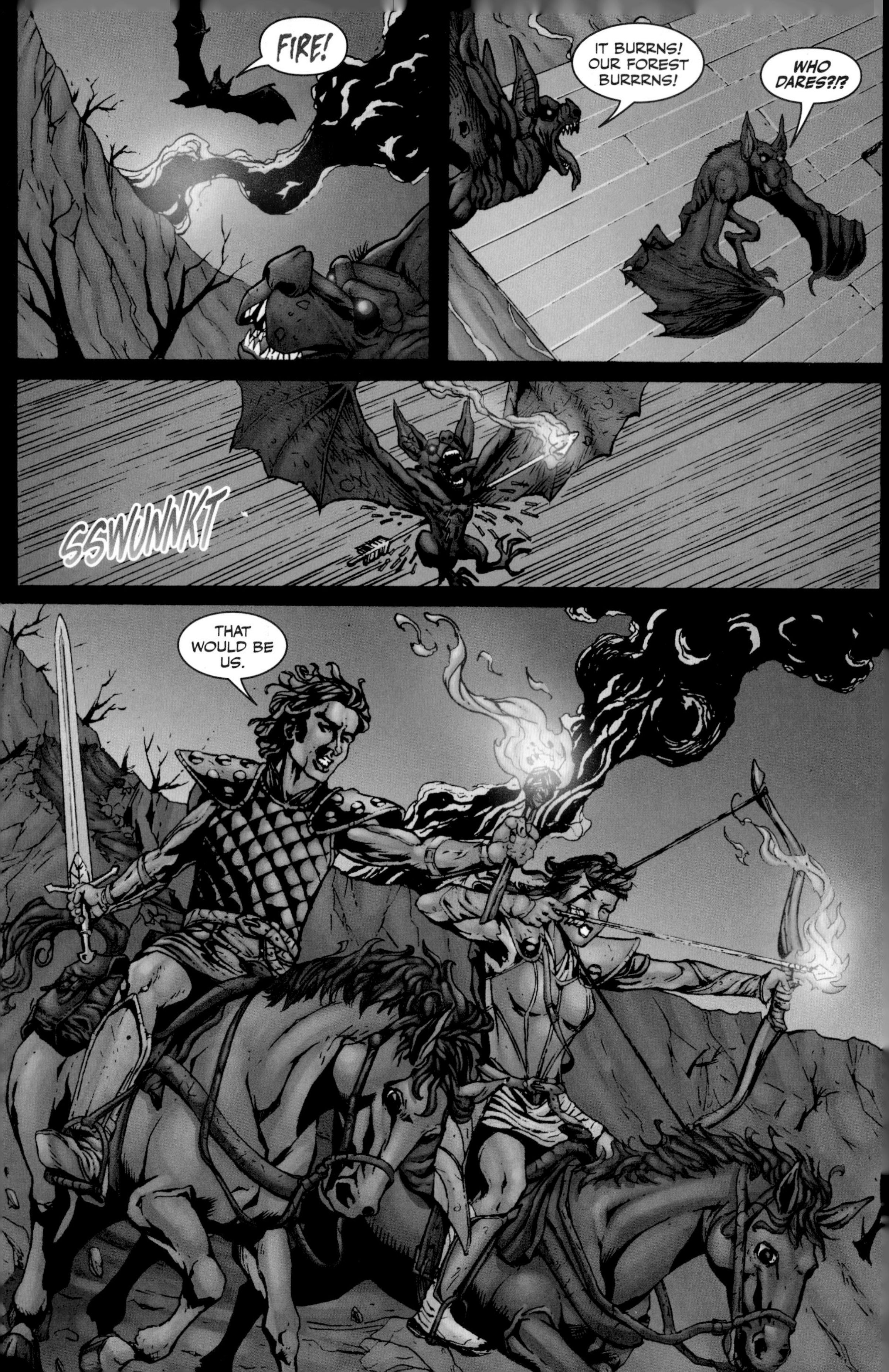
FIRE!
IT BURRNS! OUR FOREST BURRRNS!
WHO DARES?!?
SSWUNNKT
THAT WOULD BE US.

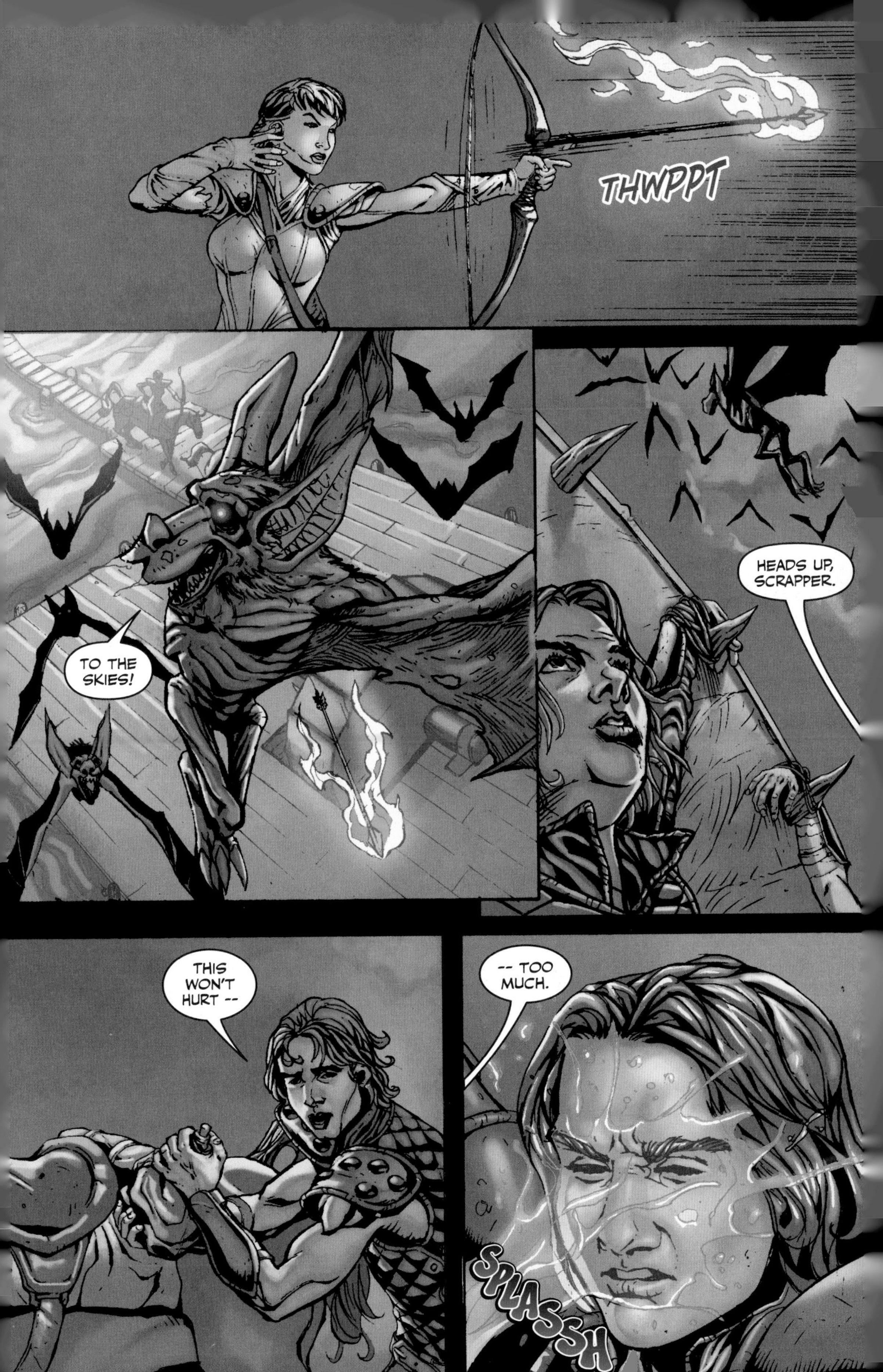
THWPPT
TO THE SKIES!
HEADS UP, SCRAPPER.
THIS WON'T HURT --
-- TOO MUCH.
SPLASSH

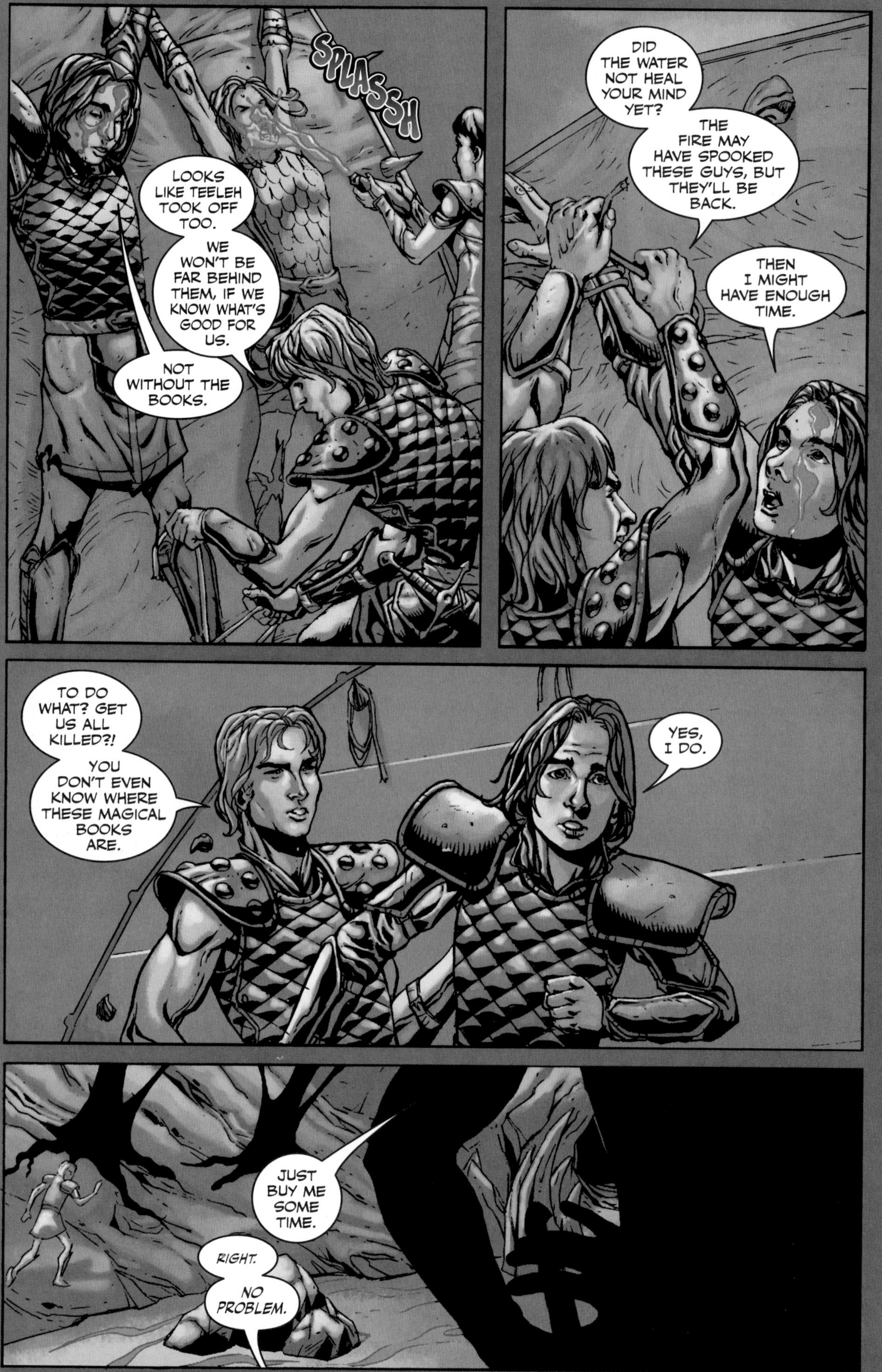
SPLASSSH
LOOKS LIKE TEELEH TOOK OFF TOO.
WE WON'T BE FAR BEHIND THEM, IF WE KNOW WHAT'S GOOD FOR US.
NOT WITHOUT THE BOOKS.
DID THE WATER NOT HEAL YOUR MIND YET?
THE FIRE MAY HAVE SPOOKED THESE GUYS, BUT THEY'LL BE BACK.
THEN I MIGHT HAVE ENOUGH TIME.
TO DO WHAT? GET US ALL KILLED?!
YOU DON'T EVEN KNOW WHERE THESE MAGICAL BOOKS ARE.
YES, I DO.
JUST BUY ME SOME TIME.
RIGHT.
NO PROBLEM.

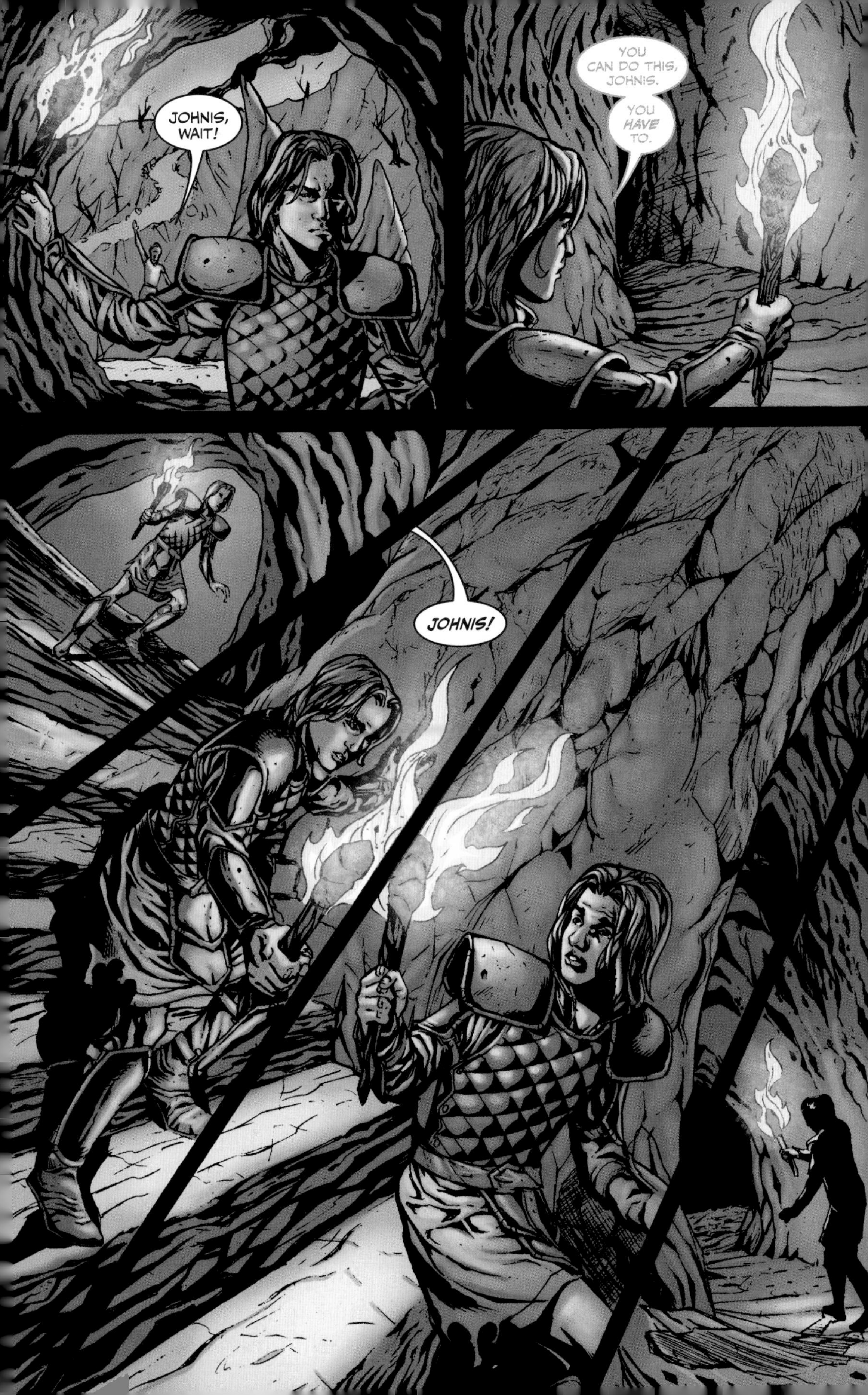
JOHNIS, WAIT!
YOU CAN DO THIS, JOHNIS.
YOU *HAVE* TO.
JOHNIS!

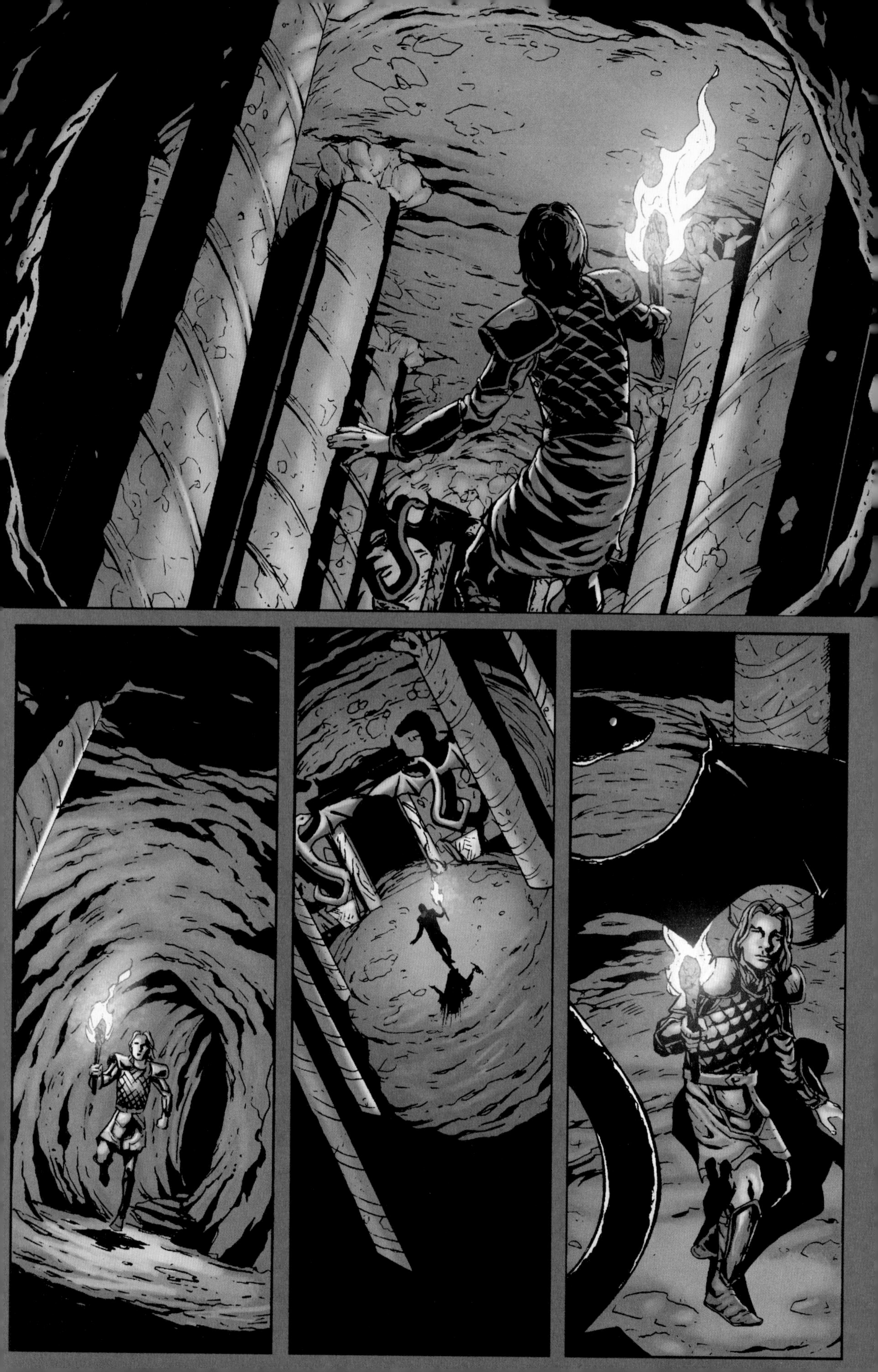

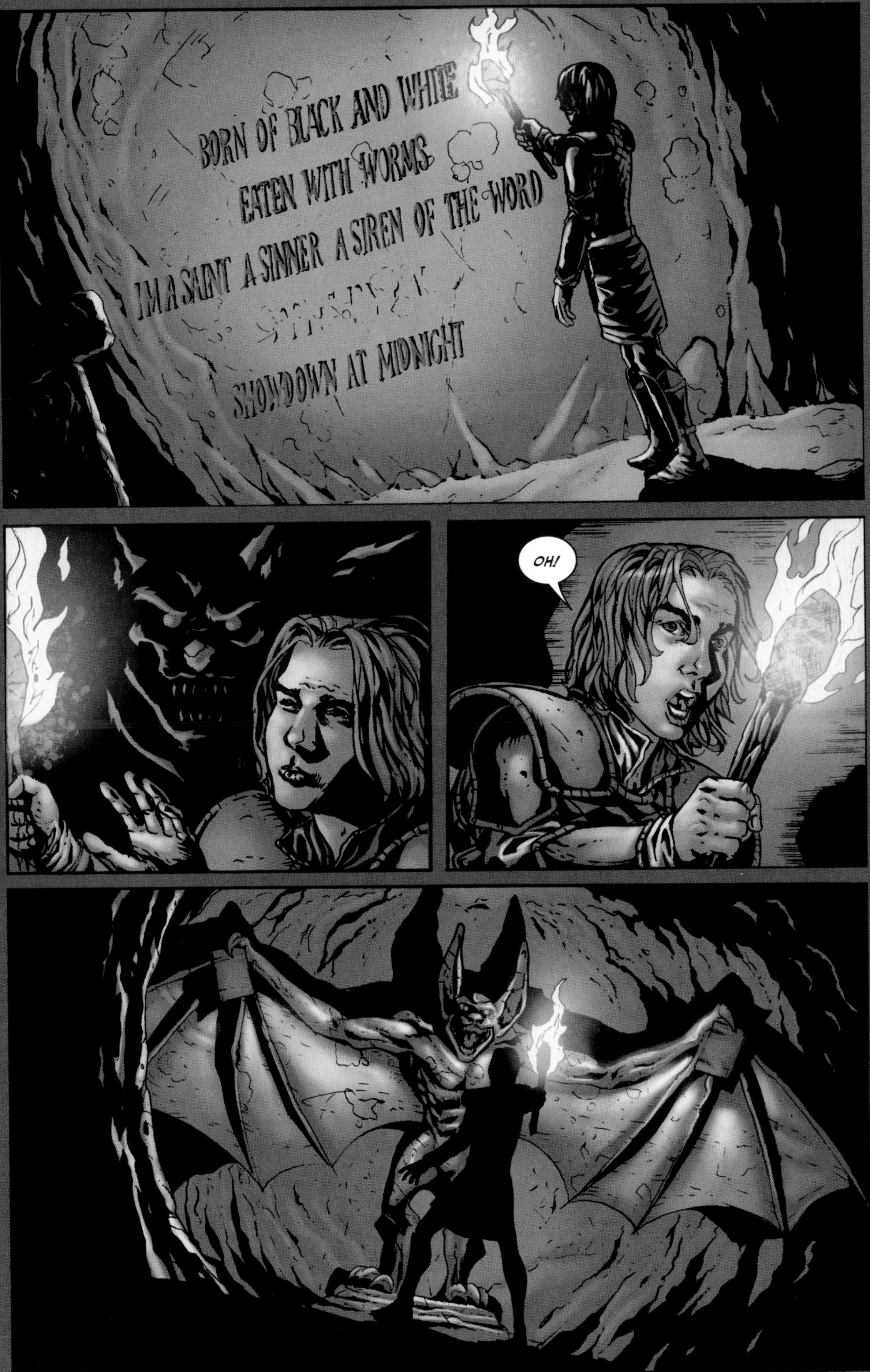
BORN OF BLACK AND WHITE
EATEN WITH WORMS
I'M A SAINT A SINNER A SIREN OF THE WORD
SHOWDOWN AT MIDNIGHT
OH!

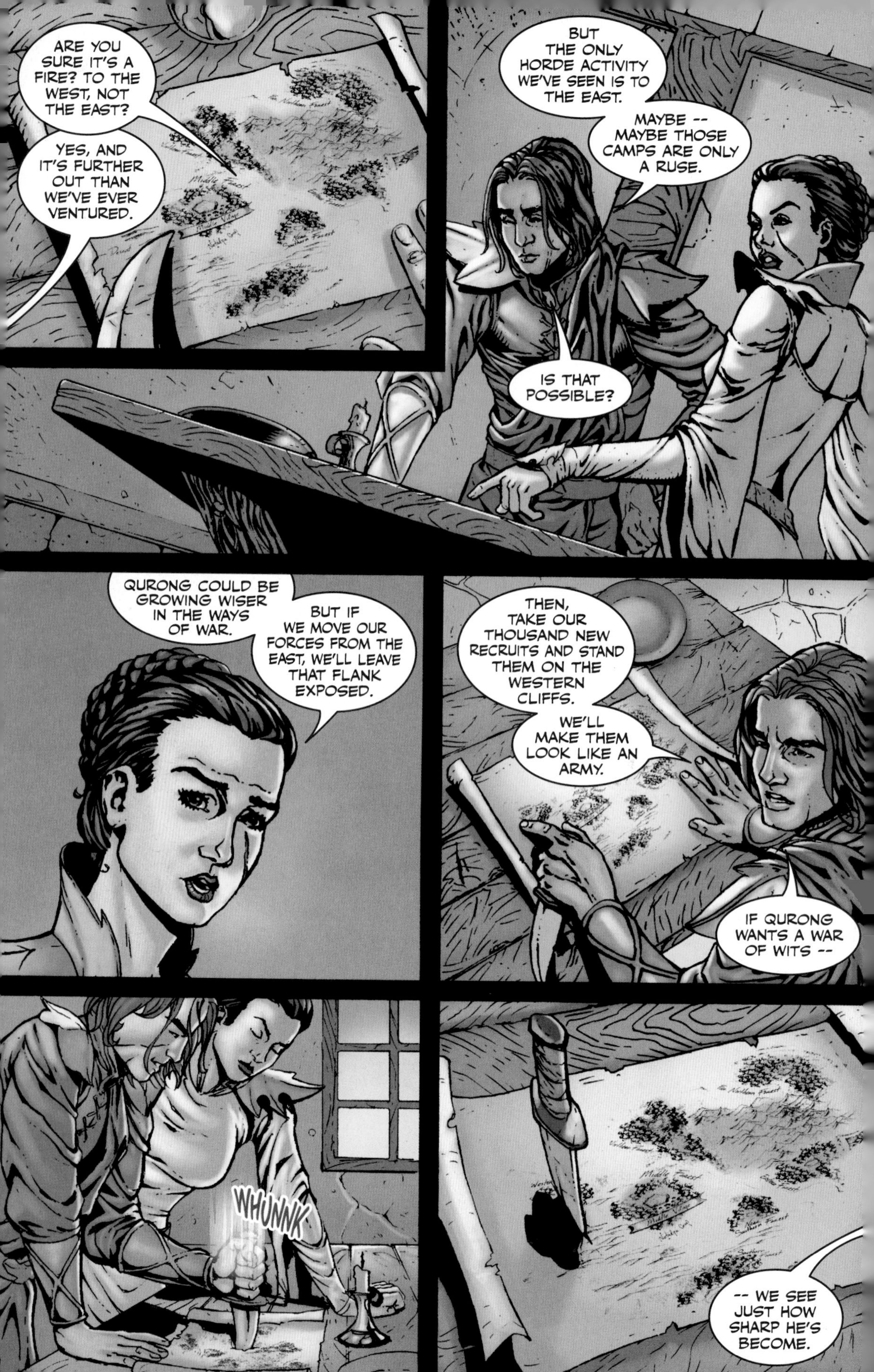
ARE YOU SURE IT'S A FIRE? TO THE WEST, NOT THE EAST?
YES, AND IT'S FURTHER OUT THAN WE'VE EVER VENTURED.
BUT THE ONLY HORDE ACTIVITY WE'VE SEEN IS TO THE EAST.
MAYBE -- MAYBE THOSE CAMPS ARE ONLY A RUSE.
IS THAT POSSIBLE?
QURONG COULD BE GROWING WISER IN THE WAYS OF WAR.
BUT IF WE MOVE OUR FORCES FROM THE EAST, WE'LL LEAVE THAT FLANK EXPOSED.
THEN, TAKE OUR THOUSAND NEW RECRUITS AND STAND THEM ON THE WESTERN CLIFFS.
WE'LL MAKE THEM LOOK LIKE AN ARMY.
IF QURONG WANTS A WAR OF WITS --
WHUNNK
-- WE SEE JUST HOW SHARP HE'S BECOME.

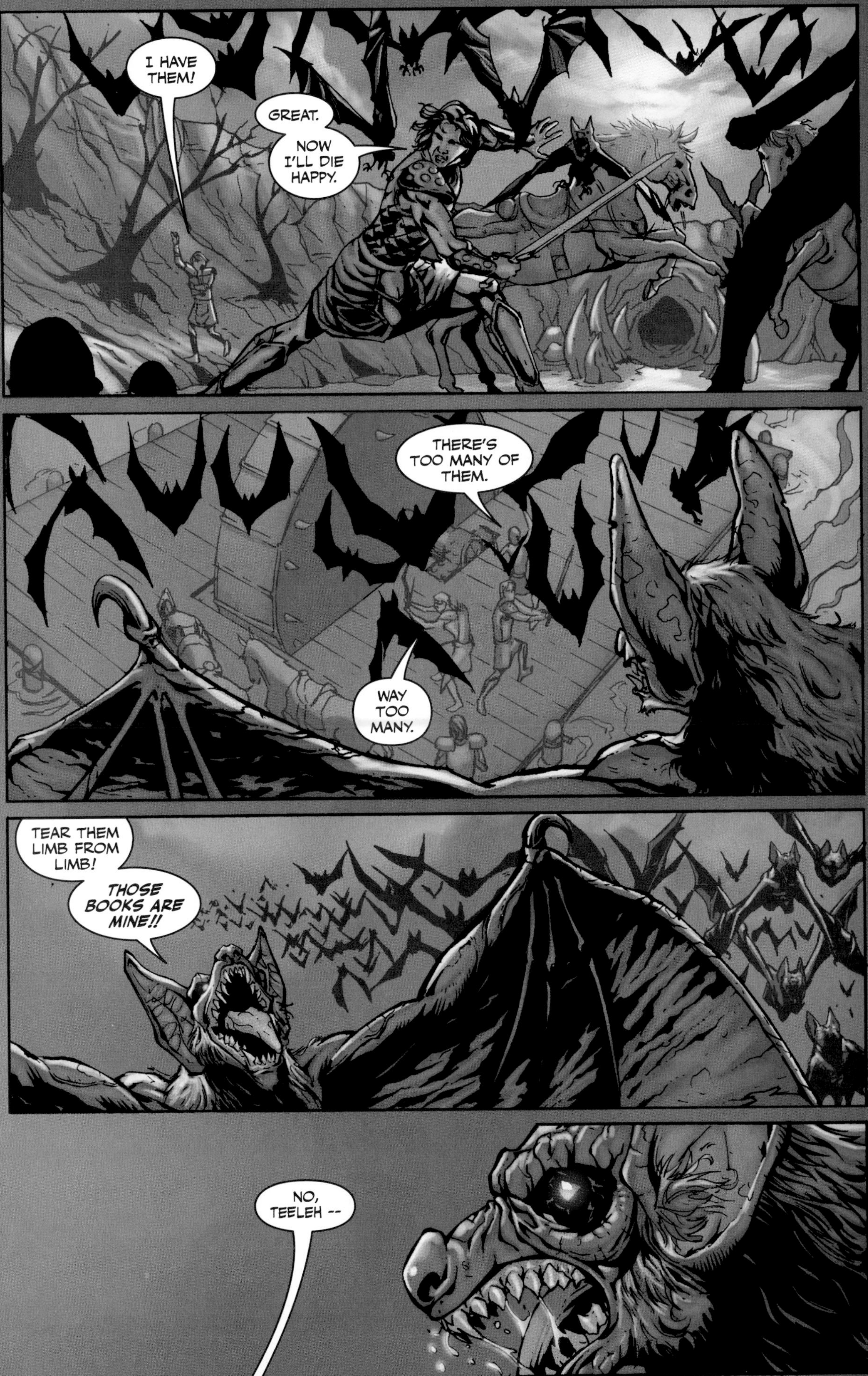

I HAVE THEM!
GREAT.
NOW I'LL DIE HAPPY.
THERE'S TOO MANY OF THEM.
WAY TOO MANY.
TEAR THEM LIMB FROM LIMB!
THOSE BOOKS ARE MINE!!
NO, TEELEH --

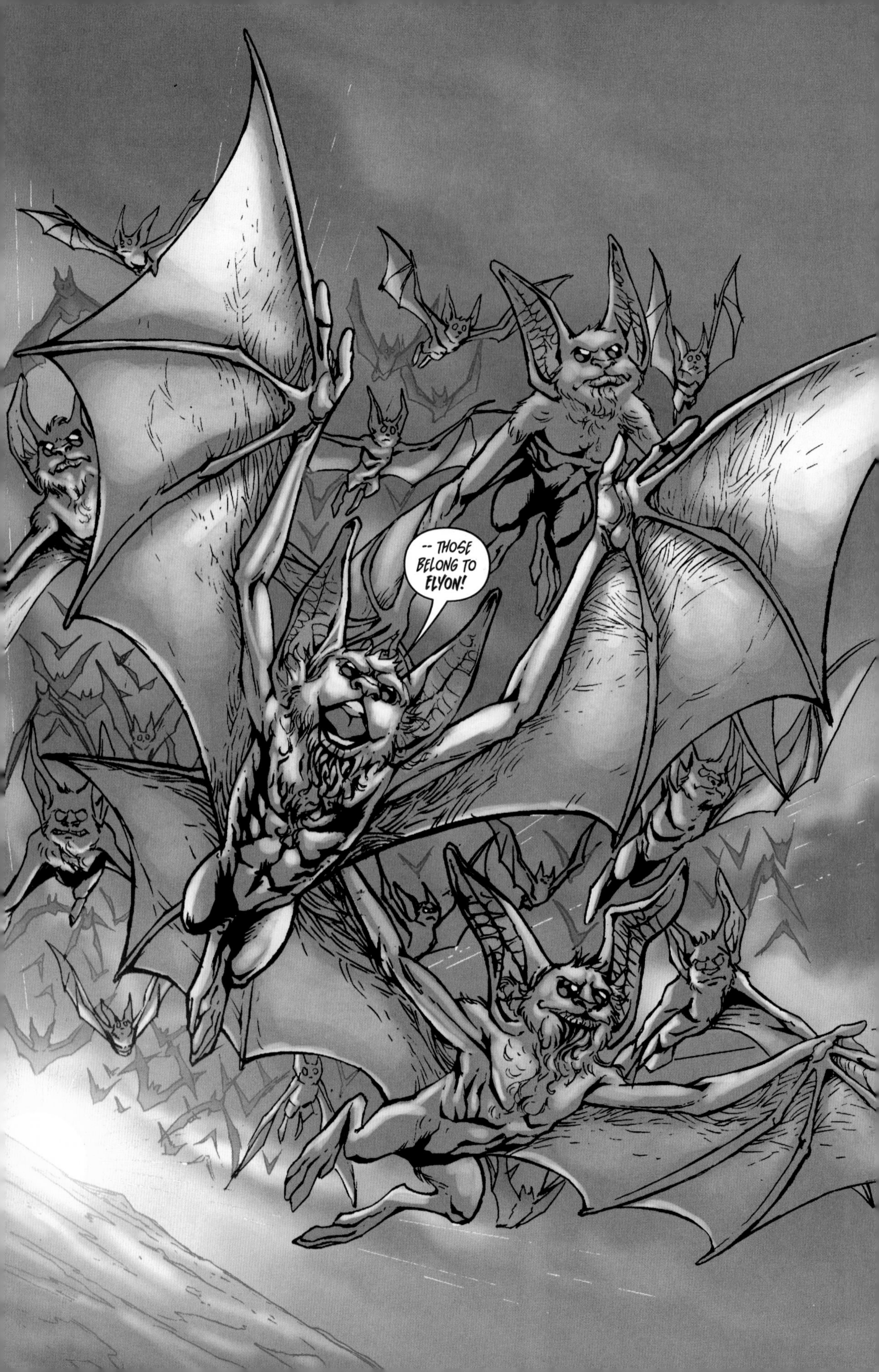
-- THOSE BELONG TO ELYON!

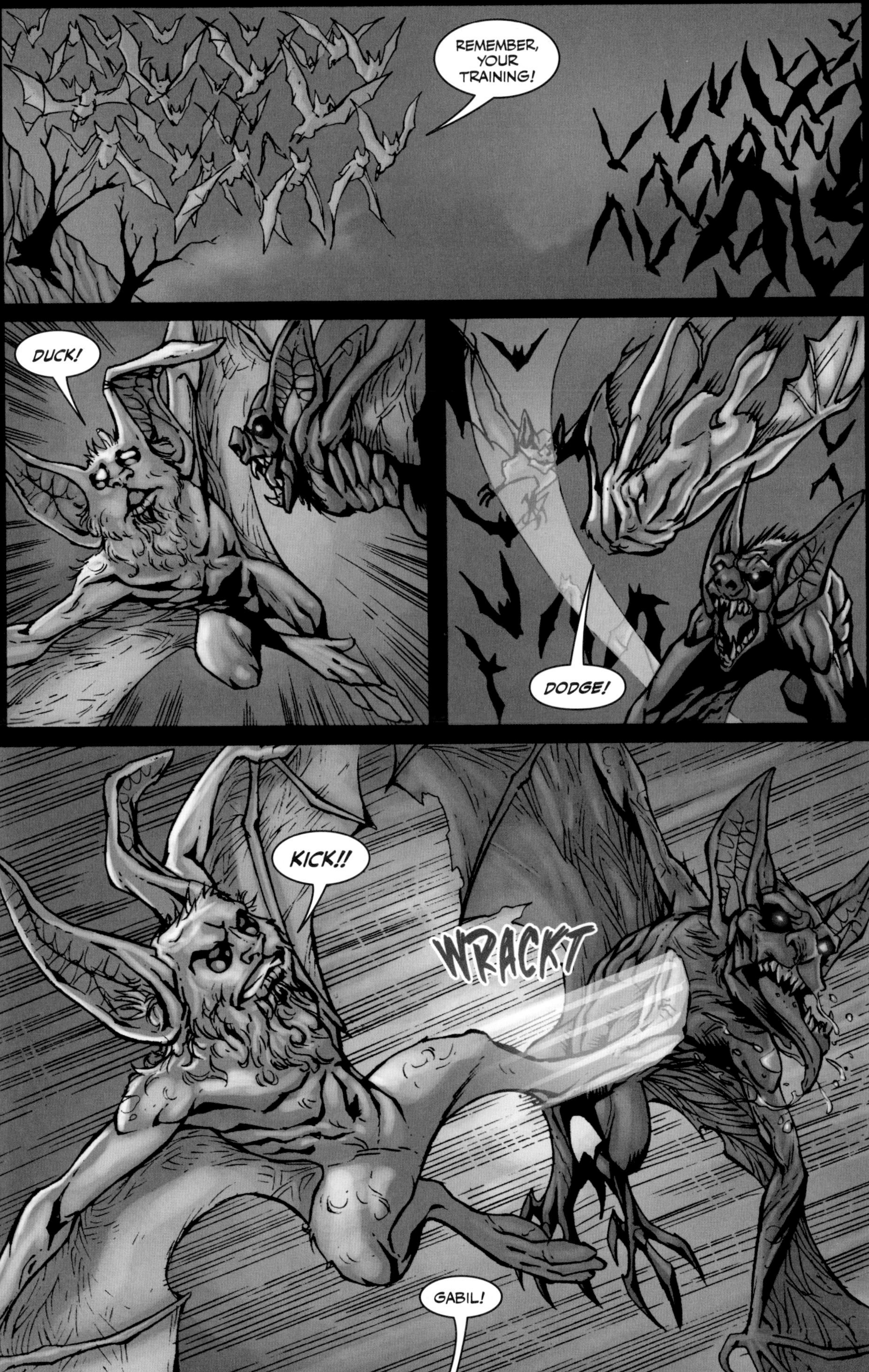
REMEMBER, YOUR TRAINING!
DUCK!
DODGE!
KICK!!
WRACKT
GABIL!

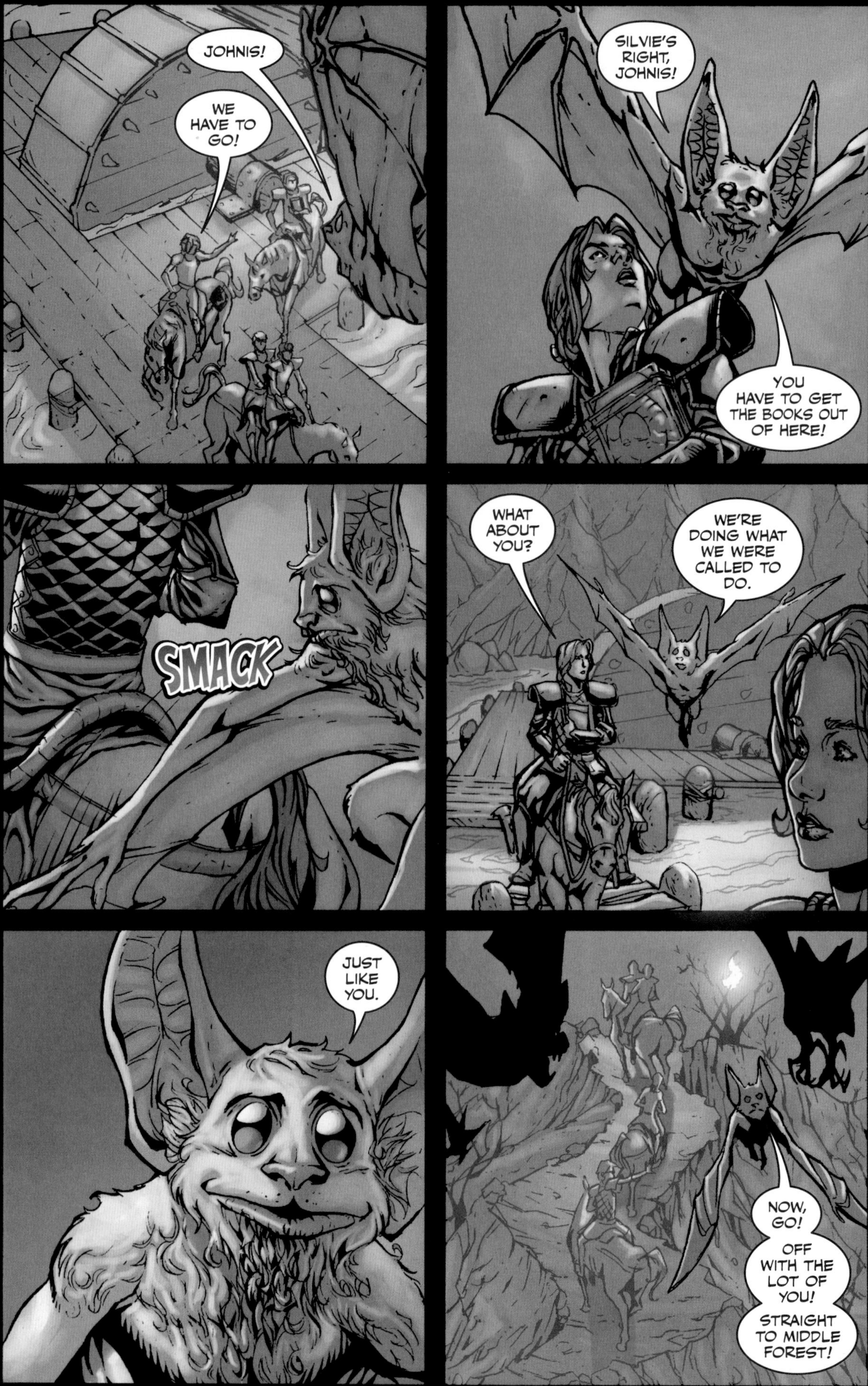
JOHNIS!
WE HAVE TO GO!
SILVIE'S RIGHT, JOHNIS!
YOU HAVE TO GET THE BOOKS OUT OF HERE!
SMACK
WHAT ABOUT YOU?
WE'RE DOING WHAT WE WERE CALLED TO DO.
JUST LIKE YOU.
NOW, GO!
OFF WITH THE LOT OF YOU!
STRAIGHT TO MIDDLE FOREST!

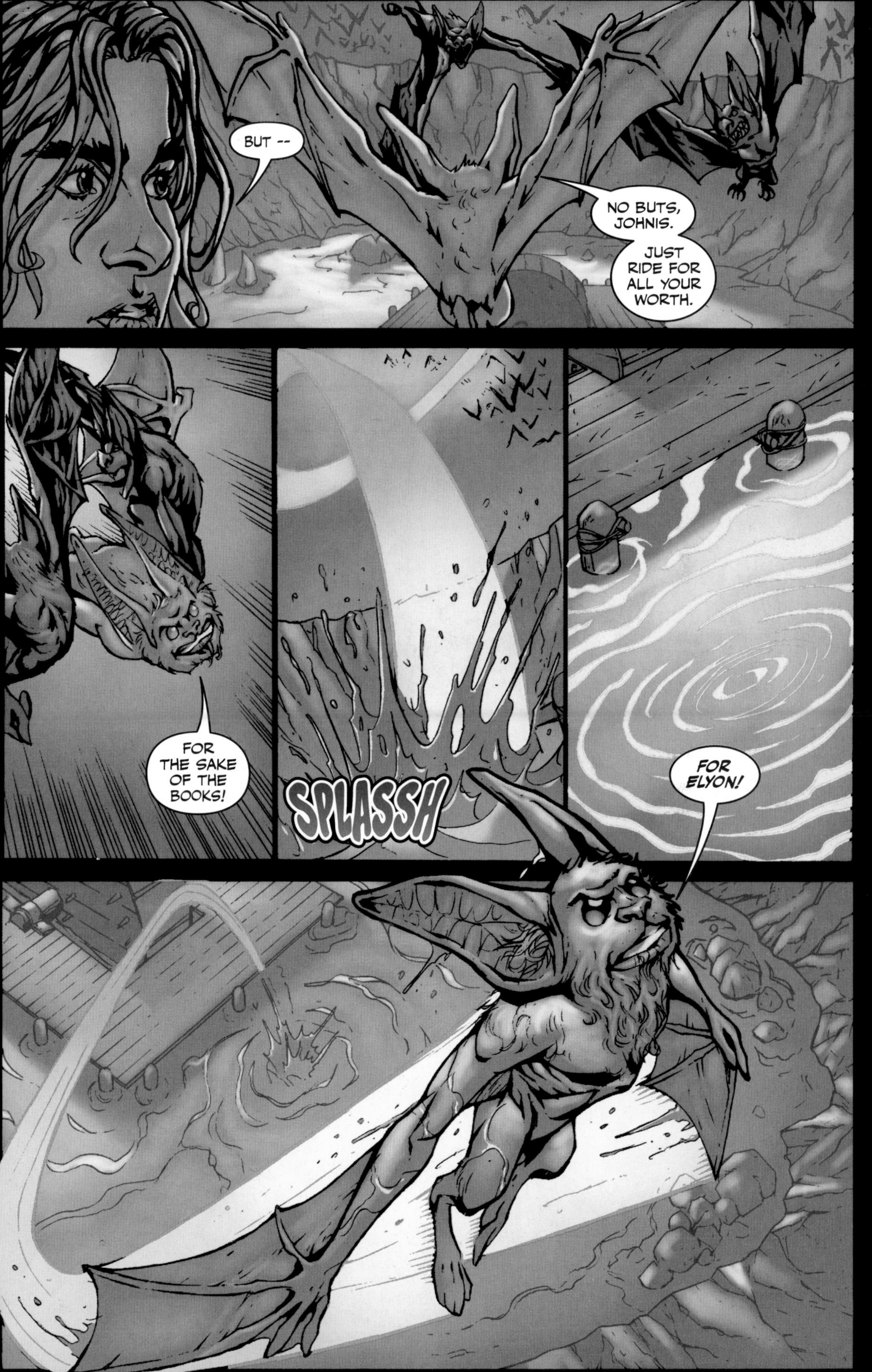
BUT --
NO BUTS, JOHNIS.
JUST RIDE FOR ALL YOUR WORTH.
FOR THE SAKE OF THE BOOKS!
SPLASSH
FOR ELYON!

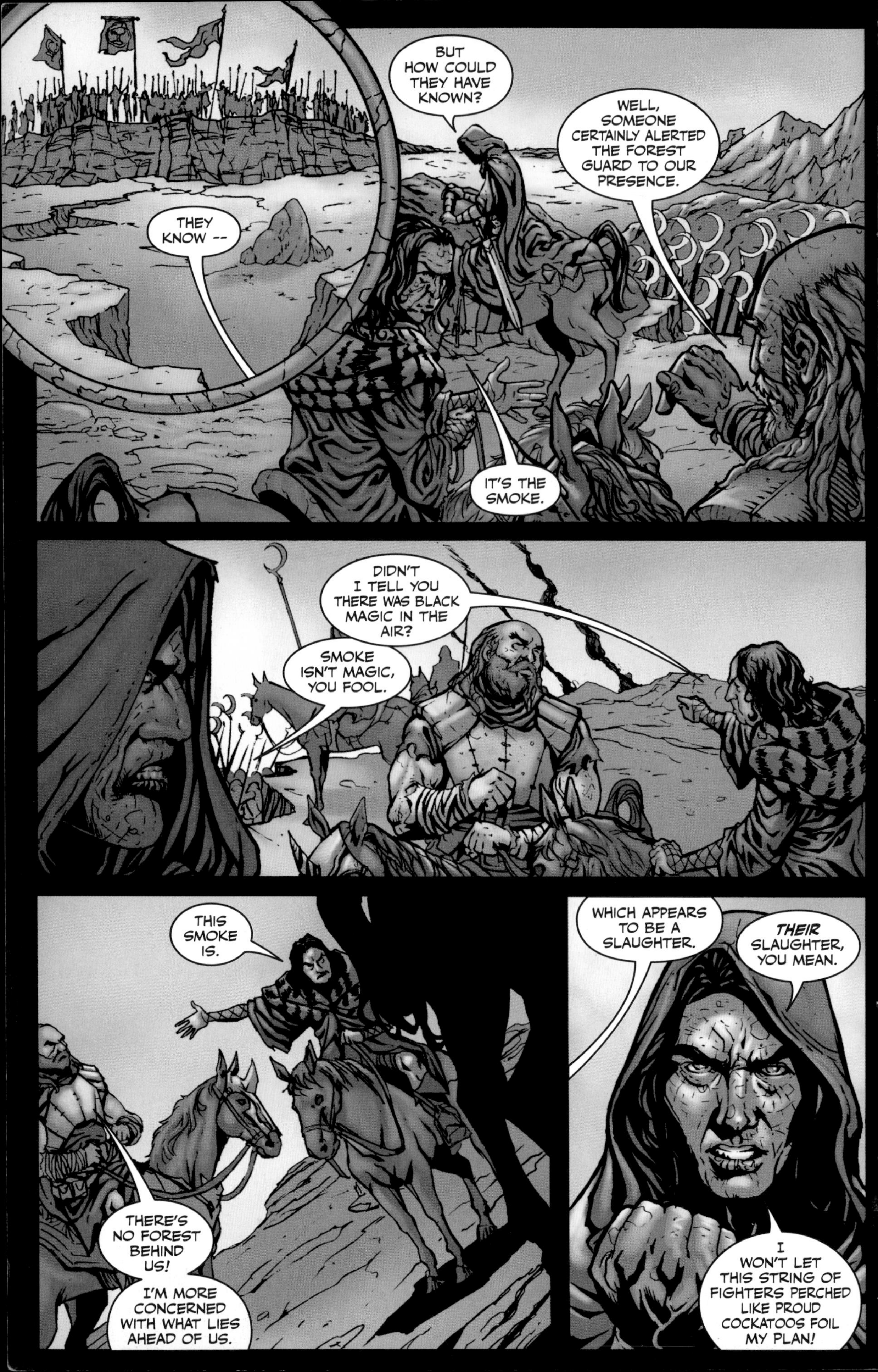
THEY KNOW --
BUT HOW COULD THEY HAVE KNOWN?
WELL, SOMEONE CERTAINLY ALERTED THE FOREST GUARD TO OUR PRESENCE.
IT'S THE SMOKE.
DIDN'T I TELL YOU THERE WAS BLACK MAGIC IN THE AIR?
SMOKE ISN'T MAGIC, YOU FOOL.
THIS SMOKE IS.
THERE'S NO FOREST BEHIND US!
I'M MORE CONCERNED WITH WHAT LIES AHEAD OF US.
WHICH APPEARS TO BE A SLAUGHTER.
THEIR SLAUGHTER, YOU MEAN.
I WON'T LET THIS STRING OF FIGHTERS PERCHED LIKE PROUD COCKATOOS FOIL MY PLAN!

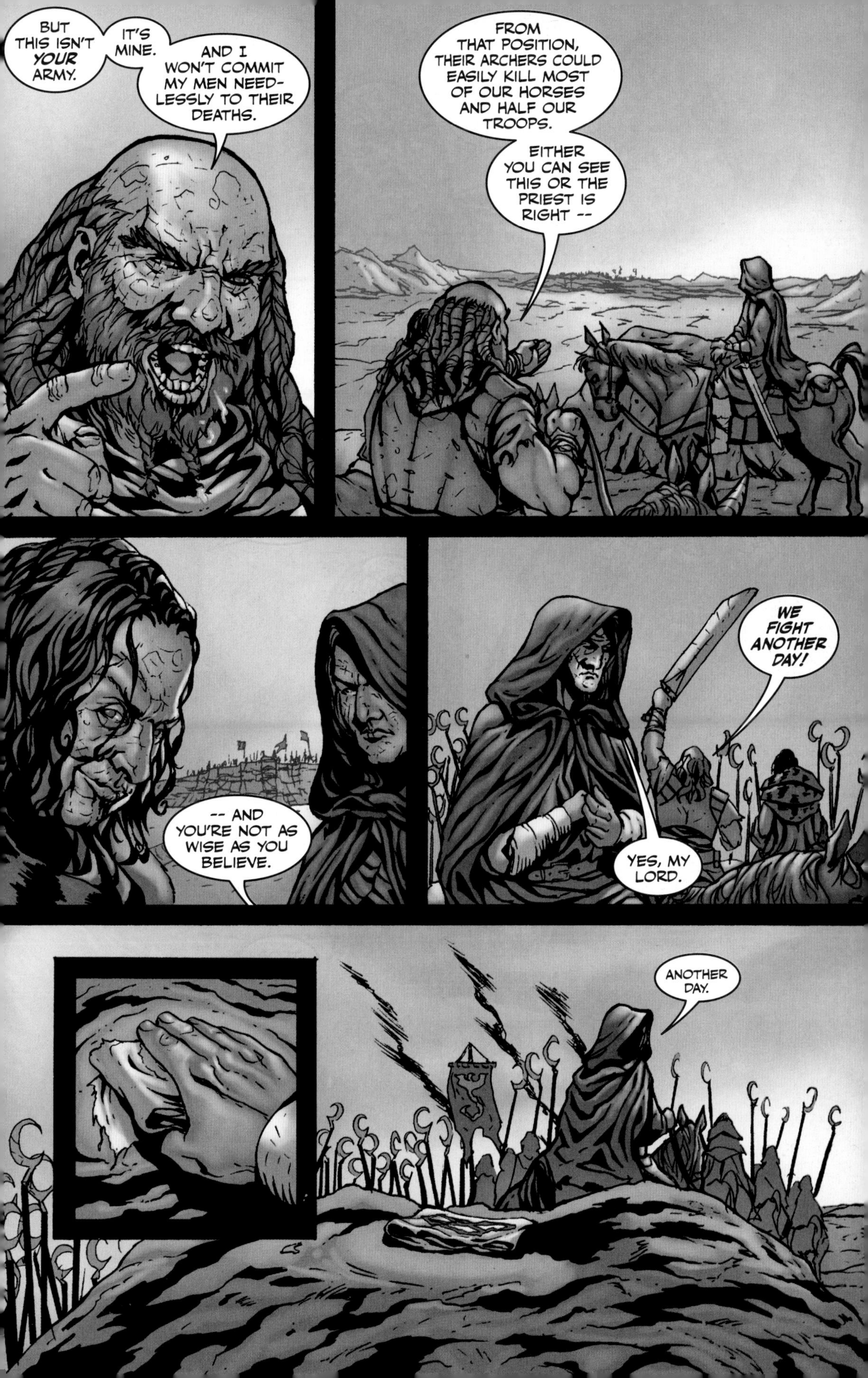
BUT THIS ISN'T *YOUR* ARMY.
IT'S MINE.
AND I WON'T COMMIT MY MEN NEEDLESSLY TO THEIR DEATHS.
FROM THAT POSITION, THEIR ARCHERS COULD EASILY KILL MOST OF OUR HORSES AND HALF OUR TROOPS.
EITHER YOU CAN SEE THIS OR THE PRIEST IS RIGHT --
-- AND YOU'RE NOT AS WISE AS YOU BELIEVE.
WE FIGHT ANOTHER DAY!
YES, MY LORD.
ANOTHER DAY.

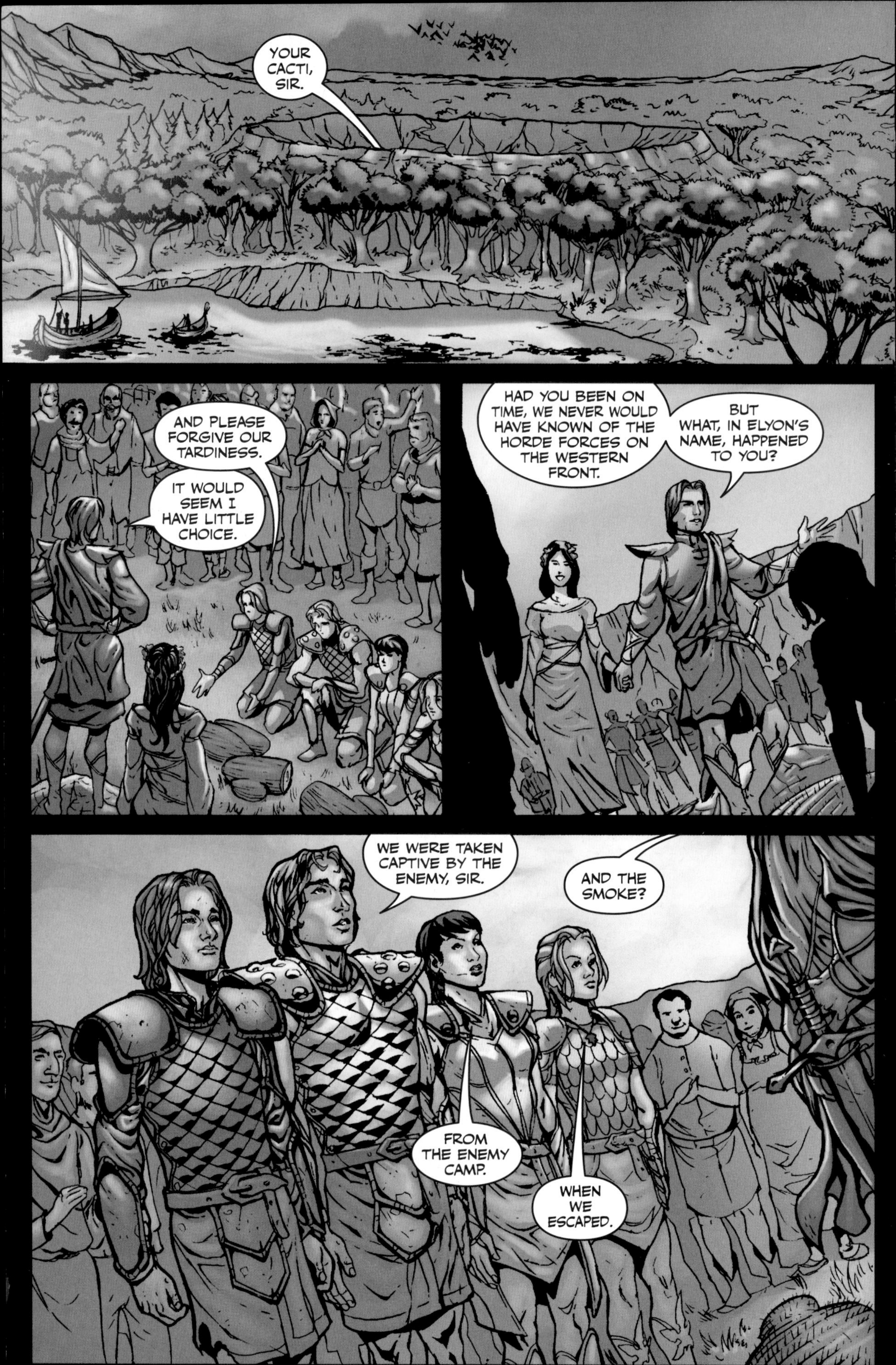
YOUR CACTI, SIR.
AND PLEASE FORGIVE OUR TARDINESS.
IT WOULD SEEM I HAVE LITTLE CHOICE.
HAD YOU BEEN ON TIME, WE NEVER WOULD HAVE KNOWN OF THE HORDE FORCES ON THE WESTERN FRONT.
BUT WHAT, IN ELYON'S NAME, HAPPENED TO YOU?
WE WERE TAKEN CAPTIVE BY THE ENEMY, SIR.
AND THE SMOKE?
FROM THE ENEMY CAMP.
WHEN WE ESCAPED.

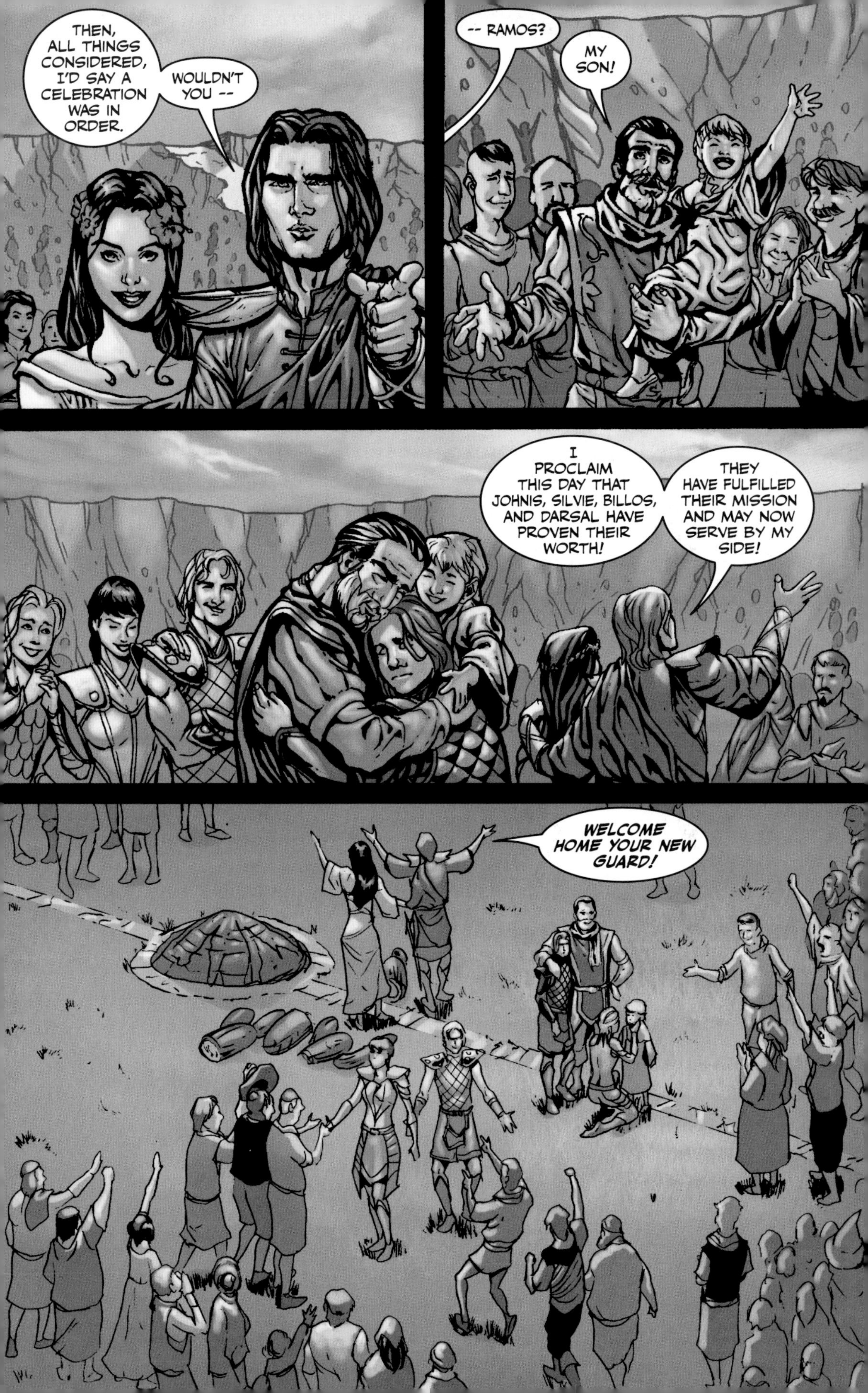
THEN, ALL THINGS CONSIDERED, I'D SAY A CELEBRATION WAS IN ORDER.
WOULDN'T YOU --
-- RAMOS?
MY SON!
I PROCLAIM THIS DAY THAT JOHNIS, SILVIE, BILLOS, AND DARSAL HAVE PROVEN THEIR WORTH!
THEY HAVE FULFILLED THEIR MISSION AND MAY NOW SERVE BY MY SIDE!
WELCOME HOME YOUR NEW GUARD!

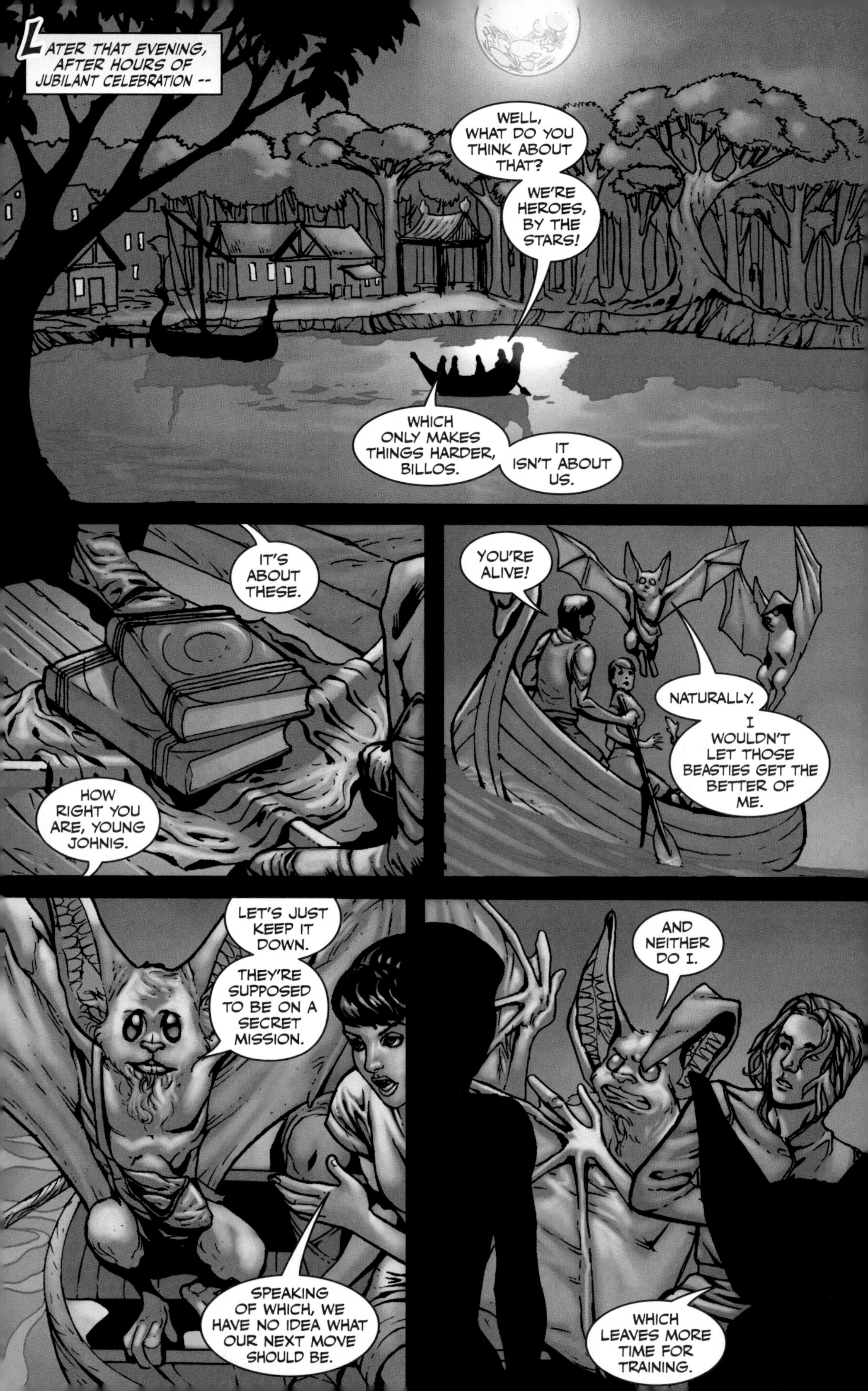
LATER THAT EVENING, AFTER HOURS OF JUBILANT CELEBRATION --
WELL, WHAT DO YOU THINK ABOUT THAT?
WE'RE HEROES, BY THE STARS!
WHICH ONLY MAKES THINGS HARDER, BILLOS.
IT ISN'T ABOUT US.
IT'S ABOUT THESE.
HOW RIGHT YOU ARE, YOUNG JOHNIS.
YOU'RE ALIVE!
NATURALLY.
I WOULDN'T LET THOSE BEASTIES GET THE BETTER OF ME.
LET'S JUST KEEP IT DOWN.
THEY'RE SUPPOSED TO BE ON A SECRET MISSION.
SPEAKING OF WHICH, WE HAVE NO IDEA WHAT OUR NEXT MOVE SHOULD BE.
AND NEITHER DO I.
WHICH LEAVES MORE TIME FOR TRAINING.

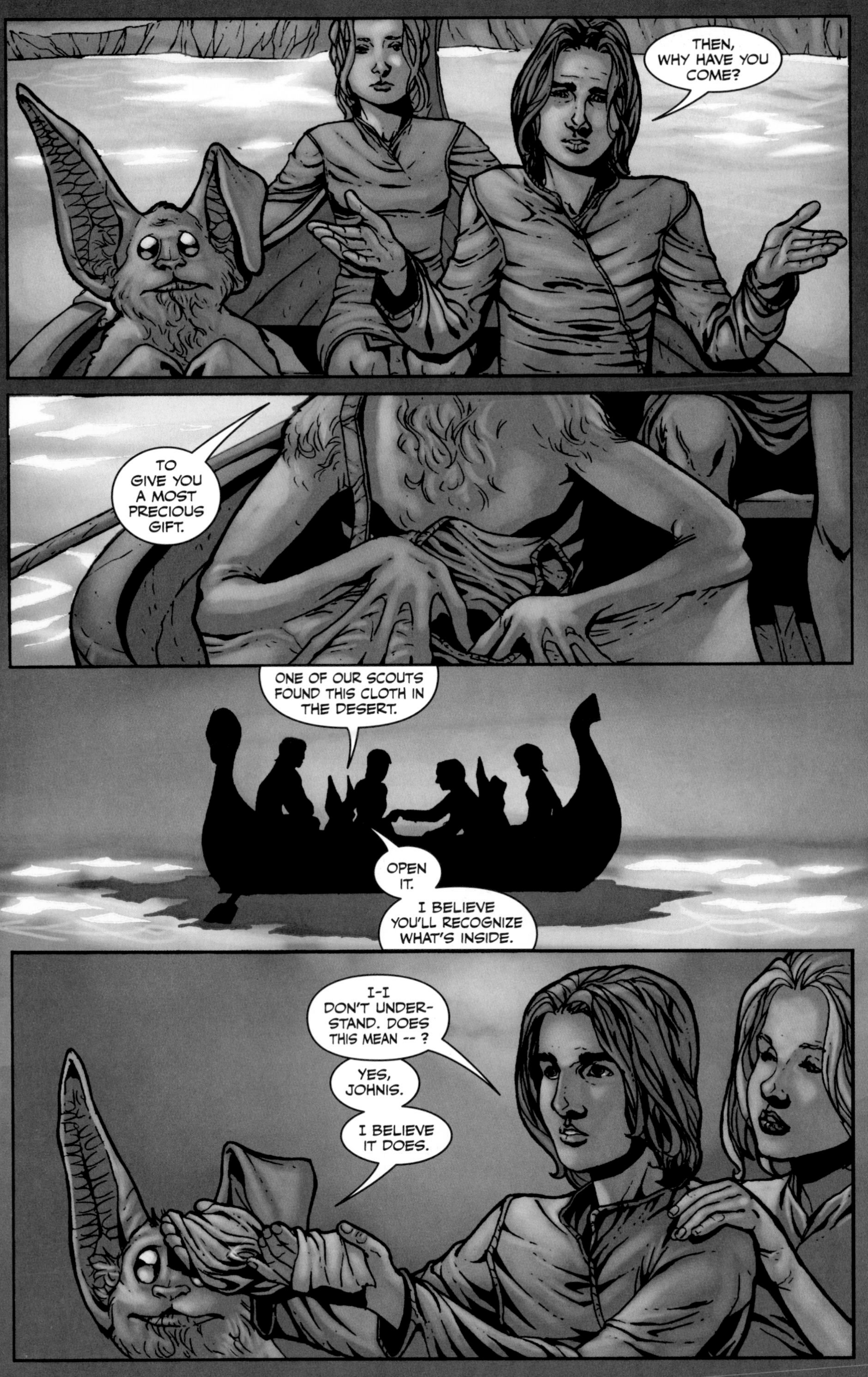
THEN, WHY HAVE YOU COME?
TO GIVE YOU A MOST PRECIOUS GIFT.
ONE OF OUR SCOUTS FOUND THIS CLOTH IN THE DESERT.
OPEN IT.
I BELIEVE YOU'LL RECOGNIZE WHAT'S INSIDE.
I-I DON'T UNDER-STAND. DOES THIS MEAN -- ?
YES, JOHNIS.
I BELIEVE IT DOES.

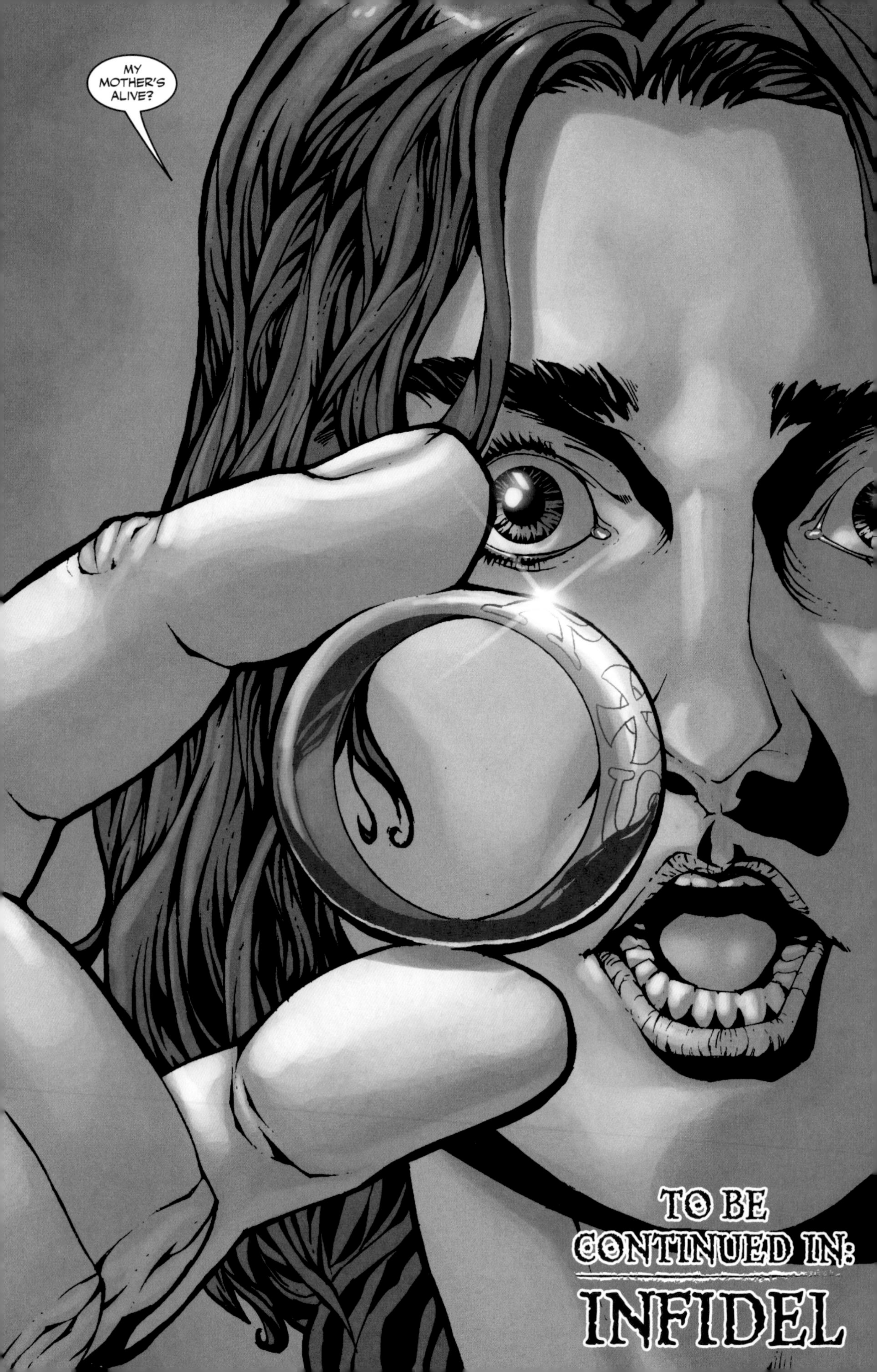
MY MOTHER'S ALIVE?
TO BE CONTINUED IN:
INFIDEL

WRITTEN BY TED DEKKER

ADAPTATION BY J.S. EARLS AND KEVIN KAISER

EDITED BY KEVIN KAISER AND JOCELYN BAILEY

ILLUSTRATIONS BY CAIO REIS

COLORS BY SALVATORE AIALA AND ROMULO FAJARDO

LETTERED BY ZACH MATHENY

FRONT COVER ART BY EDUARDO PANSICA

PUBLISHED IN NASHVILLE, TENNESSEE, BY THOMAS NELSON. THOMAS NELSON IS A REGISTERED TRADEMARK OF THOMAS NELSON, INC.

THOMAS NELSON, INC. TITLES MAY BE PURCHASED IN BULK FOR EDUCATIONAL, BUSINESS, FUND-RAISING, OR SALES PROMOTIONAL USE. FOR INFORMATION, PLEASE E-MAIL SpecialMarkets@ThomasNelson.com.

Library of Congress Cataloging in Publication Data

Dekker, Ted, 1962–
    Chosen / by Ted Dekker.
        p. cm. — (The lost books ; bk. 1)
    "Story by Ted Dekker. Adapted by J.S. Earls"—T.p. verso.
    Summary: As the land of the Forest Dwellers is increasingly decimated by the Horde, Thomas Hunter, supreme commander of the Forest Guard, choses four sixteen-year-old recruits for a special mission--to find the seven lost Books of History that have power over the past, present, and future.
    ISBN 978-1-59554-603-6 (softcover)
    1. Graphic novels. [1. Graphic novels. 2. Fantasy. 3. Christian life—Fiction.] I. Title.
PZ7.7.D45Ch 2008
741.5'973—dc22   2008036861

Printed in Canada
08 09 10 11 12 QW 5 4 3 2 1

TWO REALITIES ONE EXPERIENCE
ENTER ANYWHERE

AVAILABLE NOW

COMING JUNE 2009

AVAILABLE NOW

KEEP READING FOR AN EXCERPT FROM BLACK GRAPHIC NOVEL

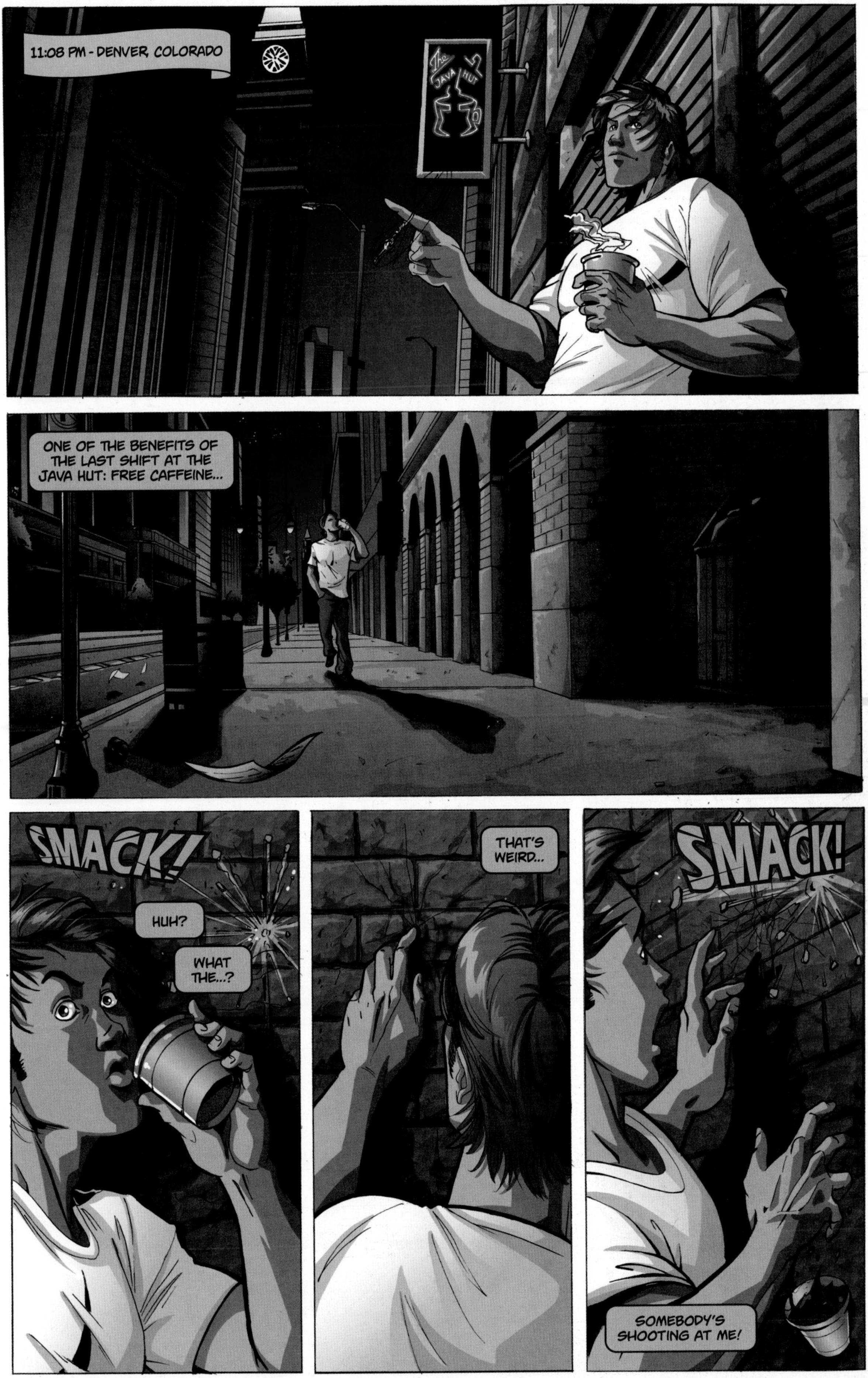
11:08 PM - DENVER, COLORADO
The JAVA HUT
ONE OF THE BENEFITS OF THE LAST SHIFT AT THE JAVA HUT: FREE CAFFEINE...
SMACK!
HUH?
WHAT THE...?
THAT'S WEIRD...
SMACK!
SOMEBODY'S SHOOTING AT ME!

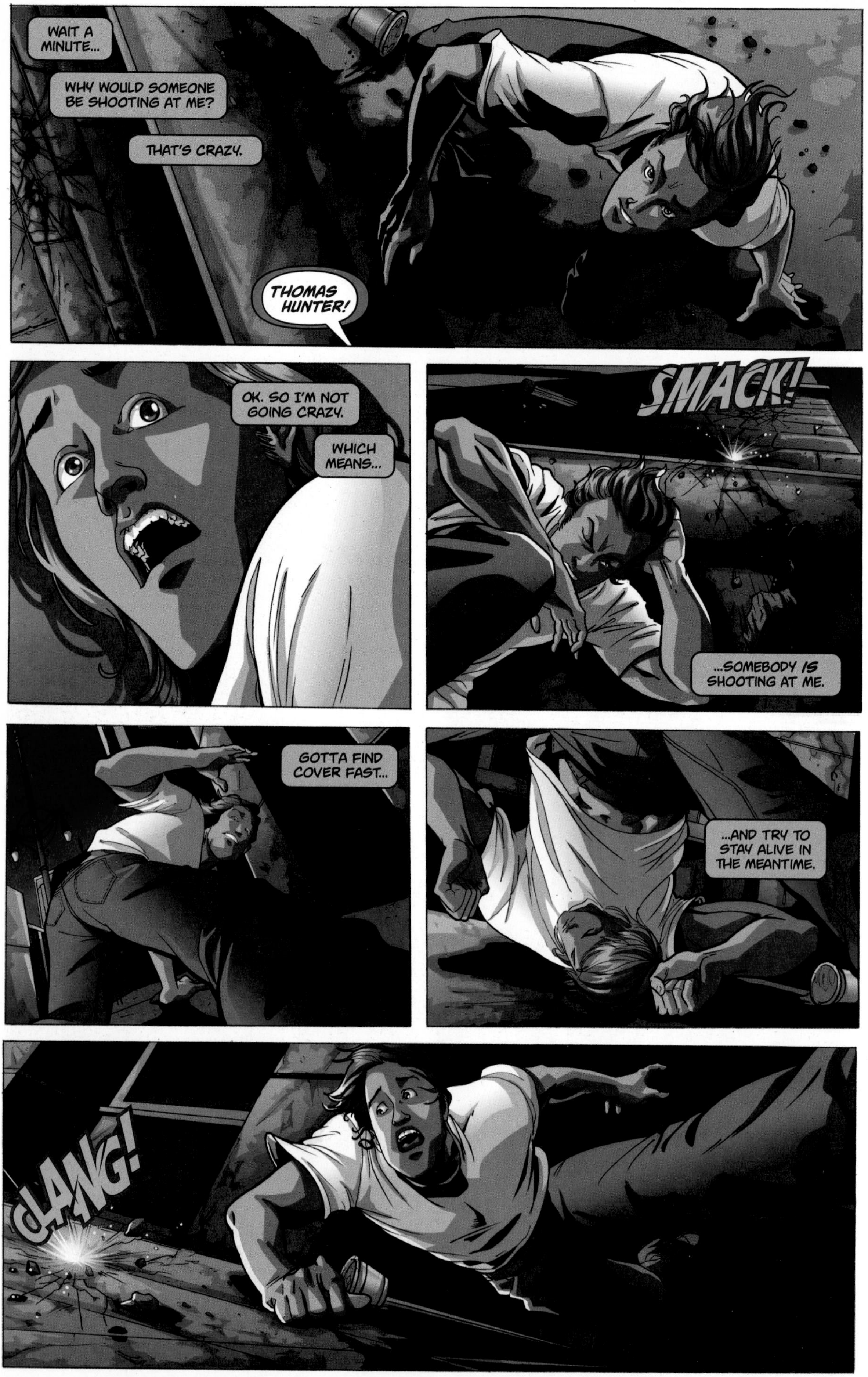
WAIT A MINUTE...
WHY WOULD SOMEONE BE SHOOTING AT ME?
THAT'S CRAZY.
THOMAS HUNTER!
OK. SO I'M NOT GOING CRAZY.
WHICH MEANS...
SMACK!
...SOMEBODY *IS* SHOOTING AT ME.
GOTTA FIND COVER FAST...
...AND TRY TO STAY ALIVE IN THE MEANTIME.
CLANG!

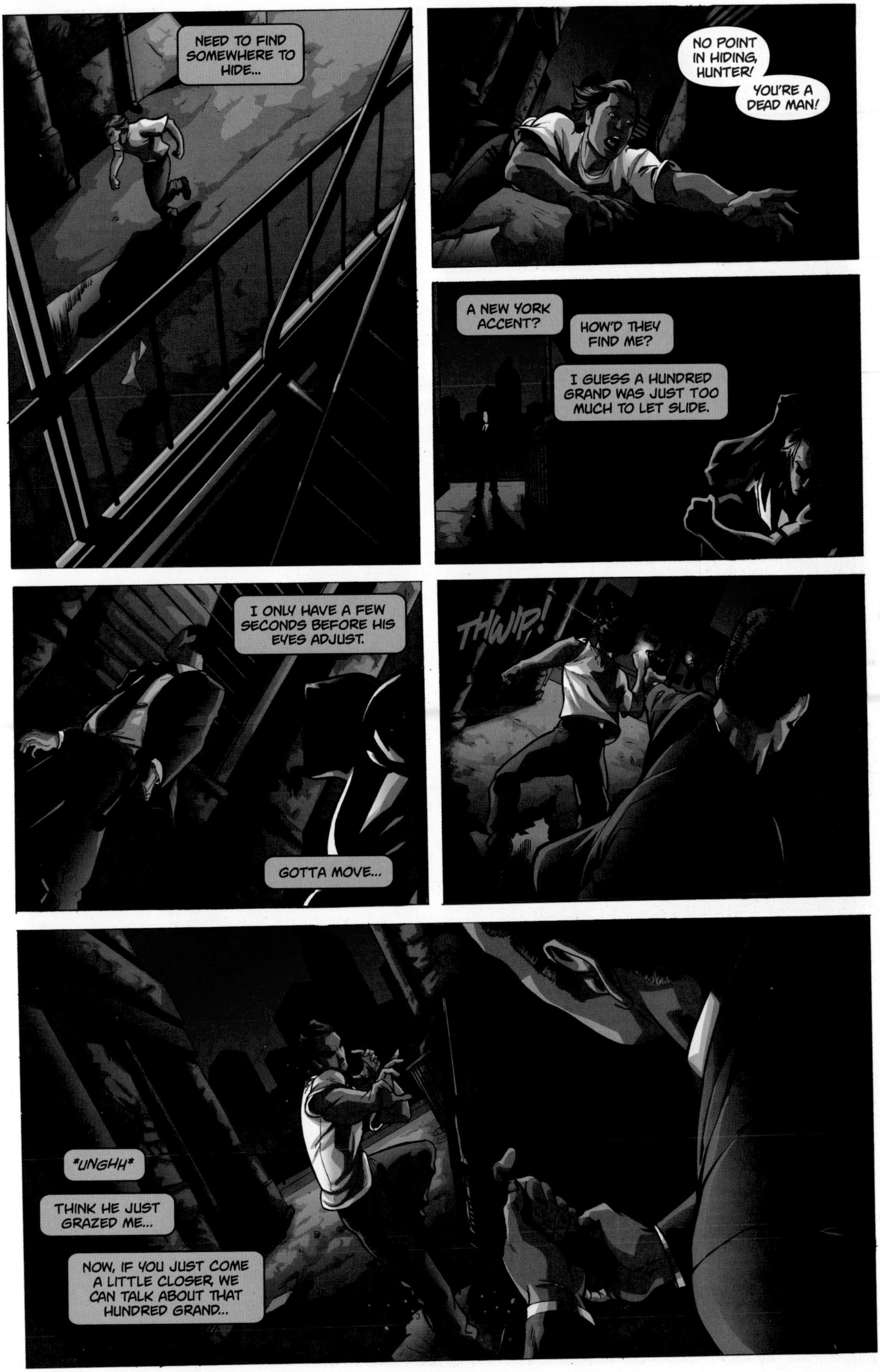
NEED TO FIND SOMEWHERE TO HIDE...
NO POINT IN HIDING, HUNTER!
YOU'RE A DEAD MAN!
A NEW YORK ACCENT?
HOW'D THEY FIND ME?
I GUESS A HUNDRED GRAND WAS JUST TOO MUCH TO LET SLIDE.
I ONLY HAVE A FEW SECONDS BEFORE HIS EYES ADJUST.
GOTTA MOVE...
THWIP!
UNGHH
THINK HE JUST GRAZED ME...
NOW, IF YOU JUST COME A LITTLE CLOSER, WE CAN TALK ABOUT THAT HUNDRED GRAND...

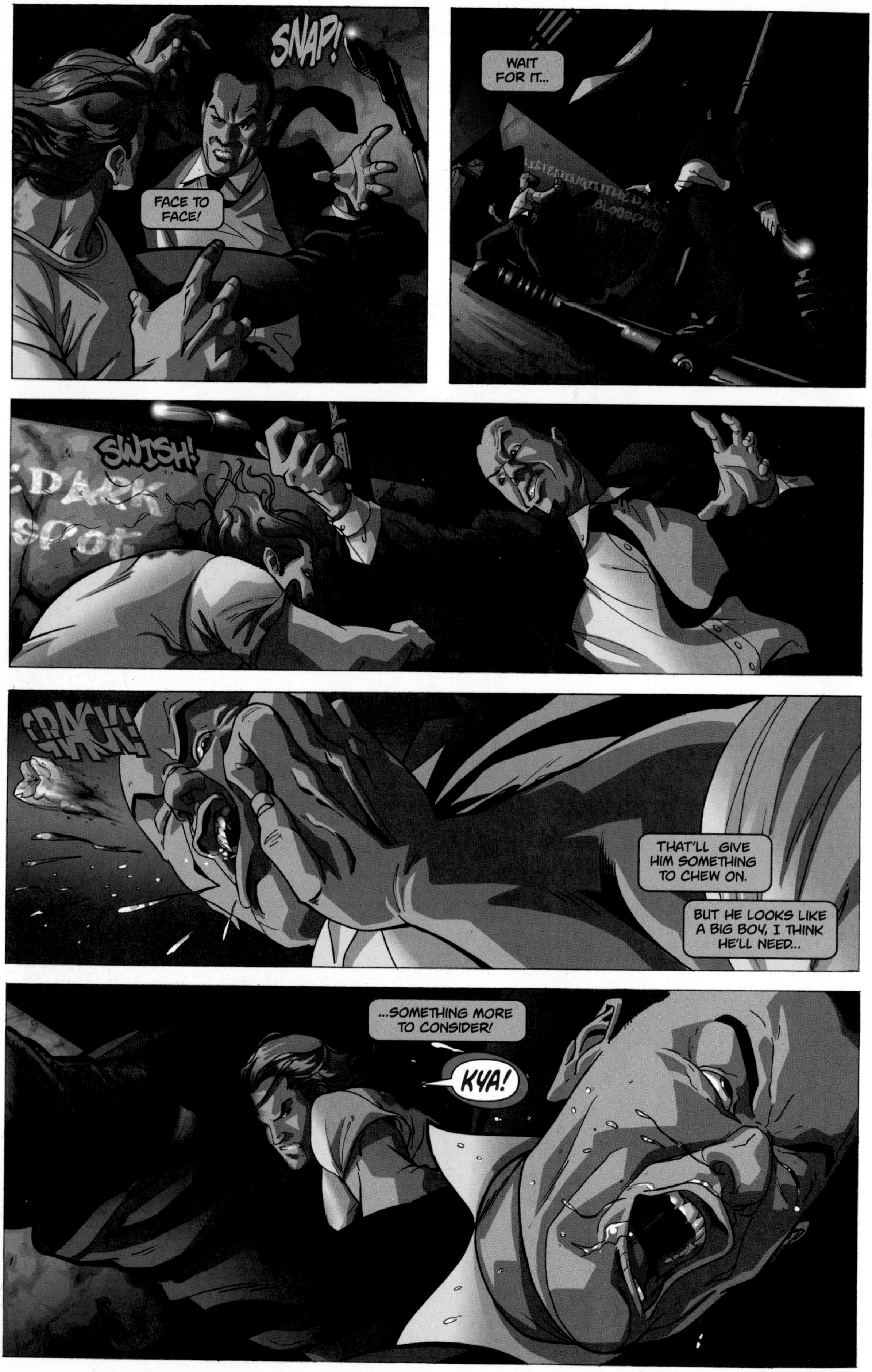
SNAP!
FACE TO FACE!
WAIT FOR IT...
SWISH!
CRACK!
THAT'LL GIVE HIM SOMETHING TO CHEW ON.
BUT HE LOOKS LIKE A BIG BOY, I THINK HE'LL NEED...
...SOMETHING MORE TO CONSIDER!
KYA!

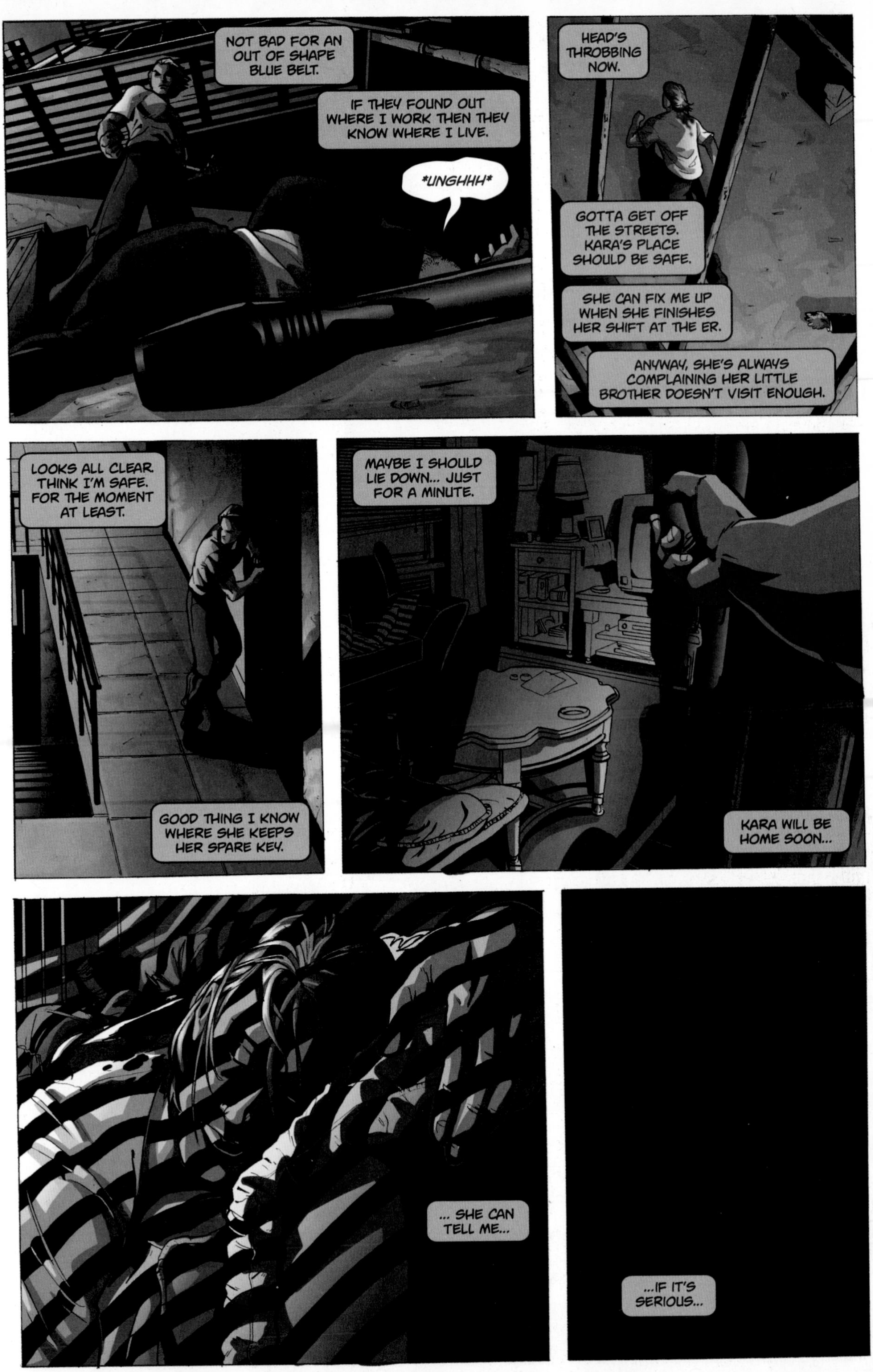
NOT BAD FOR AN OUT OF SHAPE BLUE BELT.
IF THEY FOUND OUT WHERE I WORK THEN THEY KNOW WHERE I LIVE.
UNGHHH
HEAD'S THROBBING NOW.
GOTTA GET OFF THE STREETS. KARA'S PLACE SHOULD BE SAFE.
SHE CAN FIX ME UP WHEN SHE FINISHES HER SHIFT AT THE ER.
ANYWAY, SHE'S ALWAYS COMPLAINING HER LITTLE BROTHER DOESN'T VISIT ENOUGH.
LOOKS ALL CLEAR. THINK I'M SAFE. FOR THE MOMENT AT LEAST.
GOOD THING I KNOW WHERE SHE KEEPS HER SPARE KEY.
MAYBE I SHOULD LIE DOWN... JUST FOR A MINUTE.
KARA WILL BE HOME SOON...
... SHE CAN TELL ME...
...IF IT'S SERIOUS...

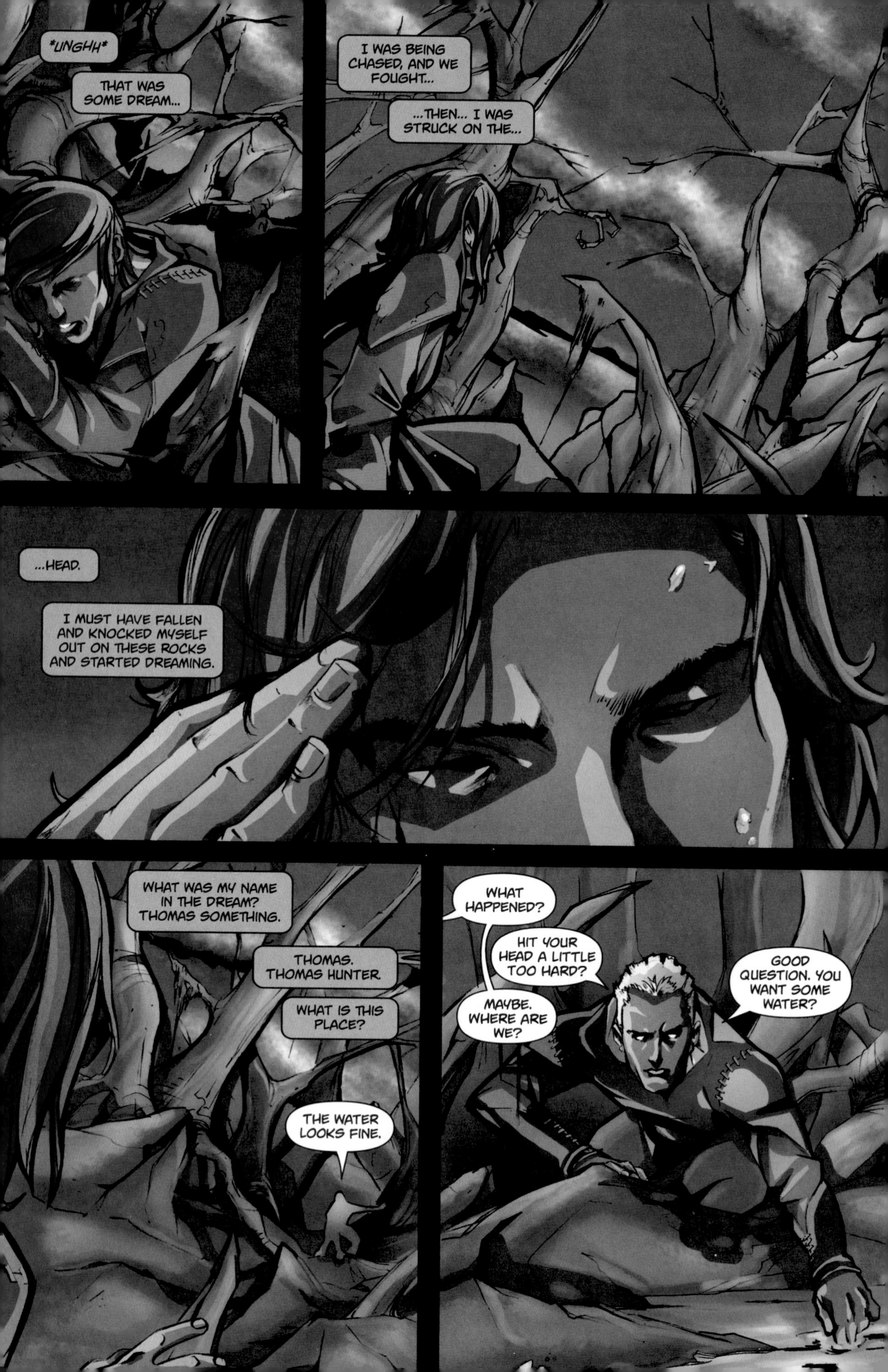
UNGHH
THAT WAS SOME DREAM...
I WAS BEING CHASED, AND WE FOUGHT...
...THEN... I WAS STRUCK ON THE...
...HEAD.
I MUST HAVE FALLEN AND KNOCKED MYSELF OUT ON THESE ROCKS AND STARTED DREAMING.
WHAT WAS MY NAME IN THE DREAM? THOMAS SOMETHING.
THOMAS. THOMAS HUNTER.
WHAT IS THIS PLACE?
THE WATER LOOKS FINE.
WHAT HAPPENED?
HIT YOUR HEAD A LITTLE TOO HARD?
MAYBE. WHERE ARE WE?
GOOD QUESTION. YOU WANT SOME WATER?

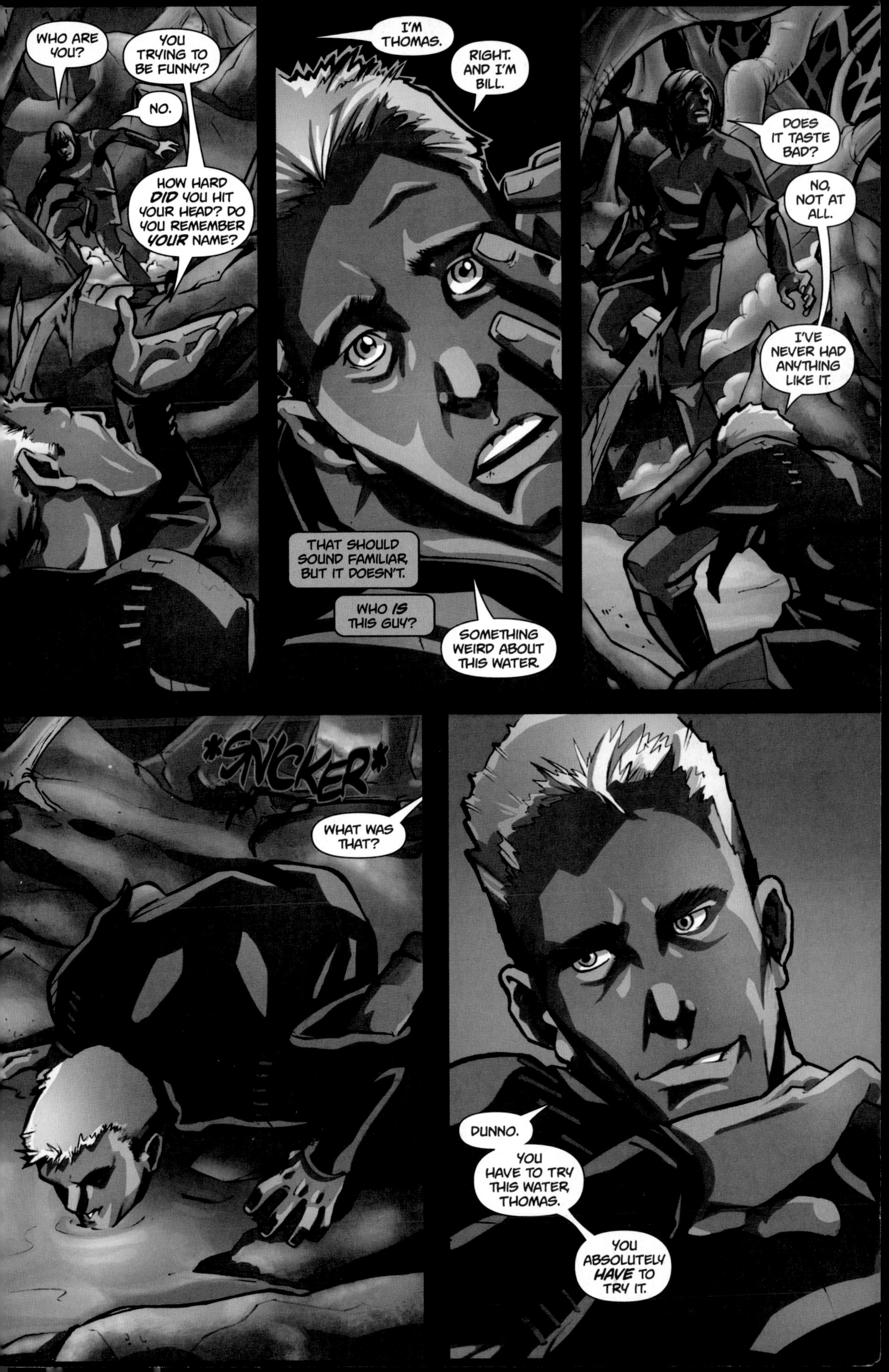

WHO ARE YOU?
YOU TRYING TO BE FUNNY?
NO.
HOW HARD *DID* YOU HIT YOUR HEAD? DO YOU REMEMBER *YOUR* NAME?
I'M THOMAS.
RIGHT. AND I'M BILL.
THAT SHOULD SOUND FAMILIAR, BUT IT DOESN'T.
WHO *IS* THIS GUY?
SOMETHING WEIRD ABOUT THIS WATER.
DOES IT TASTE BAD?
NO, NOT AT ALL.
I'VE NEVER HAD ANYTHING LIKE IT.
SNICKER
WHAT WAS THAT?
DUNNO.
YOU HAVE TO TRY THIS WATER, THOMAS.
YOU ABSOLUTELY *HAVE* TO TRY IT.

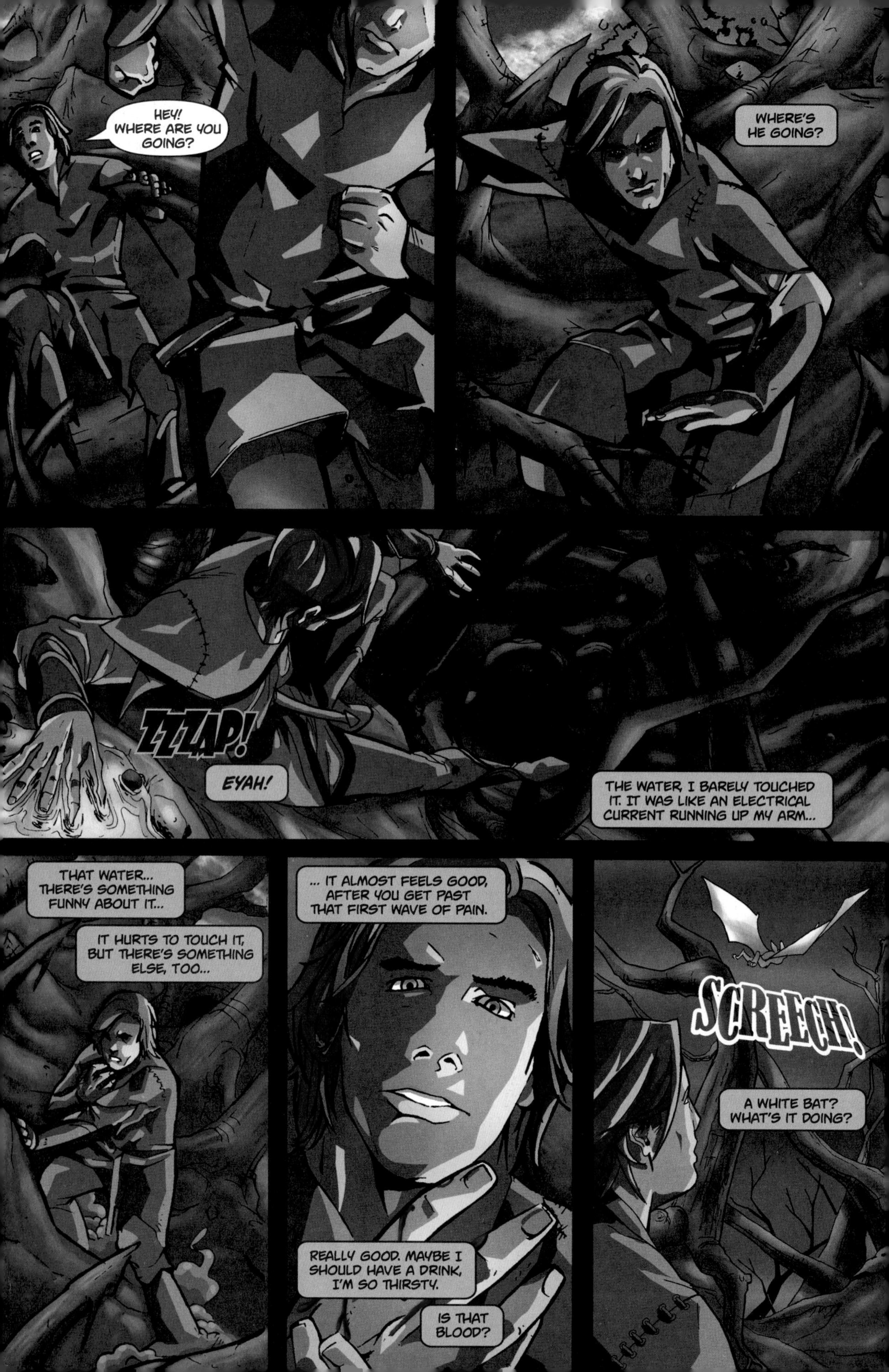
HEY! WHERE ARE YOU GOING?
WHERE'S HE GOING?
ZZZAP!
EYAH!
THE WATER, I BARELY TOUCHED IT. IT WAS LIKE AN ELECTRICAL CURRENT RUNNING UP MY ARM...
THAT WATER... THERE'S SOMETHING FUNNY ABOUT IT...
IT HURTS TO TOUCH IT, BUT THERE'S SOMETHING ELSE, TOO...
... IT ALMOST FEELS GOOD, AFTER YOU GET PAST THAT FIRST WAVE OF PAIN.
REALLY GOOD. MAYBE I SHOULD HAVE A DRINK, I'M SO THIRSTY.
IS THAT BLOOD?
SCREECH!
A WHITE BAT? WHAT'S IT DOING?

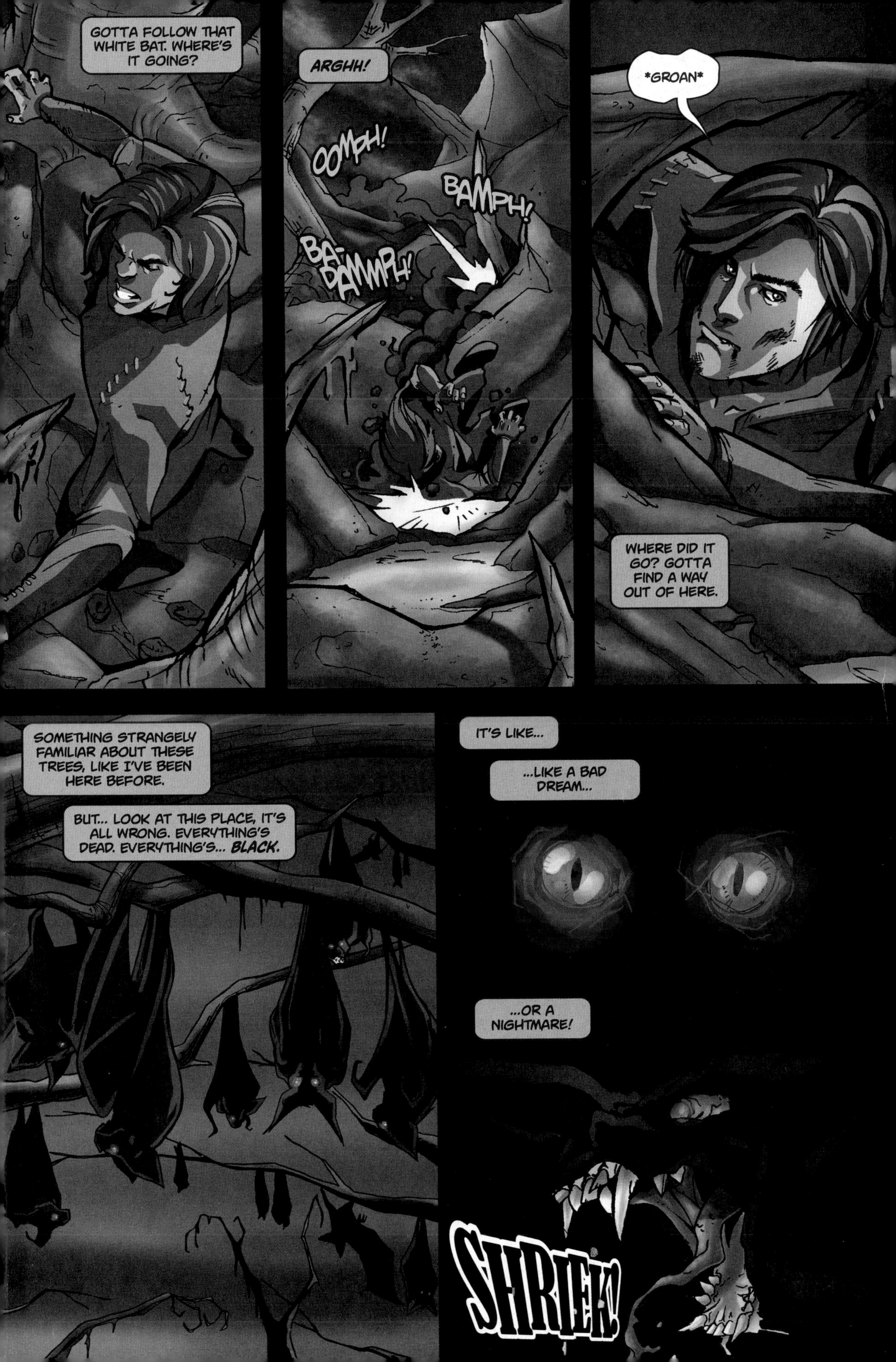
GOTTA FOLLOW THAT WHITE BAT. WHERE'S IT GOING?
ARGHH!
OOMPH!
BAMPH!
BA-DAMMPH!
GROAN
WHERE DID IT GO? GOTTA FIND A WAY OUT OF HERE.
SOMETHING STRANGELY FAMILIAR ABOUT THESE TREES, LIKE I'VE BEEN HERE BEFORE.
BUT... LOOK AT THIS PLACE, IT'S ALL WRONG. EVERYTHING'S DEAD. EVERYTHING'S... BLACK.
IT'S LIKE...
...LIKE A BAD DREAM...
...OR A NIGHTMARE!
SHRIEK!

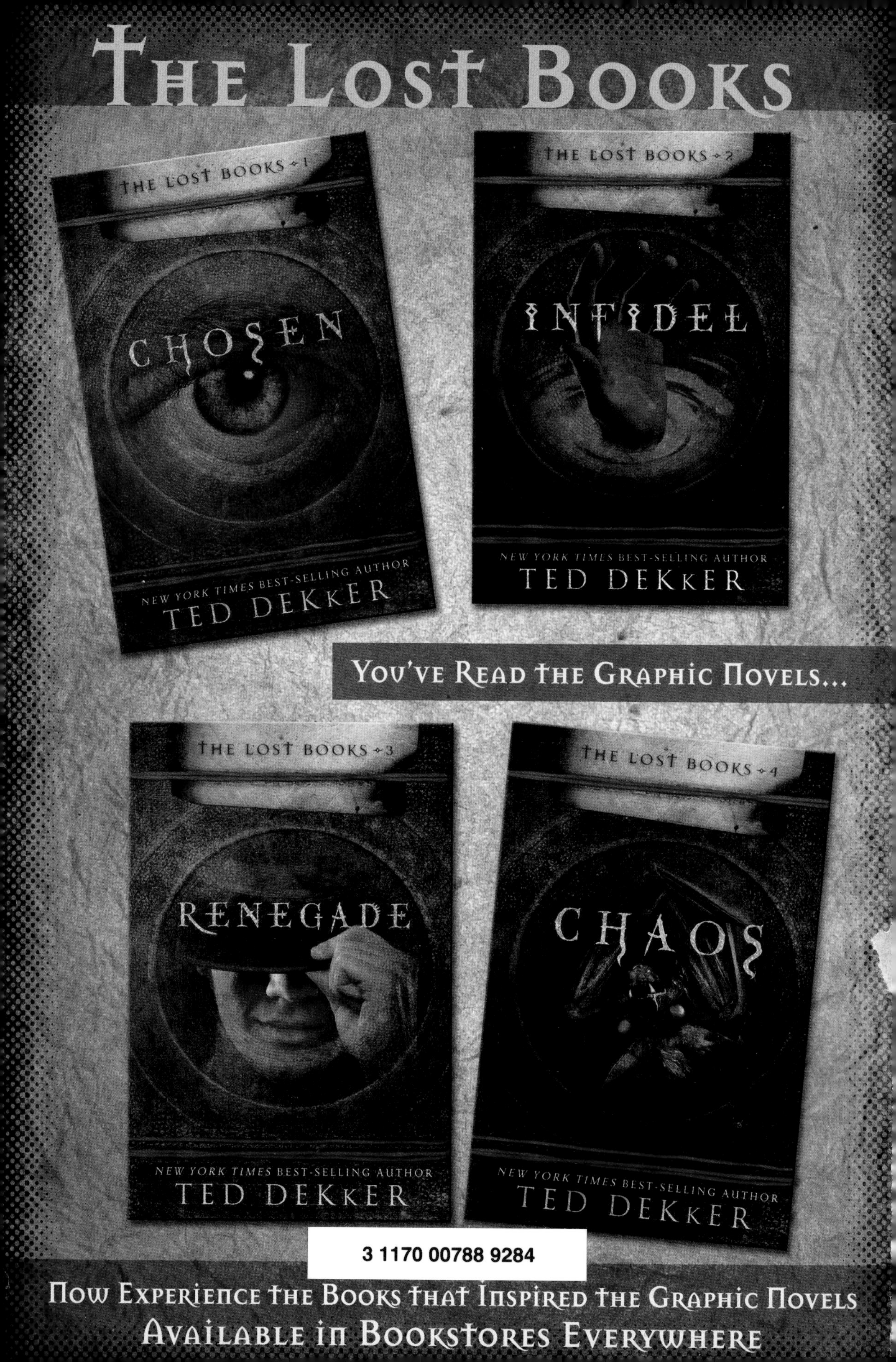

THE LOST BOOKS
THE LOST BOOKS • 1
CHOSEN
NEW YORK TIMES BEST-SELLING AUTHOR
TED DEKKER
THE LOST BOOKS • 2
INFIDEL
NEW YORK TIMES BEST-SELLING AUTHOR
TED DEKKER
YOU'VE READ THE GRAPHIC NOVELS...
THE LOST BOOKS • 3
RENEGADE
NEW YORK TIMES BEST-SELLING AUTHOR
TED DEKKER
THE LOST BOOKS • 4
CHAOS
NEW YORK TIMES BEST-SELLING AUTHOR
TED DEKKER
NOW EXPERIENCE THE BOOKS THAT INSPIRED THE GRAPHIC NOVELS
AVAILABLE IN BOOKSTORES EVERYWHERE